D0825359

The Myth of Self-Esteem

THE MYTH OF SELF-ESTEEM

HOW RATIONAL EMOTIVE
BEHAVIOR THERAPY
CAN CHANGE YOUR
LIFE FOREVER

ALBERT
ELLIS

Prometheus Books

59 John Glenn Drive
Amherst, New York 14228-2119

Published 2005 by Prometheus Books

The Myth of Self-Esteem: How Rational Emotive Behavior Therapy Can Change Your Life Forever. Copyright © 2005 by Albert Ellis. All rights reserved. No part of this publication may be reproduced, stored in a retrieval system, or transmitted in any form or by any means, digital, electronic, mechanical, photocopying, recording, or otherwise, or conveyed via the Internet or a Web site without prior written permission of the publisher, except in the case of brief quotations embodied in critical articles and reviews.

Inquiries should be addressed to
Prometheus Books
59 John Glenn Drive
Amherst, New York 14228–2119
VOICE: 716–691–0133, ext. 210
FAX: 716–691–0137
WWW.PROMETHEUSBOOKS.COM

22 21 20 19   14 13 12 11

Library of Congress Cataloging-in-Publication Data

Ellis, Albert, 1913–
     The myth of self-esteem : how rational emotive behavior therapy can change your life forever / Albert Ellis.
          p. cm.
     Includes bibliographical references and index.
     ISBN 978-1-59102-354-8 (pbk. : alk. paper)
     1. Self-esteem. 2. Self-acceptance. 3. Rational emotive behavior therapy.
I. Title.

RC489.S43E55 2006
158.1—dc22

2005017482

Printed in the United States on acid-free paper

CONTENTS

CONTENTS

CONTENTS

To Debbie Joffe, who has been of tremendous help in getting out this book. Immense thanks!

ACKNOWLEDGMENTS

To Kevin Everett Fitzmaurice, Emmett Velten, James McMahon, and Shawn Blau, who read this book in manuscript, made valuable contributions, but are of course not responsible for any of its contents, and to Tim Runion, who did a fine word-processing and compiling job.

INTRODUCTION
Is Self-Esteem a Sickness?

Is self-esteem a sickness? That's according to the way you define it. In the usual way it is defined by people and by psychologists, I'd say that it is probably the greatest emotional disturbance known to man and woman: Even greater than hating other people, which seems somewhat worse, but is perhaps a little better.

Why does hating and damning other people seem worse than self-esteem, which almost always leads to self-hatred? Well, it obviously results in fighting, acting against, war, and genocide. Pretty dramatic! While self-hatred produces more subtle results—like despising yourself but not necessarily committing suicide. *Living* with your self-lambasting.

Let me spend some time trying to clearly define self-esteem and self-disesteem. This won't be easy, since definitions have been vague and overlapping for the past century. But for the purposes of this book, here goes!

Self-esteem: You rate your self, your being, your personality, your essence, your totality, in terms of two main goals: (1) Your achieving success or effectiveness in your accomplishments. Your school, your work, your projects. When you succeed in getting what you want (and avoiding what you don't want), you say *that* is good. Great! But you also rate yourself and say, "I am a good person for succeeding!" When you fail to satisfy your achievement goals, you say, "That is bad; and *I* am bad."

(2) When your goal is relating well to other people and you actually relate well and win their approval, if you tie up your relating to your self-esteem—your worth as a *person*—then you tell yourself, "*That* is good!" and also, "I am a good and worthy person!" If you fail to win the approval of significant others, you then rate your *effort* and your *self* as *un*worthy.

That seems quite clear—and clearly gets you into trouble. As a fallible human, you can't help failing at work and at love, so your self-esteem is at best temporary. Even when it is high, you are in real danger of failing next time and of plummeting down again. Worse yet, since you know this after awhile, and you know that your worth as a person *depends* on your success, you make yourself anxious about important achievements—and, very likely, your anxiety interferes with your performances and makes you more likely to fail.

Rotten go! Your need for self-esteem makes you less likely to achieve it and more anxious when you do. Unless, of course, you are perfect—which is highly unlikely.

Realizing this some centuries ago, some philosophers—Asian and Greek and Roman, among others—invented self-acceptance. They said you could constructively *choose* to always have what is called unconditional self-acceptance (USA) by merely strongly *deciding* to have it—and keep it. Simple!

To achieve USA, you still pick an important goal—such as work or love—and you evaluate its achievement as good or bad, successful or unsuccessful. But—watch it now!—you refuse to rate or measure your self, your being, as "good" or "bad." You realize, along with a modern philosopher, Alfred Korzybski, that your performance is *part* of you, but certainly not *all* of you. You did it and are largely *responsible* for it. But it is a single performance, can easily change (be better or worse) tomorrow, and is always—yes, always—one ever-changing *aspect* of you. As Korzybski said, you *are* not your behavior. You are that and thousands of other behaviors—good, bad, and indifferent.

So you accurately tell yourself, "I did that desirable or undesirable act. It certainly did not do itself! I did it with my little hatchet; and I will—because of my talents and fallibilities—do many more desirable and undesirable behaviors. But I *am* not my acts—just a *person* who behaves well and badly."

Period. You evaluate the efficacy of your thoughts, feelings, and actions; but you don't rate or measure your *total* self or efficacy. In fact, you can't—because you are a *changeable* individual. You are not *static*. You grow, develop, progress—and retrogress. Why? Because you do.

Is this the only way you can get unconditional self-acceptance? No. You can get it indirectly, by convincing yourself that somebody gives it to you gratuitously—say God, your fairy godmother, your mother, a therapist, or someone else. But, first of all, you would have to *prove* that that spirit or person gives you USA. Otherwise, you really give it to yourself—which, fortunately, you can do. Instead of saying that God (or the devil!) gave you USA, why not merely say that you did? That's more honest! You *saw* that conditional self-acceptance (CSA) wouldn't work, so you *decided* to give USA to yourself *un*conditionally. Why not?

The main thing is: You take it, get it, keep it by *choice*. Go right ahead. Be my guest. Then no one can take it away from you—but *you*! Neat. You decide (1) "I can take it." (2) "I will take and keep it." (3) "I am the master of my fate. I am the captain of my soul."

In other words: "I accept myself, my existence, my being *with* my fallibility. Too bad about it. But I'm still okay. To define myself as non-okay—worthless—is silly and will make me *more* fallible. I'm okay because I think I am. Or, more accurately, I am a *person* who has many good and many bad traits. Let me rate *them*, such as they are, and not rate *me*."

Both self-esteem and self-acceptance, then, can be had definitionally—for the asking, for the choosing. Take one or the other. Choose! Better yet, take no *global* rating. Choose your goals and values and rate how you experience them—well or badly. Don't rate yourself, being, entity, personality at all. Your totality is too complex and too changing to measure. Repeatedly acknowledge *that*.

Now stop farting around and get on with your *life*!

CHAPTER 1
Nathaniel Branden and Self-Esteem

Nathaniel Branden became a *guru* of self-esteem when he published, in 1969, *The Psychology of Self-Esteem: A New Concept of Man's Psychological Nature.* Actually, it wasn't entirely new, since it devoutly followed the philosophy of Ayn Rand, from which Branden, at that time, was beginning to break. Rand, in *Atlas Shrugged* (1957) and several other books, deified reason and competence and was fanatically one-sided about that—as was her prophet, Branden.

Under the heading of "the basic conditions of self-esteem," Branden placed the first and fundamental requirement: that "He preserve an *indomitable will to understand.*" People with self-esteem had to be clear, intelligible, able to comprehend that which falls within the range of awareness and which is the guardian of their mental health and intellectual growth. The two requisites of self-esteem were self-confidence—or what Albert Bandura (1987) later called self-efficacy—and self-respect.

Actually, the two are *not* necessarily related. You can respect yourself for a number of reasons, one of which encompasses achievement, efficacy, and competence; and this is the reason that Rand and Branden deified and deemed necessary for *real* self-respect.

To his credit, Branden was not as rigid as Rand, and over the years began to see that self-respect and self-acceptance could be linked to other human characteristics. In *The Six Pillars of Self-Esteem*, Branden (1994) becomes more liberal and lists six essentials of self-esteem:

The practice of living consciously
The practice of self-acceptance
The practice of self-responsibility
The practice of self-assertiveness
The practice of living purposely
The practice of personal integrity

Now this is more like it—and includes a lot more than living competently, achievingly, productively, and with reason. It includes character traits, such as honesty, integrity, and being *socially* responsible—which Rand and Branden originally neglected. You live with *others* and had better respect yourself *while* honoring others. This overlaps with the existentialist views of Martin Buber, Jean-Paul Sartre, Martin Heidegger, Alfred Adler, and Rational Emotive Behavior Therapy (REBT).

Peculiarly enough, however, Branden places self-acceptance *under* self-esteem. Branden at times *sees* what unconditional acceptance is but also *sees* it partially. Thus, he says in *Six Pillars of Self-Esteem*, that you can do self-acceptance exercises morning, noon, and night by fully (and presumably unconditionally) accepting your body, your feelings, your conflicts, your thoughts, your actions, your assets and shortcomings, your fears, your pain, your anger, your sexuality, your joy, your perceptions, your knowledge, and your excitement.

18

I couldn't put it better myself! Oddly enough, Branden keeps *conditional* self-acceptance, but makes it *part of unconditional* self-esteem—which is what USA is. He tells you that you can unreservedly accept yourself (which you of course can) by *first* setting up conditions of achievement and social character—which, he somehow fails to see, *vitiate* your full self-acceptance.

So Branden almost, but not *quite*, stays in the CSA instead of the USA camp. He rightly—along with Rand—shows how useful and "rational" are competence and social character. Then, in a typical Randian manner, he says that you *have to, absolutely must*, achieve them *in order to* accept and respect your *self*, your *totality*.

Why *must* you? How can you *unconditionally* accept important *conditions*? Because achievement and social integrity are distinctly important, Branden makes them *necessary* and *sacred*. That is why, in my book *Ayn Rand: Her Fanatical, Fascistic, and Devoutly Religious Philosophy*, I show how this philosophy is unworkable.

As for Branden, I think that he could define his terms more clearly and *un*contradictably as follows:

Conditional self-esteem: Defining your thoughts, feelings, and actions as "good" and "commendable" when they help you (and others) achieve your main goals (such as good health, longevity, and happiness). When you achieve these outcomes, you rate yourself, your totality, as "good." Your self-rating is thereby *dependent* on your "good" achievements.

Unconditional self-acceptance: Choosing goals and values that help you (and others) but determinedly accepting or respecting your self or totality *whether or not* you perform well and gain the approval of others. You respect or approve of *you* even when you view your behaviors as undesirable and against your chosen goals.

Rating or evaluating your thoughts, feelings, and behaviors but not your self or totality: Telling yourself, "It is good to achieve my goals and purposes, because I *desire* to fulfill them. But I am *never* a good person *or* a bad *person*, no matter what I do. I don't have to rate my *self* at all—only what I think, feel, and do."

Actually, as I shall keep showing in this book, the third form of evaluation—nonrating of your self—is most difficult to achieve, because you are born and reared with a tendency to (inaccurately) make *global* ratings, and cannot easily give it up. So Korzybski was correct—we are naturally overgeneralizers as well as generalizers. But we can largely *stop* our overgeneralizing if we work hard at it.

Branden—like most psychologists and most people—doesn't seem to think we can stop our damnation of our *self* along with damning our ineffectual *behavior*. So he really seems to be saying, "By all means damn your good and bad traits, but somehow give yourself self-acceptance." Nice trick, if you can do it. I and Korzybski say, instead, "Berate some of your traits but *still* give yourself USA by recognizing that the *part* of you never can equal the whole."

Now it obviously can't—since two wrongs cannot make *you* totally wrong—but even some REBTers fail to see that a great wrong—like murdering an innocent child or killing a large group of people—is *so* heinous that it makes the murderer *totally* reprehensible and an *evil person*. No—no matter how bad are your acts, they still don't *equal* your totality. They can't. Even if you *only* committed murders, you as a human could change and not murder again. This won't do your victims much good, but it will preserve your humanity. If you were Jesus, would you forgive Hitler and Stalin? Yes, if you thought straight. And you might spend the rest of your days helping genocide victims and their relatives.

Which brings us to UOA—unconditional other-acceptance. Branden and, especially, Rand had no concept of UOA. He never forgave her and she certainly never forgave him for their treacherous actions. Unconditional other-acceptance holds that you condemn others' iniquitous thoughts, feelings, and actions, but you always adopt the Christian philosophy of accepting—not liking!—the sinner but not his or her sins.

Now this is damned difficult. We see that Hitler, Stalin, and Rand do evil deeds; and even though they were strongly born and reared to tend to do them, they are still partly responsible for their hostile acts. They have *some* degree of "free will"—like practically all humans have. And they *could* have, perhaps, behaved less vilely. But they wrongly chose to act the ways they did and *did* behave that way. No great excuses! Still, to save ourselves from raging, to ward off future crimes, and to make the world at least a little *less* evil, we had better not forget but still forgive.

How can the lessons learned from this violence lead us to peace? Not, again, easily, but in the long run. In fact, we have very little choice. As I pointed out in an invited address to the American Counseling Association in 1985, and as I stress in my writings since then—especially in my book *The Road to Tolerance*—the invention of mass weapons of destruction like nuclear warheads and biological warfare practically *forces* us to give up deadline revengefulness. If we use our vast stockpiles of nuclear weapons against, say, a Hitler, he will likely retaliate in kind—and there goes millions of people and maybe the inhabitable world. No matter how *just* we convince ourselves that retaliation is, who will soon be left to start and finish their "just" cause? Maybe the insects!

All-out "just revenge" with today's—and tomorrow's—weapons *just* won't work. Violence, today, can be doubly genocidal. World tribunals (if they still exist) prove that Hitler, Stalin, and others were wrong, unfair, and cruel. It may well be a little too late!

Although, according to many philosophers and to REBT, absolute absolutes don't really exist—"It *must always* be right or wrong under all conditions at all times!"—we can posit a few conditional absolutes: "If people absolutely condemn other people's thoughts, feelings, and actions, and also condemn others 'injustices,' there is a good likelihood that one group will use its deadliest weapons to destroy a dissenting group and that the dissenting group will do the same; and, pretty quickly, a world holocaust will ensue." Therefore, all powerful groups had better *peacefully* disagree with other powerful groups.

Ergo: Have disagreements and differences, but not *embattled* ones. Vigorously conciliate!

If I am on the right track so far, people who achieve USA (unconditional self-acceptance) will self-protectively strive to achieve UOA (unconditional other-acceptance). They will not only fully accept themselves with their failings and "sins" but also will accept sinful and failing *others*. They will often disagree but rarely *fight about* their disagreements. And sometimes, after discussion, they will open-mindedly *agree*. But they can still largely *noncombatively* disagree.

While we are at it, we can briefly extend USA and UOA to ULA—unconditional life-acceptance. This means that when things go wrong in our lives and we have done little or nothing to *make* them bad—such as loss of loved ones, physical disabilities, hurricanes, and floods—we honestly can hate these Adversities and do our best to rectify them, still *accept* it when they can't be presently rectified, and have the wisdom to see the difference—as Reinhold Niebuhr said in the 1950s. We can clearly see the difference between *liking* Adversities—which is difficult—and *accepting* them, which is still difficult but doable.

As I shall show later, we then create the ABCs of REBT philosophy, feeling, and action. At A (Adversity), we do our best to change unfortunate conditions. At C (Consequence), we experience the healthy emotions of sorrow, regret, and frustration—and, often, the unhealthy emotions of panic, depression, and rage. We often blame C (Consequence) on A (Adversity): "*You* treated me unfairly," and "*You* made me angry!"

No. You may well have treated me unfairly (at A) but at B (my

Belief System) *about* A, I *chose* to make myself sorry ("I wish A had not occurred and I don't like it but can live with it."); and I *chose* to make myself angry and depressed ("You *absolutely should not, must not* treat me unfairly and you are a *rotten person* for doing so!") *I* made me angry and depressed by *demanding* that you (and others) act fairly. Therefore—at B, my Belief System—I largely made *myself* angry at you. I can now *accept* your unfairness and go back to making myself feel healthfully sorry and disappointed in your *behavior* but not unhealthfully angry at *you*.

More of this later. To momentarily review: You can choose to (1) keenly *dislike* your, other people's, and life's happenings (As) and still *accept* those Adversities that you cannot now change. You can thereby *create* Consequences (Cs) of USA, UOA, and ULA instead of disapproving and damning yourself, other people, and life.

As you can see, Branden (and Rand) originally condemned himself for his achievement inadequacies and then had to make up for them by having responsible *character*. Still conditional. He talks about but never gets close to *un*conditional acceptance. Philosophically, it's still foreign territory to him.

CHAPTER 2
Carl Rogers and Unconditional Positive Regard

Carl Rogers was one of the first psychologists and psychother-apists to strongly advocate unconditional self-acceptance. At first, he was largely psychoanalytic, but in the 1950s he became remarkably client-centered or person-centered. He stressed, almost obsessively-compulsively, that the therapists listen intently to clients; see things (and feel things) from *their* framework; fully understand their thoughts, feelings, and behaviors; give clients unconditional positive regard; and be honest, congruent, and inte-grated in their relationships with clients (Rogers 1957).

I immediately saw that Rogers was correct in listing his six "necessary and sufficient" conditions for personality change—*if* he called them *desirable* or *advantageous*, but not if he called them imperative. I had created Rational Emotive Behavior Therapy in 1955 (Ellis 1957, 1958) and wrote a paper for the *Journal of Coun-seling Psychology* objecting to Rogers's necessitizing. My objec-tions never convinced Rogers but did convince many other psy-chologists. Briefly, they were:

1. Two persons had to be in personal psychological contact. No. People *could* figure out sensible philosophies by themselves and/or through lectures, recordings, sermons, novels, plays, and the like.

2. Clients are in a state of incongruence, are anxious or vulnerable. Usually yes. But some people benefit considerably by therapy or advice when they are unusually congruent, less anxious, and little vulnerable. They can still learn and grow.

3. The therapist "should be within the confines of this relationship, a congruent, genuine, integrated person." Very preferably! But many therapists aren't—in fact, few are!—and they sometimes help people enormously.

4. The therapist must experience *unconditional positive regard* for clients—"a caring for the client, but not in a possessive way, or in such a way as to simply satisfy the therapist's needs." Good, in fact, very good. But obviously not *necessary.* Occasionally, clients have been benefited by *non*caring therapists. Or, again, by therapists who were *dead* when the clients "related" to them by reading them or listening to their tapes.

5. The sufficient and necessary condition for personality change "is that the therapist is experiencing an accurate, empathic understanding of the client's awareness of his own experience." Most likely beneficial!—but still not necessary. Inaccurate and *un*empathic therapists still—occasionally!—help their clients. Not as well as accurate and empathic ones, you may say, but still definitely.

6. "The client perceives, to a minimal degree, the acceptance and empathy which the therapist experiences for him." Yes. But the client may perceive this when it doesn't exist! Even when they work very well—which they frequently do—acceptance and empathy are *perceived* by the client and not necessarily *given.* I have known a few clients—since I

supervise many recorded sessions—where the clients deliberately did their homework and improved considerably because they hated the therapist for *lack* of empathy and acceptance and were motivated to change in spite of this perception.

As you can see from the above points, I have not argued with the *value* of Rogers's six necessary and sufficient requisites for effective therapy, but with their dogmatism. Therapists still largely endorse them—as "good" but hardly necessary. Rogers's main directive, for which he'd best be given considerable support, is his fourth point—the therapist's unconditional accepting of clients with their numerous faults and failings—including clients' resistance to her or him. Rogers clearly does not, like Branden, demand that clients be competent, productive, and bright; nor that they be responsible, honest, and have good character. He *likes* these traits and really helps clients to achieve them. But no insistence. If they don't, they don't. He still fully accepts them. "By acceptance," he writes in *On Becoming a Person* (1961), "I mean a warm regard for him as a person of unconditional self-worth—of value no matter what his condition, his behavior, or his feelings." Very clever—and the same as the REBT position.

Exactly where Rogers got this USA position is not clear. He went to Union Theological Seminary for two years, almost becoming a minister. He must have met there Paul Tillich, the famous professor of theology, who wrote *The Courage to Be* in 1953, before Rogers became something of an existentialist. But he never seems to mention Heidegger, Sartre, and Tillich. Strange!

Fortunately, I read Tillich in 1953 and immediately became devoted to unconditional self-acceptance. Rogers *may* have got this unusual concept from his *experiencing* himself and others, as he implies. But I doubt it and still suspect Tillich's influence. Maybe he didn't want to *admit* that he got it by being *taught* to have it. He clearly said that it could not merely be *taught* but had to be empathically *experienced*. I of course disagree—since I learned it from Tillich and other existentialists—and *then* I worked on myself—and with others—to experience it.

Anyway, I differ from Rogers and many other existentialists in that I hold that teaching and being taught *is* experiencing—and that they include both emphasizing *and* understanding. In fact, Rogers says, "Acceptance does not mean much until it involves understanding" (p. 34). So does empathy; so does teaching.

Where I significantly differ from Rogers in regard to self-acceptance, is his statement on page 35 of *On Becoming a Person*: "When the other person can, to some degree, experience these attitudes [of my fully accepting him], then I believe that change and constructive personal development will *invariably* occur—and I include the word 'invariably' only after long and careful consideration."

Ah! This is exactly why Rogers and I closely agree on what is USA but why our therapies radically differ, with REBT having much more of an active-directive *teaching* approach. I discovered, in giving my clients UOA—that is, thoroughly accepting them with their failings and virtues—that I did *not* help some of them to achieve USA. I also saw a number of ex-clients of Rogers and his followers, who had been given unconditional positive regard by them and—what do you know!—they were far from achieving USA. In fact, they rarely achieved UOA. As a result of their therapy experience, they did not unconditionally accept others. They still pummeled themselves for their own mistakes—and lambasted others for theirs.

Dorothy, for example, a thirty-three-year-old depressive whom I saw for ten months in the 1960s, finally accepted the fact that I never blamed her for her hostility to her parents (and many other people). But for almost a year I made little headway in having her achieve

28

USA—even when I got her to accept her parents with their abusive behaviors. UOA—by myself and by Dorothy—did not lead her to experience USA. In fact, she castigated herself mightily for hating her parents until I used general semantics theory to convince her that they often *acted* badly but could not therefore be *bad people.*

My therapy experiences—and that of other therapists who followed Rogers's methods—helped me to see that both UOA and USA could be believed by clients separately, together, or not at all. Giving clients UOA usually works best to help them gain USA— but not always! So I gave my clients UOA and taught it to them philosophically and I *also* over and over taught them the virtues of USA and how to achieve them. As is usual in REBT, I simultaneously gave my clients, as homework and during sessions, a number of emotive-experiential exercises and several behavioral assignments. All three. As you may imagine, when one set of methods didn't work too well to help them achieve USA, UOA, and ULA, another set sometimes did the trick.

My main differences in technique with Carl Rogers are that I teach *and* relate; I am active-directive *and* (at times) nondirective; I am very involved in my sessions and quiet homework-assigning. My therapy goals are often the same as were Rogers's; but my techniques are much more varied. I would be delighted to see several therapy experiments performed to discover if Rogers's and the regular REBT technique seem to help clients acquire more or less USA, UOA, and ULA.

I predict that if such experiments were done, REBT and Rogers's PCT (person-centered therapy) would both help clients considerably; and, at first, PCT might help them be less depressed, self-downing, and angry than REBT. Because, I hypothesize, clients normally turn their gaining other-acceptance from therapists into personal acceptance and love. When therapists deliberately give them full approval, they see him/her as personally caring for them; and they *conditionally* tell themselves, "I thought I was unlovable, but now that my *therapist* accepts/approves of me, I am lovable and *therefore* I am a good person." Still conditional self-esteem!

Clients who are helped with PCT therefore often *feel* better but not *get* better; while clients who are helped with REBT more often *un*conditionally accept themselves and *get* better. An interesting hypothesis to test!

Another experiment: Let fifty clients use Rogerian PCT with a problem of severe depression and fifty depressed clients use PCT *plus* a therapist's teaching them how to consciously acquire USA and UOA *philosophically*—as they could do *without* a therapist, from reading my, Korzybski's, Tillich's, and other existentialists' books. Elliott Cohen, who is a philosopher who does REBT, could show them how to do this!

To conclude this chapter, Carl Rogers has made some outstanding contributions to acceptance therapy. With him, clients experienced an important part of the game. I suggest that PCT clients be additionally *taught* to unconditionally accept themselves and others by thinking through the *philosophy* of acceptance by themselves.

CHAPTER 3
Albert Ellis and Unconditional Self-Acceptance

As I have described in my books—especially, *Rational Emotive Behavior Therapy: It Works for Me, It Can Work for You*—I had conditional self-esteem until I was twenty-four, and suffered from periods of performance anxiety and occasional depression. Usually, I wasn't too anxious or depressed but with my first wife, Karyl, was constantly worried about: Did she love me *really, enough, and for the future?* And what a ninny I was for putting up with her perilously unsteady feelings!

I worried—endlessly!—through and through and one night after seeing her—and getting nowhere with my "Does she love me, does she not?" rosary, I went for an hour's walk in the Bronx Botanical Gardens and came up with a wonderful antianxiety pill: Whether or not Karyl *really* loved me, I didn't *need* her love, I only *wanted* it. There!

Wanting and not needing changed me forever. I was still *conscious* about doing well and being loved by Karyl. But not *over*concerned, *anxious*. At bottom, too, I realized that I didn't *need* her—or anyone's—love because my *self*-acceptance didn't depend on it.

My pleasure, yes; my dependence, no. I saw this more thoroughly later. But I saw the essence of it at twenty-four. I didn't *need* anything, except a few things—food, water, shelter—for survival. Love, success, sex all *added* to my life. They didn't *make* it.

That one new idea was revolutionary. That is why REBT, along with feelings and behaviors, stresses (more than even the other cognitive behavior therapies, which copy it) ideas, thoughts, cognitions, and philosophies. A single new idea can make you radically different in many ways. For example, "You don't *need* the approval you *want*; your worth doesn't depend on it!"

That idea probably got me to become a therapist—so I could help others get it, too. I immediately started doing volunteer therapy with my friends and relatives—including Karyl!—and three years later enrolled in graduate school in clinical psychology.

From the time I became an accredited psychologist—in 1943, at the age of twenty-nine—I quickly and forcefully began to teach my clients how to *desire* but not *need* what they wanted, and was very happy about that. Then I read Paul Tillich's *The Courage to Be* and saw the existentialist position much clearer than in Sartre and Heidegger and in some ways better than Korzybski's position. Tillich (1953), who was a hedonist himself, very much *wanted* but didn't *need* sex. He particularly saw that his worth as a person didn't *depend* on accomplishing his goals. Oh!! He was right. I would never give up wanting—desiring, lusting—but I would give up *attaching* it to my rating of my *self*, my totality. Promptly!

I began to see clearly: not *needing* success and love and failing to get them didn't make me—or anyone!—a lesser person. It merely made me a *person who*—for the time being—wasn't getting all I wanted. Tough! I reread Heidegger, Sartre, and other existentialists; became more than ever a constructivist; and thoroughly didn't *need* Karyl's love. Ironically, she madly loved and respected me, for many years later, even after we got divorced!

Albert Ellis and Unconditional Self-Acceptance

Soon after I became a fully accepting therapist and teacher, I also found other thinkers who independently accepted people unconditionally—especially philosopher Robert S. Hartman, who wrote a brilliant book, *The Philosophy of Value*, in 1969, and with whom I had several talks and correspondence. Hartman distinguished between your extrinsic value (to other people), which depended on your acting the way they wanted you to act, and your intrinsic value (to yourself), because you were alive and kicking. You had a choice!—and, as Korzybski said, you *were* not what you *did*. Although your extrinsic value could be measured and rated—by different people at different times—your intrinsic value could not be accurately assessed. It was too complex and changing! Of course!

Following Tillich, the existentialists, Hartman, Martin Buber, and a few therapists like Alfred Adler, Preston Lecky, and Rollo May, I pointed out in *Reason and Emotion in Psychotherapy* (1962) and in all my subsequent writings that self-acceptance was definitional; you could choose to have it or not have it. It helped you greatly, but it still was up to you. Choose or not choose!

What is more, your choosing unconditional self-acceptance, and your profoundly thinking, feeling, and acting on it, healthfully affected you in many ways, and could improve your life and was the basic antidote to much of your depressed self-downing feelings. It almost miraculously worked.

I made USA an invariable, strong, and persistent method of REBT, while other cognitive behavior therapies—like those of Aaron Beck, Donald Meichenbaum, and David Barlow—sometimes criticized me for my emotive and repetitive philosophy. That didn't exactly stop me!

In 1972 I was asked to write a chapter in a book honoring the work of Robert S. Hartman. So I wrote a long chapter, "Psychotherapy and the Value of a Human," which I think accurately and thoroughly presented my views on unconditional self-acceptance. Professor Hartman was delighted with my chapter and said that if I were writing my PhD thesis in philosophy, he would be glad to give me my doctorate on the basis of that paper alone. It was "excellent and original."

Naturally, I was pleased to hear that. Our Albert Ellis Institute published a separate pamphlet of *Psychotherapy and the Value of a Human* in 1973, and a great number of my and the institute's other clients read it and said that they benefited from it. Here, slightly revised and updated, is this seminal paper on REBT and its theory of unconditional self-acceptance. I still strongly subscribe to it, and have kept it as a cornerstone that goes into the details of why USA works and why self-esteem or conditional self-acceptance does so much damage. If you think it a little long-winded—as do some of my clients—read it lightly and go on to the next chapter, "REBT Diminishes Much of the Human Ego."

CHAPTER 4
Psychotherapy and the Value of a Human

Almost all modern authorities in psychotherapy believe that people's estimation of their own value, or worth, is exceptionally important and that if they seriously denigrate themselves or have a poor self-image, they will impair their normal functioning and make themselves miserable in many significant ways. Consequently, one of the main functions of psychotherapy, it is usually held, is to enhance individuals' self-respect (or "ego strength," "self-confidence," "self-esteem," "feelings of personal worth," or "sense of identity") so that they may thereby solve the problem of self-evaluation (Adler 1926; Ellis 1962; Ellis and Harper 1961; Kelly 1955; Lecky 1943; Rogers 1961).

When people do not value themselves very highly, innumerable problems result. They frequently will focus so intensely on what a rotten person they are that they will distract themselves from problem solving and will become increasingly inefficient. They may falsely conclude that rotters such as they can do virtually

Reprinted by permission from *Value and Valuation: Axiological Studies in Honor of Robert S. Hartman*, edited by John William Davis (Knoxville: University of Tennessee Press, 1972).

nothing right, and may stop trying to succeed at the things they want to accomplish. They may look at their proven advantages with a jaundiced eye and tend to conclude that they are phonies and that people just haven't as yet seen through them. Or they may become so intent on "proving" their value that they will be inclined to grovel for others' favors and approval and will conformingly give up their own desires for what they think (rightly or wrongly) they want them to do (Ellis 1962; Hoffer 1955; Lecky 1943). They may tend to annihilate themselves, either literally or figuratively, as they desperately try to achieve or to please (Watzlawick 1978). They may favor noncommitment and avoidance, and become essentially "nonalive" (May 1969). They may sabotage many or most of their potentialities for creative living. They may become obsessed with comparing themselves to others and their achievements and tend to be status seeking rather than joy exploring. They may frequently be anxious, panicked, terrified (Ellis 1962). They may tend to be short-range hedonists and to lack self-discipline (Hoffer 1955). Often they may become defensive and thus act in a "superior," grandiose way (Low 1967). They may compensatingly assume an unusually rough or "masculine" manner (Adler 1926). They may become quite hostile toward others. They may become exceptionally depressed. They may withdraw from reality and retreat into fantasy. They may become exceptionally guilty. They may present a great false front to the world. They may sabotage a number of special talents which they possess. They may easily become conscious of their lack of self-approval, may berate themselves for having little or no confidence in themselves, and may thereby reduce their self-image even more than they have done previously (Ellis and Harper 1961a, 1961b). They may become afflicted with numerous psychosomatic reactions, which then encourage them to defame themselves still more.

This list is hardly exhaustive since almost the entire psychotherapeutic literature of the last fifty years is more or less concerned with the harm individuals may do themselves and how badly they may maim or destroy their relations with others when they condemn themselves, make themselves feel guilty or ashamed about their acts or inactions, and otherwise lower their self-images. This same literature illustrates the corollary proposition almost endlessly; namely, that when human beings somehow manage to accept, respect, and approve of themselves, in most instances their behavior changes remarkably for the better: their efficiency considerably improves; their anxiety, guilt, depression, and rage lessen; and they become less emotionally disturbed.

An obvious question therefore presents itself: If the individual's perception of his own value, or worth, so importantly affects his thoughts, emotions, and actions, how is it possible to help him consistently to appraise himself so that, no matter what kind of performances he achieves and no matter how popular or unpopular he is in his relations with others, he almost invariably accepts or respects himself? Oddly enough, modern psychotherapy has not often posed this question—at least not in the form just stated. Instead, it has fairly consistently asked another, and actually almost antithetical, question: Since the individual's self-acceptance seems to depend on (1) her succeeding or achieving reasonably well in society and on (2) her having good relations with others, how can she be helped to accomplish these two goals and thereby to achieve self-esteem?

Self-acceptance and self-esteem may seem, at first blush, to be very similar; but actually, when they are clearly defined, they are quite different. Self-esteem—as it is fairly consistently used by Branden (1969), Rand (1956), and other devotees of Ayn Rand's objectivist philosophy—means that the individual values himself because he has behaved intelligently, correctly, or competently. When taken to its logical extremes, it "is the consequence, expression and reward of a mind *fully* committed to reason" (Branden

1969; italics mine); and "an *unbreached rationality*—that is, an unbreached determination to use one's mind to the fullest extent of one's ability, and a refusal *ever* to evade one's knowledge or act against it—is the *only* valid criterion of virtue and the *only* possible basis of authentic self-esteem" (Branden 1969; italics mine).

Self-acceptance, on the other hand, means that the individual fully and unconditionally accepts herself whether or not she behaves intelligently, correctly, or competently and whether or not other people approve, respect, or love her (Bone 1968; Ellis 1962, 1966; Rogers 1961). Whereas, therefore, only well-behaving (not to mention perfectly behaving) individuals can merit and feel self-esteem, virtually all humans are capable of feeling self-acceptance. And since the number of consistently well-behaving individuals in this world appears usually to be exceptionally small and the number of exceptionally fallible and often ill-behaving persons appears to be legion, the consistent achievement of self-esteem by most of us would seem to be remote while the steady feeling of self-acceptance would seem to be quite attainable.

Those psychotherapists, therefore, who think and practice in terms of their clients' achieving a high measure of self-esteem or of highly conditional, positive self-regard are clearly misguided. What they had better more realistically aim for would be to help these clients attain self-acceptance or *un*conditional positive regard. But even the very term *unconditional positive regard*, which was originally coined by Carl Rogers and Stanley Stendhal (Rogers 1951), tends to have misleading overtones, since, in our culture, we usually regard someone positively because of a good thing that he has done, for some beauty or strength of character he possesses, or for some talent or particular achievement. Rogers, however, really seems to mean that the individual can be accepted, and can accept himself, without reference to *regard* or achievement; or that, as I have noted elsewhere, he can accept himself just because he is he, because he is alive, because he exists (Ellis 1962; Ellis and Gullo 1971).

It is mainly philosophers, and existentialist philosophers in particular, who have honestly and determinedly tackled the problem of human value and who have tried to determine what the individual can do to see herself as a worthwhile being even when she is not behaving in a notably competent, successful, or supposedly deserving way. Among these philosophers, Robert S. Hartman has led all the rest. No one has given more time and thought to the general problem of value than he; and no one, to my knowledge, has come up with a better explication of intrinsic value, or a human being's worth to himself, than has Hartman.

According to Hartman's theory "value is the degree in which a thing fulfills its concept. There are three kinds of concepts—*abstract, construct,* and *singular.* Correspondingly, there are three kinds of value: (1) *systemic* value, as the fulfillment of the construct; (2) *extrinsic* value, as the fulfillment of the abstract; and (3) *intrinsic* value, as the fulfillment of the singular concept. The difference between these three concepts is that a construct is *finite,* the abstract is *denumerably infinite,* and the singular is *non-denumerably infinite*" (Hartman 1959, p. 18).

By sticking to these highly original and well-delineated concepts of value, Hartman is able to concentrate upon the exceptionally important idea of intrinsic value and, by its use, to prove, as well as I have ever seen anyone prove, that the human individual is fully and unconditionally acceptable in his own right, as a unique and singular person; that he always has value to himself, as long as he is alive; and that his intrinsic worth, or self-image, need not depend in any way on his extrinsic value, or worth to others. Hartman gives several reasons why an individual may invariably accept himself, or consider himself good or valuable in spite of his talents and achievements or lack thereof. These reasons include:

1. A thing is good if it fulfills the definition of its concept. A "good man," therefore, is a person who fulfills the definition of a man—that is, one who is alive; who has arms, legs, eyes, a mouth, a voice, etc. In this sense a Martian might well not be a good person, but virtually every alive Earthian would be (Hartman 1967, p. 103).

2. "It is infinitely more valuable, in the strictly defined sense of infinity, to be a morally good person than to be a good member of society, say a good conductor, baker, or professor. To be sincere, honest, or authentic in whatever one does is infinitely more important than what one does" (Hartman 1967, p. 115). As long, therefore, as a woman is sincere, honest, and authentic—as long as she is truly herself—she has great intrinsic value, no matter what others may think of her.

3. A man can think about an infinite number of items in the universe and he may think *that* he is thinking about each of these items. He can also think that his thoughts about his thinking are being thought, and so on ad infinitum. Hence he is essentially infinite—"a spiritual *Gestalt* whose cardinality is that of the continuum. This cardinality, however, is that of the entire space-time universe itself. The result of this axiological proof of the value of man is that every individual person is as infinite as the whole space-time universe" (Hartman 1967, pp. 117–18). In any axiological system, therefore, man's intrinsic value is above all other values, and he must be conceived of as being valuable or good.

4. "Being is extensionally the totality of all beings. Intensionally, it is the totality of all consistently thinkable properties; it is that than which nothing richer in properties can be thought. But if Being is this totality, then by the definition of good given by the Axiom, Being is good. For if Being is

the totality of all consistently thinkable properties, its goodness is the secondary property defined by this totality—good is a property of the set of properties that define Being" (Hartman 1967).

5. If a person does not accept the intrinsic value of a human being as more important than her extrinsic value to others, if she does not learn that "intrinsic value has nothing to do with what a person does, but only with what she is," she will not see the injustices that she does to herself and others, will lose out on life and love, and will create a world of death and desolation. Pragmatically, therefore, for her own self-preservation and happiness, she had best fully accept the premise that she is good because she exists (Hartman 1960, p. 22).

6. "I have moral value in the degree that I fulfill my own definition of myself. This definition is: 'I am I.' Thus, in the degree that I *am* I, I am a morally good person. Moral goodness is the depth of man's own being himself. That is the greatest goodness in the world" (Hartman 1962, p. 20).

7. "Who gives me my definition of myself? Of course, nobody can give me the definition of myself but myself. So, I defined woman as *the being that has its own definition of itself within itself. . . .* Now, then, I know I am human if I have my own definition of myself within myself. What then is the property I have to fulfill to be a good myself? Precisely this: to be conscious of myself, to define myself—for to define myself, to be conscious of myself—that *is* the definition of myself. *The more, therefore, I am conscious of myself, the more, and the more clearly,* I define myself—the more I am a good person." All one has to do, then, to be good, is to be conscious of herself" (Hartman 1967, p. 11).

8. "This is the important thing, you cannot fully be systemic or extrinsic unless you are fully intrinsic, fully yourself. In other words, the moral man will also be a better accountant, pilot, or surgeon. The value dimensions are within each other. The systematic, the social, and the human envelop each other. The human contains the social, and the social the systematic. The lower value is within the higher. The systemic is within the extrinsic, and the extrinsic within the intrinsic. The more fully you are yourself, the better you will be at your job and in your social role, and in your thinking. Out of your intrinsic being you summon the resources to be anything you want to be. Thus, the intrinsic, the development of your inner self, is not a luxury. It is a necessity for your own being yourself in all three dimensions" (Hartman 1967).

9. "Man as personality, as intrinsic value, is in a dimension which makes him not more valuable—for the intrinsic value is not comparable—but incomparably valuable in comparison to the whole extrinsic world, the physical universe. This world is *nothing* compared to the intrinsic value of one person" (Hartman 1967).

10. Extrinsic value of an individual depends on her fulfilling an abstract concept of what a human being should be, while intrinsic value depends on her fulfilling a singular concept. Her intrinsic or personal value, therefore, cannot be measured in extrinsic terms; and she is, consequently, good within her own right, as a singular person (Hartman 1967).

11. "A person's arrival in the world is a cosmic event because of the unlimited possibilities of the human person" (Hartman 1967, p. 2). Consequently, if the world has any value, the person and his existence should have as much or more value.

12. "Once one starts with the axiom of value, namely that value is richness of properties, then, since woman is an infinity of properties, it is impossible to say that she may be bad. All thus depends on the definition of 'good,' and this is a definition in value theory which has to be accepted or else a new value theory has to be designed" (Hartman 1967).

Although these arguments of Hartman may not be definitive or unchallengeable, they certainly provide much useful material which any philosophically oriented psychotherapist may use to combat his/her clients' overwhelming fears that their traits and abilities are far from ideal, that many people whom they encounter more or less disapprove of them, and that therefore their intrinsic value, or self-worth (which they wrongly correlate with their extrinsic value, or worth to others), is abysmally low. I have used Hartman's kind of existential arguments with self-deprecating clients for a good many years now, and I have usually found that they work rather well. For if disturbed individuals insist that they are worthless and hopeless, it does not take me very long to show them that this "fact" is really a hypothesis and that although they may think they can substantiate it with some kind of evidence, they actually cannot. Since, moreover, their stubbornly maintaining this hypothesis inevitably leads them to dismal results, they had damned well better give it up—and they usually, at least to some degree, do.

As Hartman himself notes, however, especially when he admits that a man's accepting himself as a good person "all . . . depends on the definition of 'good,'" the basic argument in favor of the theory that man has intrinsic value and that he cannot possibly be worthless is essentially tautological and definitional. There is really no empirical evidence to back (or confute) it, and it looks very much as though there never will be any. True, it has a strong pragmatic appeal; for if the opposite point is made, and it is held that women in general or a woman in particular is bad or unworthy of her own or others' respect, dire consequences will ensue. Therefore, she had better accept her "goodness" rather than her "badness," if she is to survive long and happily.

I am hardly opposed to this pragmatic argument, as I doubt any effective psychotherapist would be. The trouble, however, is with the inelegance of the philosophic premise that goes with it. Granted that man's thinking of himself as bad or worthless is usually pernicious and that his thinking of himself as good or worthwhile is more beneficial, I see no reason why these two hypotheses exhaust the possibilities of useful choices. I believe, instead, that there is a third choice that is much more philosophically elegant, less definitional, and more likely to conform to empirical reality. And that is the seldom-posited assumption that value is a meaningless term when applied to a person's being, that it is invalid to call him either "good" or "bad," and that if educators and psychotherapists can teach people to give up all "ego" concepts and to have no "self-images" whatever, they may considerably help the human dilemma and enable men and women to be much less emotionally disturbed than they now tend to be.

Must a person actually be a self-evaluator? Yes and no. On the yes side, she clearly seems to be the kind of animal who is not merely reared but is also born with strong self-evaluating tendencies. For nowhere in the world, to my knowledge, does civilized woman simply accept that she is alive, go about the business of discovering how she can enjoy herself more and discomfort herself less, and live her century or so of existence in a reasonably unself-conscious, nondamning, and nondeifying manner. Instead, she invariably seems to identify and rate her *self* as well as her *performances*, to be highly ego-involved about accomplishing this and

44

avoiding that deed, and to believe and feel strongly that she will end up in some kind of heaven or hell if she does the "right" and eschews the "wrong" thing.

Take, for example, the extremely permissive, hedonistic-oriented people of Polynesia and, especially, of Tahiti. The Polynesians, as Danielsson (1956) reports, are still pleasure-seeking and careless, are outspoken in sex matters, are premaritally free, have erotic dances, delight in sexual games, practice free love without legal weddings, and are fairly free extramaritally; and in the not-too-distant past they also practiced polygyny and wife-lending, danced in the nude, engaged in sexual intercourse in public, had pleasure houses for young people, permitted periodic sexual liberty, and encouraged deflowering ceremonies.

At the same time, however, the Polynesians have many taboos, the violation of which makes them feel utterly ashamed and self-hating. To this day, for instance, they seriously adhere to circumcision rites when the male reaches puberty; they have separate eating and sleeping houses; and they cling to rigid division of work between the sexes. In the past, moreover, they have practiced sexual privileges based on birth and rank, obligatory marriage of widows, ritual continence, the forbidding of women to concern themselves with religious matters, and the isolation of females during periods of menstruation. Religiously and politically they have been very strict: "The Polynesian chiefs and nobles would certainly never have been able to maintain their provocative privileges in the long run if they had not had an effective support in religion. According to the Polynesian religious doctrine they were descended from gods and were thus holy and unassailable. . . . The Polynesian gods required sacrifices, on many islands even human sacrifices. Nothing, therefore, was easier and more natural for a devout chief than to get rid of all troublesome persons by sacrificing them. . . . In Tahiti the most powerful rulers were always carried by a servant when they wanted to go anywhere, for if they touched the earth the owner would not be able to tread on it in future.... Certain Hawaiian potentates were so holy that subjects had to stop working at once, throw themselves flat on the ground and remain in that position so long as the rulers were in sight; so in order not to paralyze the food supply the rulers inspected the fields by night. Most Polynesian chiefs could not eat with their families, and on certain islands they were actually so full of mana that they could not eat at all, but had to be fed" (Danielsson 1956, pp. 52–53).

General discipline in Polynesia, moreover, has been and still, to a considerable degree, is based on exceptionally ego-raising and ego-debasing rules: "Polynesian ethics were certainly far from being as charitable as the Christian, and what was permitted a chief was often forbidden to his subjects, but on the other hand the existing rules were infinitely better observed than they are with us. The cause of this strict discipline was, of course, that public opinion in the small Polynesian communities or tribes had a strength and importance which even a newly arrived schoolmistress or a curate in a remote country district can hardly imagine. Public disapproval was in Polynesia simply intolerable, and there was as a rule no possibility of moving to another district or island on account of the enmity between the different tribes. Good behavior was therefore a primary necessity.... Although contrary views have sometimes been expressed, the Polynesians were not moral anarchists, but rather slaves of custom" (Danielsson 1956, p. 55).

I have quoted at length here to show that even among one of the most sexually permissive and easygoing groups of which we have knowledge, rules and rites of "proper" conduct are the norm rather than the exception, and humans become so ego-involved in following these rules and so ashamed to break them that they literally hurt or kill themselves and easily permit themselves to be severely punished or sacrificed when they flout these publicly approved regulations. If there ever was a culture in which practically all the members did not similarly denigrate themselves and bring severe emotional or physical penalties on their own heads for engaging in "wrong" or "bad" behavior, I have never heard of it and would be delighted to learn about it.

The reason, I believe, for this practically universal tendency of people to put themselves down, as well as to rate some of their ineffective performances negatively, is their biological predisposition to be what we call self-conscious. Certainly many of the "lower" animals (especially the mammals and primates) seem to be somewhat aware of "themselves," in that they "know" or "learn" that one kind of behavior (e.g., going where food is likely to be) is more "rewarding" or "reinforcing" than another kind of behavior (e.g., randomly exploring their environment). But these animals act much more instinctively than humans do, meaning that they "think" about their actions much less than humans do; they rarely, if ever, appear to think about thinking about their thinking. In the usual sense of the word, therefore, they have no "selves," and are not particularly aware that "they" are responsible for their own "good" or "bad" acts and that, consequently, "they" are "good" or "bad" individuals. In other words, they are only to a limited degree, if at all, what we call ego-involved in their performances.

People, on the contrary, not only have a strong "self-awareness" or "ego" but also have an exceptionally strong, and I again think innate, tendency to tie it up with their deeds. Since they are thin-skinned and highly vulnerable animals (as compared, say, to the rhinoceros, which can be quite careless about its behavior and is not likely to suffer ill effects) and since humans rely so heavily on cognition rather than instinct for their survival, it is greatly to their advantage that they observe and appraise their actions to see whether they are satisfaction- or pain-producing and to keep modifying them in one direction or another. Unfortunately, however, just as people protectively rate their performances in relation to their own survival and happiness, they also dysfunctionally tend to rate their selves; and they thereby almost inevitably harm themselves.

Let me graphically illustrate this human tendency with a typical case of *Rational Emotive Behavior Therapy*, which is a system of therapy based on the hypothesis that people become emotionally disturbed by foolishly rating or giving report cards to their selves as well as their deeds. Mr. Richard Roe comes to see me because he is terribly depressed about his work and because he frequently becomes enraged at his wife and acts cruelly to her when she has her minor lapses of decorum. I first show him perhaps in a session or two of psychotherapy, how and why he is *making* himself depressed. At point A, an *Adversity* exists—he is not doing well at his work and his boss is consistently bringing his poor performance to his attention. At point C—the emotional *Consequence*—he is becoming depressed. Quite wrongly he concludes that the Adversity at point A is causing his disturbed emotional reaction, or consequence, at point C: "Because I am working inefficiently and because my boss is displeased and may fire me, I am depressed." But if A really caused C, I quickly show him, magic or voodoo would exist: for how can an external event (his inefficiency or his boss's disapproval) cause him to think or to feel anything?

Obviously, Roe is doing something about these outside Adversities to make himself suffer the consequence of depression. Probably he is first observing them (noticing that his performance is inefficient and that his boss is disapproving) and then reflecting on them (thinking about their possible effects and appraising how he would dislike these effects). Moreover, he is appraising these possible results in a highly negative way. For if he were not noticing his poor work or if he were appraising it as a good thing (because it would enable him to get fired from a job he really did not want), he would hardly feel depressed. In fact, he might feel elated!

It is highly probable, therefore, that Roe is signaling, imagining, or telling himself something at point B (his *belief system*) to produce his depressed reactions at point C. Most probably, he is first telling himself a rational belief (at point RB): "I see that I am working inefficiently and that my boss may fire me; and if he did, that would be unfortunate. I certainly wouldn't like being fired." This RB belief is rational because, in all probability, it would be unfortunate if he were fired. He would then (1) be without income, (2) have to look for another job, (3) possibly have to put up with a displeased wife, and (4) perhaps have to take a worse or lower-paying position. There are several good, empirically ascertainable reasons why it would not be pleasant if he were fired. Therefore, his RB hypothesis that it would be unfortunate for him to keep working inefficiently is an empirically verifiable proposition.

If, moreover, Roe held rigorously to his RB conclusion, he would most probably never feel depressed. Instead, he would feel the *rational consequences* (RC) of displeasure, disappointment, sorrow, regret, annoyance, or feeling of frustration. These are all negative emotions but are far from the feeling of depression. In order to make himself feel the *irrational consequence* (IC) of depression, he would have to add to his rational belief an unhealthy, self-defeating, self-denigrating *irrational belief* (IB): "If I keep working inefficiently and am fired, that would be awful. I couldn't stand my boss disapproving of me and firing me. Not only would that action show that my work is poor, but it would also conclusively prove that I am pretty worthless; that I can never do well on a job like this; and that I deserve to be poor, unloved, and otherwise punished for the rest of my life for being such a slob!"

Roe's irrational belief is unhealthy for several reasons: (1) it is definitional and unverifiable. However unfortunate his working inefficiently and his being fired may be, it is only "awful," "terrible," or "catastrophic" because he thinks it is. Actually, it is still only unfortunate or inconvenient. (2) It is an overgeneralization. Because he doesn't like being fired hardly means that he can't stand it. Because his work is inefficient does not prove that he, a human being, is no good. Because he now works poorly is not evidence that he will always do so. (3) It is a non sequitur. If he really were a worthless individual who could never succeed at any job, why should he deserve to be unloved and punished? Being thus handicapped, he might well be said to deserve an unusual degree of love and help from the rest of us less-handicapped humans. What just person or deity would ever condemn him for having been born and reared to be deficient? (4) It almost invariably leads to dreadful and even more unfortunate results than those which Roe may naturally derive from his inefficient work behavior. For if he thinks it awful to be disapproved of and cannot stand being dismissed, he will probably make himself so anxious that his job efficiency will deteriorate rather than improve, and he will stand even less chance of keeping his job. Moreover, if his boss lets him go and he concludes that, therefore, he is worthless, he will tend, on future jobs, to act as if he were unable to perform, and he will bring about his self-fulfilling prophecy—he will not do well and will be dismissed again (thereby falsely "proving" his original hypothesis).

As a Rational Emotive Behavior Therapist, therefore, I will clearly show Roe what his rational beliefs and irrational beliefs are; I will try to help him discriminate his sensible RB from his foolish IB hypotheses; and I will indicate how he can keep his RB appraisals of his performances and feel healthy consequences (sorrow, regret, displeasure, increased effort to work more efficiently) and to minimize or eliminate his IB appraisals and their unhealthy consequences (feelings of panic, depression, increased inefficiency, etc.).

Similarly, I will explain and help change Roe's feelings of rage against his wife. I will show him that when her actions, at point A, are inconsiderate, impolite, or unjust, he is probably first signaling himself the rational belief "I don't like her behavior; I wish she would change it; what a nuisance!" At point RC, he is consequently experiencing the healthy consequences—that is, emotions of dissatisfaction, disappointment, frustration, and annoyance. At point IB, he has the irrational belief "Because she is acting badly, I can't stand it. She is a horrible person. I'll never be able to forgive her for acting like that. She deserves to suffer for the awful way she is treating me!" He, consequently, at point IC, feels the unhealthy consequences of rage and self-pity. If I can induce Roe to retain his sensible RB hypotheses and to surrender his condemnatory IB hypotheses, he will tend to feel displeasure but not rage, and he will probably have a better chance of helping his wife change her unpleasing behavior.

The main point here is that the Adversities that occur in Roe's (or anyone's) life at point A do not cause or make him feel depressed or enraged at point C. Rather, his thoughts, appraisals, and evaluations—his beliefs at point B—also create these feelings. To a large degree he has a choice at point A about what he will feel at point C regarding the actions or agents in his life—as long as he thinks about his thinking, challenges some of his IB conceptions and conclusions, and returns to his empirically based RB hypotheses. Being, however, born and raised a human, he easily and naturally tends to make a magical jump from RB to IB conclusions; and, much more often than not, he confuses his self, his total personality, with his performances, and he automatically evaluates and rates the former along with the latter. Consequently, he very frequently ends up by damning himself and other people (that is, denigrating his and their intrinsic value) rather than merely appraising the efficacy or desirability of his or their performances (his and their extrinsic value). He thereby gets into all kinds of needless difficulties, or emotional problems, with himself and with others.

Again, I ask: Must woman be a self-evaluator? And again I answer: Yes, to some degree she must, since it is biologically and sociologically almost impossible for her not to do so. In terms of self-preservation, if she did not constantly evaluate her performances, she would soon be dead: for before she can safely drive a car, climb a mountain, or cultivate a certain kind of food, she had better know how competent she is likely to be in these respects, else she will maim or kill herself. So, to survive, she really has to assess her deeds and her potentials.

Self-appraisal, moreover, has distinct advantages as well as disadvantages. If you (unempirically and unscientifically) rate your self, your being, as "good," "great," or "noble" when you succeed in love, work well on your job, or paint a fine canvas, you will tend, at least for awhile, to be much happier than if you merely rate your performance in a similar manner. If you (unrealistically) appraise your girlfriend or your wife as being a "glorious," "marvelous," or "goddesslike" person when you (more accurately) really mean that she has some highly desirable and pleasing traits, you will also tend to feel ecstatic about your relations with her. People, as May (1969) has strongly pointed out, largely live with demons and deities, and it is silly to think that they do not gain much by doing so.

But is it really worth it? Do people absolutely have to rate themselves as a person and evaluate others as people? My tentative answer to both these questions, after sixty years busily engaged as a psychotherapist, writer, teacher, and lecturer, is no. People have an exceptionally strong, inborn, and socially acquired tendency to be a self- and an other-appraiser; but by very hardheaded thinking, along with active work and practice, they can persistently fight against and minimize this tendency; and if they do, they will, in all probability, be considerably healthier and happier than they usually are. Instead of strongly evaluating their and other people's selves, they can pretty rigorously stick to rating only performances; instead of damning or deifying anyone or anything, they can adhere to reality and be truly demonless and godless; and instead of inventing demands and needs, they can remain with desires and preferences. If they do so, I hypothesize, they will not achieve utopia (which itself is changeless, absolutistic, and unrealistic) but they most probably will achieve more spontaneity, creativity, and satisfaction than they have ever previously achieved or presently tend to attain. Some of the main reasons for my espousing people's taking a non-evaluative attitude toward themselves (while still evaluating many of their traits and performances) are as follows:

1. Both positive and negative self-evaluation are inefficient and often seriously interfere with problem solving. If you elevate or defame yourself because of your performances, you will tend to be self-centered rather than problem-centered, and these performances will, consequently, tend to suffer. Self-evaluation, moreover, is usually ruminative and absorbs enormous amounts of time and energy. By it you may possibly cultivate your "soul" but hardly your garden!
2. Self-rating only works well when you have many talents and few flaws; but, statistically speaking, few are in that class. It also tends to demand universal competence. But, again, few can measure up to such a demand.
3. Self-appraisal almost inevitably leads to one-upmanship and one-downmanship. If you rate yourself as being "good," you will usually rate others as being "bad" or "less good." If you rate yourself as being "bad," others will be seen as "less bad" or "good." Thereby you practically force yourself to compete with others in "goodness" or "badness" and constantly feel envious, jealous, or superior. Persistent individual, group, and international conflicts easily stem from this kind of thinking and feeling; and love, coop-

eration, and other forms of fellow-feeling are minimized. To see yourself as having a better or worse *trait* than another person may be unimportant or even beneficial (since you may use your knowledge of another's superior trait to help achieve that trait yourself). But to see yourself as being a better or worse *person* than another is likely to cause trouble for both.

4. Self-evaluation enhances self-consciousness and therefore tends to shut you up within yourself, to narrow your range of interests and enjoyments. "It should be our endeavor," said Bertrand Russell, "to aim at avoiding self-centered passions and at acquiring those affections and those interests which will prevent our thoughts from dwelling perpetually upon ourselves. It is not the nature of most men to be happy in a prison, and the passions which shut us up in ourselves constitute one of the worst kinds of prisons. Among such passions some of the commonest are fear, envy, the sense of sin, self-pity, and self-admiration" (Russell 1965).

5. Blaming or praising yourself, the whole individual, for a few of your acts is an unscientific overgeneralization. "I have called the process of converting a child mentally into something else, whether it be a monster or a mere nonentity, *pathogenic metamorphosis*," Jules Henry declared. "Mrs. Portman called [her son] Pete 'a human garbage pail'; she said to him, 'you smell, you stink'; and she kept the garbage bag and refuse newspapers on his high chair when he was not in it; she called him Mr. Magoo, and never used his right name. Thus he was a stinking monster, a nonentity, a buffoon" (Henry 1963). But Henry failed to point out that had Mrs. Portman called her son, Pete, "an angel" and said to him, "you smell heavenly," she would have equally seen him, by the process of pathogenic meta-

morphosis, into something he was not; namely, a godlike being. Peter is a human person who sometimes smells bad (or heavenly); he is not a *bad-smelling* (or heavenly smelling) *person.*

6. When human selves are lauded or condemned there is a strong implication that people should be rewarded or punished for being "good" or "bad." But, as noted above, if there were "bad" people, they would already be so handicapped by their "rottenness" that it would be thoroughly unfair to punish them further for being "rotten." And if there were "good" people, they would already be so favored by their "goodness" that it would be superfluous or unjust to reward them for it. Human justice, therefore, is very badly served by self-evaluations.

7. To rate a person high because of his good traits is often tantamount to deifying him; conversely, to rate him low because of his bad traits is tantamount to demonizing him. But since there seems to be no way of validating the existence of gods and devils and since man can well live without this redundant hypothesis, it merely clutters human thinking and acting and probably does much more harm than good. Concepts of god and the devil, moreover, obviously vary enormously from person to person and from group to group; they add nothing to human knowledge; and they usually serve as obstructions to precise intrapersonal and interpersonal communication. Although it is possible that people who behave stupidly and weakly may derive benefits from inventing supernatural beings, there is no evidence that those who act intelligently and strongly have any need of them.

8. Bigotry and lack of respect for individuals in their own right are consequences of self- and other-evaluation. For if you

accept A because he is white, Episcopalian, and well educated and reject B because he is black, Baptist, and a high school dropout, you are clearly not respecting B as a human—and, of course, are intolerantly disrespecting millions of people like him. Bigotry is arbitrary, unjust, and conflict-creating; it is ineffective for social living. As George Axtelle has noted, "Men are profoundly social creatures. They can realize their own ends more fully only as they respect one another as ends in themselves. Mutual respect is an essential condition of effectiveness both individually and socially. Its opposites, hatred, contempt, segregation, exploitation, frustrate the realization of values of all concerned and hence they are profoundly destructive of all effectiveness" (Axtelle 1956). Once you damn an individual, including yourself, for having or lacking any trait whatever, you become authoritarian or fascistic; for fascism is the very essence of people-evaluation (Ellis 1965a, 1965b).

9. By evaluating an individual, even if only in a complimentary way, you are often trying to change her or trying to control or manipulate her; and the kind of change envisioned may or may not be good for her. "Often," Richard Farson notes, "the change which praise asks one to make is not necessarily beneficial to the person being praised but will redound to the convenience, pleasure or profit of the praiser" (Farson 1966). Evaluation may induce the individual to feel obligated to her evaluator; and to the degree that she lets herself feel compelled or obligated to change herself, she may be much less of the self that she would really like to be. Positive or negative evaluation of a person, therefore, may well encourage her to be less of a self or of a self-directed individual than she would enjoy being.

10. Evaluation of the individual tends to bolster the Establish-

Psychotherapy and the Value of a Human

ment and to block social change. For when one gives himself a report card he not only becomes accustomed to telling himself, "My deeds are wrong, and I think I'd better work at improving them in the future," but also, "I am wrong, I am a 'no-goodnik' for performing these poor deeds." Since "wrong" acts are largely measured by societal standards, and since most societies are run by a limited number of "upper-level" people who have a strong, vested interest in keeping them the way they are, self-evaluation usually encourages the individual to go along with social rules, no matter how arbitrary or foolish they are, and especially to woo the approval of the powers-that-be. Conformism, which is one of the worst products of self-rating, generally means conformity to the time-honored and justice-dishonoring rules of the Establishment.

11. Self-appraisal and the measuring of others tend to sabotage empathic listening. Close and authentic relationships between two people, as Richard Farson points out, are often achieved through intensive listening: "This does not merely mean to wait for a person to finish talking, but to try to see how the world looks to this person and to communicate this understanding to him. This empathic, non-evaluative listening responds to the person's feelings as well as to his words; that is, to the total meaning of what he is trying to say. It implies no evaluation, no judgment, no agreement (or disagreement). It simply conveys an understanding of what the person is feeling and attempting to communicate; and his feelings and ideas are accepted as being valid for him, if not for the listener" (Farson 1966). When, however, one evaluates a person (and oneself) as one listens to the other person, one is usually prejudicedly blocked from fully understanding and getting close to him.

12. Person-rating tends to denigrate human wants, desires, and preferences and to replace them with demands, compulsions, or needs. If you do not measure your selfness, you tend to spend your days asking yourself, "Now what would I really like to do, in my relatively brief span of existence, to gain maximum satisfaction and minimum pain?" If you do measure your selfhood, you tend to keep asking, "What do I *have* to do to prove that I am a worthwhile person?" As Richard Robertiello has observed, "People are constantly negating their right to take something just purely because they want it, to enjoy something simply because they enjoy it. They can hardly ever let themselves take anything for pure pleasure without justifying it on the basis of having earned it or suffered enough to be entitled to it or rationalizing that, though they enjoy it, it is really an altruistic act that they are doing for someone else's good. . . . It seems as if the greatest crime is to do something simply because we enjoy it and without any thought of doing good for anyone else or of serving an absolute need in us that is essential for our continued survival" (Robertiello 1964). Such is the folly born of self-deservingness!

13. Placing a value on a human being tends to sabotage her free will. One has little enough self-direction in the normal course of events!—since even her most "voluntary" activities are significantly influenced by her heredity and environment; and when she thinks that one of her thoughts, feelings, or actions is really "hers," she is ignoring some of its most important biosocial causes. As soon as one labels herself as "good" or "bad," as a "genius" or as an "idiot," she so seriously stereotypes herself that she will almost certainly bias and influence much of her subsequent behavior. For how can a "bad person" or an "idiot" determine, even

to a small degree, what her future actions will be, and how can she work hard at achieving her goals? Moreover, how can a "good person" do nongood acts, or a "genius" turn out mediocre works along with her outstanding ones? What asinine, creativity-downing restrictions one almost automatically places on herself when she thinks in terms of these general designations of her selfness!

14. To give a human an accurate global rating is probably impossible for several reasons:

   a. The traits by which he is to be rated are very likely to change from year to year, even from moment to moment. Man is not a thing or an object, but a process. How can an ever-changing process be precisely measured and rated?

   b. The characteristics by which a person is to be evaluated have no absolute scale by which they can be judged. Traits which are highly honored in one social group are roundly condemned in another. A murderer may be seen as a horrible criminal by a judge but as a marvelous soldier by a general. A man's qualities (such as his ability to compose music) may be defined fine in one century and mediocre in a later age.

   c. To rate a human globally, special weights would have to be given to each kind of positive and negative action that he performed. Thus, if a man did a friend a small favor and also worked very hard to save a hundred people from drowning, his latter act would normally be given a much higher rating than his former act; and if he told a lie to his wife and also battered a child, his second deed would be considered much more heinous than his first. But who is to give an exact weight to his various deeds, so that it could finally be determined how globally "good" or "bad" he is? It might be convenient if there existed on earth some kind of St. Peter, who would have a record of every single one of his deeds (and, for that matter, his thoughts) and who could quickly assess him as a potential angel or as hell-bound. But what is the likelihood of such a St. Peter (even in the form of an infallible computer) ever existing?

d. What kind of mathematics could we employ to arrive at a single, total rating of a human being's worth? Suppose an individual does a thousand good acts, and then she fiendishly tortures someone to death. Shall we, to arrive at a general evaluation of her being, add up all her good acts arithmetically and compare this sum to the weighted sum of her bad act? Shall we, instead, use some geometric means of assessing her "goodness" and "badness"? What system shall we employ to "accurately" measure her "value"? Is there, really, any valid kind of mathematical evaluation by which she can be rated?

e. No matter how many traits of an individual are known and employed for her global rating, since it is quite impossible for her or anyone else to discover all her characteristics and to use them in arriving at a single universal rating, in the final analysis the whole of her is being evaluated by some of her parts. But is it ever really legitimate to rate a whole individual by some (or even many) of her parts? Even one unknown, and hence unevaluated, part might significantly change and, hence, invalidate the final rating. Suppose, for example, the individual is given (by herself or others) a 91 percent general rating (that is, is considered to have 91 percent of "goodness"). If she unconsciously hated her brother most of her life and actually brought about the early demise of this brother, but if she consciously only remembers loving her brother and presumably helping to live happily, she will rate herself (and anyone but an all-knowing St. Peter will rate her) considerably higher than if she consciously admitted her hatred for her brother and causing this brother needless harm. Her "real" rating, therefore, will be considerably lower than 91 percent; but how will this "real" rating ever be known?

f. If an individual is given a very low global rating by herself and others—say, she winds up with a 13 percent general report card on herself—it presumably means that (1) she was born a worthless individual; (2) she never possibly could become worthwhile, and (3) she deserves to be punished (and ultimately roasted in some kind of hell) for being hopelessly worthless. All of these are empirically unverifiable hypotheses which can hardly be proved or disproved and which tend (as stated above) to bring about much more harm than good.

g. Measuring a human being is really a form of circular thinking. If a man is "good" because he has "good" traits, his "goodness," in both instances, is based on some kind of value system that is definitional; for who, again, except some deity, is to say what "good" traits truly are? Once his traits are defined as being "good," and his global "goodness" is deduced from his specific "goodnesses," the concept of his being globally "good" will almost inevitably prejudice one's view of his specific traits—which will then seem "more good" than they really may be. And once his traits are defined as being "bad," the concept of his being globally "bad" will almost inevitably prejudice one's view of his specific traits—which will then seem "more bad" than they really may be. If the "good" traits of a person who is rated as being globally "good" are prejudicedly seen as being "more good" than they really are, one will keep seeing him, by prejudice, as being "good," when he may not actually be. Globally rating him, in other words, includes making a prophecy about his specific "good" traits and rating his specific traits as "good" includes making a prophecy about his global "goodness." Both these prophecies, in all probability, will turn out to be "true," whatever the facts of his specific and general "goodness" actually are; for "goodness" itself can never accurately be determined, since the entire edifice of "goodness" is based, as I have said, on concepts which are largely definitional.

h. Perhaps the only sensible way of making a global rating of an individual is on the basis of her aliveness: that is, assuming that she is intrinsically good just because she is human and alive (and that she will be nongood or nonexistent when she is dead). Similarly, we can hypothesize, if we want to accept redundant and unnecessary religious assumptions, that an individual is good because she is human and because Jehovah, Jesus, or some other deity in whom she believes accepts, loves, or gives grace to all humans. This is a groundless assumption, since we know (as well as we know anything) that the individual who believes in this assumed deity exists, while we have no way of proving the existence (or nonexistence) of the deity in which she believes. Nonetheless, such an assumption will work, in that it will refer back to the more basic assumption that a human is globally "good" just because she is human and alive. The trouble with this basic concept of general human "goodness" is that it obviously puts *all* humans in the same boat—makes them all equally "good" and leaves no room whatever for any of them to be "bad." Consequently, it is a global rating that is not really a rating, and it is entirely definitional and is rather meaningless.

i. The concept of giving any human a general or global evaluation may be an artifact of the inaccurate way in which almost all humans think and communicate with themselves and each other. Korzybski (1933) and some of his main followers, such as Hayakawa (1965) and Bourland (Bourland and Johnson 1991), have pointed out for a good many years that just as pencil$_1$ is not the same thing as pencil$_2$, so individual$_1$ is not the same as individual$_2$. Consequently, generalizing about pencils and about individuals is never entirely accurate. Bourland has especially campaigned, for many years, against our using any form of the verb *to be* when we speak about or categorize the behavior of a person. Thus, it is one thing for us to note that "Jones has (or possesses) some outstanding mathematical qualities" and another to say that "Jones is an outstanding mathematician." The former sentence is much more precise and probably "truer" than the latter. The latter sentence, moreover, implies a global rating of Jones that is hardly warranted by the facts, if these can be substantiated, of Jones's possessing some mathematical qualities. If Korzybski and his followers are correct, as they in all probability (at least to some degree) are, then global terms and ratings of humans are easily made (indeed, it is most difficult for us not to make them) but would better be fought against and transformed into more specific evaluations of their performances, talents, and traits. Such generalized (or overgeneralized) grades exist (since we obviously keep employing them), but it would be much better if we minimized or eliminated them.

j. All of people's traits are different—as apples and pears are different. Just as one cannot legitimately add and divide apples and pears and thereby get a single, accurate global rating of an entire basket of fruit, so one cannot truly add and divide different human traits and thereby obtain a single, meaningful global rating of a human individual.

What conclusions can be drawn from the foregoing observations and deductions about psychotherapy and human value? First, that self-reference and self-evaluation are a normal and natural part of humans. It seems to be much easier for them to rate their self, their being, as well as their performances, than it is for them only to assess, the latter and not the former.

When people do appraise themselves globally, they almost invariably get into trouble. When they term themselves "bad," "inferior," or "inadequate," they tend to feel anxious, guilty, and depressed, to act below their potential level of efficiency, and to falsely confirm their low estimation of themselves. When they term themselves as "good," "superior," or "adequate," they tend to feel forever unsure of maintaining their "goodness," to spend considerable time and energy "proving" how worthwhile they are, but still to sabotage their relations with themselves and others.

Ideally, it would seem wise for people to train themselves, through rigorous thinking about and working against some of their strongest inborn and environmentally bolstered tendencies, to refuse to evaluate themselves at all. They had better continue, as objectively as they can, to assess their traits, talents, and performances, so that they can thereby lead a stronger, pain-avoiding, and satisfaction-filled life. But, for many reasons which are considered in detail in this book, they would do better to also accept rather than rate their so-called self and strive for the enjoyment rather than the justification of their existence. According to Freud (1963), the individual attains mental health when he follows the rule "Where id was, there shall ego be." Freud, however, did not mean by *ego* man's self-evaluating but his self-directing tendencies. According to my own views (Ellis 1962, 2001a, 2001b, 2002, 2003) and the principles of Rational Emotive Behavior Therapy, people attain maximum understanding of themselves and others and minimum anxiety and hostility when they follow the rule "Where ego was, there shall the person be." By *ego*, of course, I mean people's self-rating and self-justifying tendencies.

For humans, as individuals living with other individuals in a world with which they interact, are too complex to be measured, or given a report card. They may be legitimately "valued," in the sense of accepting and abiding by the empirically determinable facts that (1) they exist, (2) they can suffer satisfaction and pain while existing, (3) it is usually within their power to continue to exist and to experience more satisfaction than pain, and (4) it is therefore highly probable that they "deserve" to (that is, had better) go on existing and enjoying. Or, more succinctly stated, people have value because they decide to remain alive and to value their existence. Observations and conclusions other than those based on these minimal assumptions may well be foolishly egocentric and fictional, and in the final analysis human—all too human, but still essentially inhumane.

CHAPTER 5

REBT Diminishes Much of the Human Ego

Self-esteem takes the human ego to arrogant extremes by correctly saying that it exists and incorrectly giving it—your personality—a rating. As I am about to say, you do have an ego or personality and you do normally rate it. Alas!

Not everyone does. I originally took from the Zen Buddhists and from Lao Tsu and his followers the idea that self-rating or ego-rating is misleading and had better not be made. You exist and have self-consciousness but, as Korzybski pointed out in the twentieth century, *you*, your *totality*, is too complex to be rated. The ancient Asians were sometimes a little extreme on this issue and said that ego really didn't exist—or, if it did, you had better abolish it. By doing so, you could become thoroughly enlightened, free from egocentric prejudice, and open to *live*.

I wasn't so sure. Some of the Zen Buddhists—for, remember, they have a number of different sects—seemed to hold that your *desire* was an important *part* of your self or ego, and that to give up ego, you had to surrender desire and to reach *nirvana* or desirelessness. That didn't seem real to me. My ego—which is notably prejudiced—wanted to tame or control my desire but not eliminate it. Some of it, yes; but *all* desire, no. That would include the desire to eat, drink, love, have sex—indeed, the desire to live. Not for me and the rest of the human race!

I still saw that *uncontrollable* desire was indeed ego-centered—and would not work. So I, along with Paul Tillich, the existentialists, Korzybski, and others, looked around for a less radical solution that would make better sense. I finally saw that rating and evaluating was the problem. We had better rate our important parts—our thoughts, feelings, and actions—to see how they helped or hindered us. But—damn it!—we didn't have to rate our *self*, our *being*, our *essence*. Our *self* or *personhood* was too complex to be given a global rating. We could say, for practical reasons, it was "good"—meaning it helped us to live and enjoy. Or we could say that it just didn't *have* to be rated *at all*. Use our self but not rate it!

I started to show my clients (and myself!) how to unconditionally *accept* their ego without rating it—and get the hell on with their lives. I found it *difficult* to do so in many instances, because—like the Zen Buddhists—they were *prone* to rate their egos, had done it for years, often thought it helped them, and didn't see its (to me) obvious harm. I stubbornly persisted with my teaching, relating, empathizing, and experiencing with my clients (and friends), and began to make good headway. I—or my point of view—won; and so did they.

Here it is, forty and more years later, and I am still at it—still (largely) winning. And helping. I speak, I write, I give workshops, I see individual clients, I have REBT groups—mainly to help people stop rating themselves while still evaluating what they think, feel, and do to presumably live more successfully. And I follow my own REBT lead to alleviate my own problems and increase my joy.

I have written many articles and chapters on unconditional self-acceptance (USA). The one that we most recommend at the psychological clinic of the Albert Ellis Institute is this one, "REBT Diminishes Much of the Human Ego." Try it!

Much of what we can call the human "ego" is vague and indeterminate and, when conceived of and given a global rating, interferes with survival and happiness. Certain aspects of "ego" seem to be vital and lead to beneficial results: for people do exist, or have aliveness, for a number of years, and they also have self-consciousness, or awareness of their existence. In this sense, they have uniqueness, ongoingness, and "ego." What people call their "self" or "totality" or "personality," on the other hand, has a vague, almost indefinable quality. People may well have "good" or "bad" traits—characteristics that help or hinder them in their goals of survival or happiness—but they really have no "self" that "is" good or bad.

To increase their health and happiness, Rational Emotive Behavior Therapy recommends that people had better resist the tendency to rate their "self" or "essence" and stick with only rating their deeds, traits, acts, characteristics, and performances. In some ways they can evaluate the *effectiveness* of how they think, feel, and do. Once they choose their goals and purposes, they can rate their efficacy and efficiency in achieving these goals. And, as a number of experiments by Albert Bandura and his students have shown, their *belief* in their efficacy will often help make them more productive and achieving. But when people give a global, allover rating to their "self" or "ego," they almost always create self-defeating, neurotic thoughts, feelings, and behaviors.

The vast majority of systems of psychotherapy seem intent on—indeed, almost obsessed with—upholding, bolstering, and strengthening people's "self-esteem." This includes such diverse systems as psychoanalysis, object relations, gestalt therapy, and even some of the main cognitive-behavioral therapies. Very few systems of personality change, as does Zen Buddhism, take an opposing stand, and try to help humans diminish or surrender some aspects of their egos; but these systems tend to have little popularity and to engender much dispute.

Carl Rogers tried to help people achieve "unconditional positive regard" and thereby see themselves as "good persons" in spite of their lack of achievement. Actually, however, he induced them to regard themselves as "okay" through their having a good relationship with a psychotherapist. But that, unfortunately, makes their *self*-acceptance depend on their *therapist's* acting uncritically toward them. If so, that is still highly *conditional* acceptance, instead of the *un*conditional self-acceptance that REBT teaches.

REBT constitutes one of the very few modern therapeutic schools that takes a stand against ego-rating, and continues to take an even stronger stand in this direction as it grows in its theory and its applications. This chapter outlines the up-to-date REBT position on ego-rating and explains why REBT helps people *diminish* their ego-rating propensities.

LEGITIMATE ASPECTS OF THE HUMAN EGO

REBT first tries to define the various aspects of the human ego and to endorse its "legitimate" aspects. It assumes that an individual's main goals or purposes include: (1) remaining alive and healthy and (2) enjoying himself or herself—experiencing a good deal of happiness and relatively little pain or dissatisfaction. We may, of course, argue with these goals; and not everyone accepts them as "good." But assuming that a person does have a valid "ego," "self," "self-consciousness," or "personality," we may conceive of this as something along the following lines:

1. I exist—have an ongoing aliveness that lasts perhaps eighty or more years and then apparently comes to an end, so that "I" no longer exist.

2. I exist separately, at least in part, from other humans, and can therefore conceive of myself as an individual in my "own" right.

3. I have different traits, at least in many of their details, from other humans, and consequently my "I-ness" or my "aliveness" has a certain kind of uniqueness. No other person in the entire world appears to have exactly the same traits as I have nor equals "me" or constitutes the same entity as "me."

4. I have the ability to keep existing, if I choose to do so, for a certain number of years—to have an ongoing existence, and to have some degree of consistent traits as I continue to exist. In that sense, I remain "me" for a long time, even though my traits change in important respects.

5. I have awareness or consciousness of my ongoingness, of my existence, of my behaviors and traits, and of various other aspects of my aliveness and experiencing. I can therefore say, "I have self-consciousness."

6. I have some power to predict and plan for my future existence or ongoingness, and to change some of my traits and behaviors in accordance with my basic values and goals. My "rational behavior," as Myles Friedman has pointed out, to a large extent consists of my ability to predict and plan for the future.

7. Because of my "self-consciousness" and my ability to predict and plan for my future, I can to a considerable degree change my present and future traits (and hence "existence"). In other words, I can at least partially control "myself."

8. I similarly have the ability to remember, understand, and

71

learn from my past and present experiences, and to use this remembering, understanding, and learning to predict and change my future behavior.

9. I can choose to discover what I like (enjoy) and dislike (disenjoy) and to try to arrange to experience more of what I like and less of what I dislike. I can also choose to survive or not to survive.

10. I can choose to monitor or observe my thoughts, feelings, and actions to help myself survive and lead a more satisfying, more enjoyable existence.

11. I can have confidence (believe that a high probability exists) that I can remain alive and make myself relatively happy and free from pain.

12. I can choose to act as a *short-range* hedonist who mainly goes for the pleasures of the moment and gives little consideration to those of the future, or as a *long-range* hedonist who considers both the pleasures of the moment and of the future and who strives to achieve a fair degree of both.

13. I can choose to see myself as having worth or value for pragmatic reasons—because I will then tend to act in my own interests, to go for pleasures rather than pain, to survive better, and to feel good.

14. I can choose to accept myself unconditionally—whether or not I do well or get approved by others. I can thereby refuse to rate "myself," "my totality," "my personhood" at all. Instead, I can rate my traits, deeds, acts, and performances—for the purposes of surviving and enjoying my life more, and *not* for the purposes of "proving myself" or being "egoistic" or showing that I have a "better" or "greater" value than others.

15. My "self" and my "personality," while in important ways individualistic and unique to me, are also very much part of

my sociality and my culture. An unusually large part of "me" and how "I" think, feel, and behave is significantly influenced—and even created—by my social learning and my being tested in various groups. I am far from being *merely* an individual in my *own* right. My personhood includes socialhood. Moreover, I rarely am a hermit but strongly *choose* to spend much of my life in family, school, work, neighborhood, community, and other *groups*. In numerous ways "I" am "me" and *also* a "groupie"! "My" individual ways of living, therefore, coalesce with "social" rules of living. My "self" is a personal *and* a social product—and process! My unconditional self-acceptance (USA) had better intrinsically include unconditional other-acceptance (UOA). I can—and will!—accept other people, as well as myself, with our virtues *and* our failings, with our important accomplishments *and* our nonachievements, just because we are alive and kicking, just because we are human! My survival and happiness is well worth striving for and so is that of the rest of humanity.

These, it seems to me, are some "legitimate" aspects of ego. Why legitimate? Because they seem to have some "reality"—that is, have some "facts" behind them, and because they appear to help people who subscribe to them to attain their usual basic values of surviving and feeling happy rather than miserable.

SELF-DEFEATING ASPECTS OF THE HUMAN EGO (SELF-RATING)

At the same time, people subscribe to some "illegitimate" aspects of the human "ego" or of self-rating, such as these:

1. I not only exist as a unique person, but as a *special* person. I am a *better individual* than other people because of my outstanding traits.
2. I have a superhuman rather than merely a human quality. I can do things that other people cannot possibly do and deserve to be deified for doing these things.
3. If I do not have outstanding, special, or superhuman characteristics, I am subhuman. Whenever I do not perform notably, I deserve to be devilified and damned.
4. The universe especially and signally cares about me. It has a personal interest in me and wants to see me do remarkably well and to feel happy.
5. I *need* the universe to specially care about me. If it does not, I am a lowly individual, I cannot take care of myself, and I must feel desperately miserable.
6. Because I exist, I *absolutely* have to succeed in life and I *must* obtain love and approval by all the people that I find significant.
7. Because I exist, I *must* survive and continue to have a happy existence.
8. Because I exist, I *must* exist forever and have *immortality*.
9. I *equal* my traits. If I have significant bad traits, *I* totally rate as bad; and if I have significant good traits, *I* rate as a good person.
10. I particularly equal my character traits. If I treat others well and therefore have a "good character," I am a good person; and if I treat others badly and therefore have a "bad character," I have the essence of a bad person.
11. In order to accept and respect myself, I must prove I have real worth—prove it by having competence, outstandingness, and the approval of others.
12. To have a happy existence, I *must* have—absolutely *need*—the things I really want.

The self-rating aspects of ego, in other words, tend to do you in, to handicap you, to interfere with your satisfactions. They differ enormously from the self-individuating aspects of ego. The latter involve *how* or *how well* you exist. You remain alive as a distinct, different, unique individual because you have various traits and performances and because you enjoy their fruits. But you have "ego" in the sense of self-rating because you magically think in terms of upping or downing, deifying or devil-ifying yourself *for* how or how well you exist. Ironically, you probably think that rating yourself or your "ego" will help you live as a unique person and enjoy yourself. Well, it usually won't! For the most part it will let you survive—but pretty miserably!

ADVANTAGES OF EGOISM OR SELF-RATING

Doesn't egoism (or self-rating, or self-esteem) have *any* advantages? It certainly does—and therefore, probably, it survives in spite of its disadvantages. What advantages does it have? It tends to motivate you to succeed and to win others' approval. It gives you an interesting, preoccupying *game* of constantly comparing your deeds and your "self" to those of other people. It often helps you impress others—which has a practical value, in many instances. It may help preserve your life—such as when you strive to make more money, for egoistic reasons, and thus aid your survival by means of money.

Self-rating serves as a very easy and comfortable position to fall into—humans seem to have a biological tendency to engage in it. It can also give you enormous pleasure when you rate yourself as noble, great, or outstanding. It may motivate you to produce notable works of art, science, or invention. It can enable you to feel superior to others—at times, even to feel godlike.

Egoism obviously has real advantages. To give up self-rating completely would amount to quite a sacrifice. We cannot justifiably say that it brings no gains, produces no social or individual good.

DISADVANTAGES OF EGOISM OR SELF-RATING

These are some of the more important reasons why rating yourself as either a good or a bad person has immense dangers and will frequently handicap you:

1. To work well, self-rating requires you to have extraordinary ability and talent, or virtual infallibility. For you then elevate your ego when you do well, and concomitantly depress it when you do poorly. What chance do you have of steadily or always doing well?
2. To have, in common parlance, a "strong" ego or "real" self-esteem really requires you to be above average or outstanding. Only if you have special talent will you likely accept yourself and rate yourself highly. But, obviously, very few individuals can have unusual, geniuslike ability. And will you personally reach that uncommon level? I doubt it!
3. Even if you have enormous talents and abilities, to accept yourself or esteem yourself consistently, in an ego-rating way, you have to display them virtually all the time. Any significant lapse, and you immediately tend to down yourself. And then, when you down yourself, you tend to lapse more—a truly vicious circle!
4. When you insist on gaining "self-esteem," you basically do so in order to impress others with your great "value" or "worth" as a human. But the need to impress others and to

win their approval, and thereby view yourself as a "good person," leads to an obsession that tends to preempt a large part of your life. You seek status instead of seeking joy. And you seek universal acceptance—which you certainly have virtually no chance of achieving!

5. Even when you impress others, and supposedly gain "worth" that way, you tend to realize that you do so partly by acting and falsifying your talents. You consequently look upon yourself as a phony. Ironically, then, first you down yourself for not impressing others; but then you also down yourself for phonily impressing them!

6. When you rate yourself and succeed at giving yourself a superior rating, you delude yourself into thinking you have superiority over others. You may indeed have some superior traits; but you devoutly feel that you become a truly superior person—or semigod. And that delusion gives you an artificial or false sense of "self-esteem."

7. When you insist on rating yourself as good or bad, you tend to focus on your defects, liabilities, and failings, for you feel certain that they make you into an "R.P.," or rotten person. By focusing on these defects, you accentuate them, often making them worse; interfere with changing them; and acquire a generalized negative view of yourself that frequently ends up with arrant self-deprecation.

8. When you rate your *self*, instead of only evaluating the effectiveness of your thoughts, feelings, and actions, you have the philosophy that you *must* prove yourself as good; and since there always exists a chance that you will not, you tend to remain underlyingly or overtly anxious practically all the time. In addition, you may continually verge on depression, despair, and feelings of intense shame, guilt, and worthlessness.

9. When you preoccupyingly rate yourself, even if you succeed in earning a good rating, you do so at the expense of becoming obsessed with success, achievement, attainment, and outstandingness. But this kind of concentration on success deflects you from doing what *you* really desire to do and from the goal of trying to be happy: some of the most successful people actually remain quite miserable.

10. By the same token, in mightily striving for outstandingness, success, and superiority, you rarely stop to ask yourself, "What do I really want—and want for myself?" So you fail to find what you really enjoy in life.

11. Ostensibly, your focusing on achieving greatness and superiority over others and thereby winning a high self-rating serves to help you do better in life. Actually, it helps you focus on your so-called worth and value rather than on your competency and happiness; and consequently, you fail to achieve many things that you otherwise could. Because you *have* to prove your utter competence, you often tend to make yourself less competent—and sometimes withdraw from competition.

12. Although self-rating occasionally may help you pursue creative activities, it frequently has the opposite result. For example, you may become so hung up on success and superiority that you uncreatively and obsessively-compulsively go for those goals rather than that of creative participation in art, music, science, invention, or other pursuits.

13. When you rate yourself you tend to become self-centered rather than problem-centered. Therefore, you do not try to solve many of the practical and important problems in life but largely focus on your own navel and the pseudo-problem of *proving* yourself instead of *finding* yourself.

14. Self-rating generally helps you feel abnormally self-conscious. Self-consciousness, or the knowledge that you have

an ongoing quality and can enjoy or disenjoy yourself, can have great advantages. But extreme self-consciousness, or continually spying on yourself and rating yourself on how well you do, takes this good trait to an obnoxious extreme and may interfere seriously with your happiness.

15. Self-rating encourages a great amount of prejudice. It consists of an overgeneralization: "Because one or more of my traits seem adequate, I rate as a totally adequate person." This means, in effect, that you feel prejudiced against *yourself* for some of your *behavior*. In doing this, you tend also to feel prejudiced against others for their poor behavior— or for what you consider their inferior traits. You thus can make yourself feel bigoted about African Americans, Jews, Catholics, Italians, and various other groups, which include a minority of individuals in a group.

16. Self-rating leads to necessitizing and compulsiveness. When you believe, "I must down myself when I have a crummy trait or set of performances," you usually also believe that "I absolutely *have* to have good traits or performances," and you feel compelled to act in certain "good" ways—even when you have little chance of consistently doing so.

WHY EGOISM AND SELF-RATING ARE ILLOGICAL

In these and other ways, attempting to have "ego-strength" or "self-esteem" leads to distinctly poor results: meaning, it interferes with your life and happiness. To make matters even worse, ego-ratings or self-ratings are unsound, in that accurate or "true" self-ratings or global ratings are virtually impossible to make. For a global or total rating of an individual involves the following kinds of contradictions and magical thinking:

1. As a person, you have almost innumerable traits—virtually all of which change from day to day or year to year. How can any single global rating of you, therefore, meaningfully apply to all of you—including your constantly changing traits?

2. You exist as an ongoing *process*—an individual who has a past, present, and future. Any rating of your you-ness, therefore, would apply only to "you" at single points in time and hardly to your ongoingness.

3. To give a rating to "you" totally, we would have to rate all of your traits, deeds, acts, and performances, and somehow add or multiply them. But these characteristics are valued differently in different cultures and at different times. And *who* can therefore legitimately rate or weight them, except in a given culture at a given time, and to a very limited degree?

4. If we did get legitimate ratings for every one of your past, present, and future traits, what kind of math would we employ to total them? Can we divide by the number of traits and get a "valid" global rating? Could we use simple arithmetic? Algebraic ratings? Geometric ratings? Logarithmic ratings? What?

5. To rate "you" totally and accurately, we would have to know *all* your characteristics, or at least the "important" ones, and include them in our total. But how could we ever know them all? All your thoughts? Your emotions? Your "good" and "bad" deeds? Your accomplishments? Your psychological state?

6. To say that you have no value or are worthless may involve several unprovable (and unfalsifiable) hypotheses: (1) that you have, innately, an essence of worthlessness; (2) that you never could possibly have any worth whatsoever; and (3) that you deserve damnation or eternal punishment for having the misfortune of worthlessness. Similarly, to say

that you have great worth may involve the unprovable hypothesis that (1) you just happen to have superior worth; (2) you will always have it, no matter what you do; and (3) you deserve deification or eternal reward for having this boon of great worth. No scientific methods of confirming or falsifying these hypotheses seem to exist.

7. When you posit global worth or worthlessness, you almost inevitably get yourself into circular thinking. If you *see* yourself as having intrinsic value, you will tend to *see* your traits as good, and will have a halo effect. Then you will falsely conclude that because you have these good characteristics, you have intrinsic value. Similarly, if you see yourself as having worthlessness, you will view your "good" traits as "bad," and "prove" your hypothesized lack of value.

8. You can pragmatically believe that "I am good because I exist." But this stands as a tautological, unprovable hypothesis, in the same class with the equally unprovable (and undisprovable) statement, "I am bad because I exist." *Assuming* that you have intrinsic value because you remain alive may help you feel happier than if you assume the opposite. But philosophically, it remains an untenable proposition. You might just as well say, "I have worth because God loves me," or "I have no value because God (or the Devil) hates me." These assumptions cause you to feel and act in certain ways; but they appear essentially unverifiable and unfalsifiable.

For reasons such as those just outlined, we may make the following conclusions: (1) You do seem to exist, or have aliveness, for a number of years, and you also appear to have consciousness, or awareness of your existence. In this sense, you have a human uniqueness, ongoingness, or, if you will, "ego." (2) But what you normally call your "self" or your "totality" or your "personality" has a vague, almost indefinable quality; and you cannot legitimately give it a global rating or report card. You may *have* good and bad traits or characteristics that help you or hinder you in your goals of survival and happiness and that enable you to live responsibly or irresponsibly with others. But you or your "self" really "aren't" good or bad. (3) When you give yourself a global rating, or have "ego" in the usual sense of that term, you may help yourself in various ways; on the whole, however, you tend to do much more harm than good and preoccupy yourself with rather foolish, sidetracking goals. Much of what we call emotional "disturbance" or neurotic "symptoms" directly or indirectly results from globally rating yourself and other humans. (4) Therefore, you'd better resist the tendency to rate your "self" or your "essence" or your "totality" and had better stick with only rating your deeds, traits, acts, characteristics, and performances.

In other words, you had better reduce much of what we normally call your human "ego" and retain those parts of it which can help you experiment with life, choose what you tentatively think you want to do or avoid, and enjoy what you *discover* is "good" for you and for the social group in which you choose to live.

More positively, the two main solutions to the problem of self-rating consist of an elegant answer and an inelegant one. The inelegant solution involves your making an arbitrary but practical definition or statement about yourself: "I accept myself as good or evaluate myself as good because I exist." This proposition, though absolute and arguable, will tend to provide you with feelings of self-acceptance or self-confidence and has many advantages and few disadvantages. It will almost always work; and will preclude your having feelings of self-denigration or worthlessness as long as you hold it.

More elegantly, you can accept this proposition: "I do not have intrinsic worth or worthlessness, but merely aliveness. I'd better rate my traits and acts but not my totality or 'self.' I fully *accept* myself, in the sense that I know I have aliveness, and I *choose* to survive and live as happily as possible, and with minimum needless pain. I only require this knowledge and this choice—and no other kind of self-rating."

In other words, you can decide only to rate or measure your *acts* and *performances*—your thoughts, feelings, and behaviors—by viewing them as "good" when they aid your goals and values and as "bad" when they sabotage your individual and social desires and preferences. But you can simultaneously decide not to rate your "self," "essence," or "totality" at all. Yes, *at all*!

Rational Emotive Behavior Therapy recommends this second, more elegant solution, because it appears more honest, more practical, and leads to fewer philosophical difficulties than the inelegant one. But if you absolutely insist on a "self"-rating, we recommend that you rate yourself as "good" *merely* because you are alive. That kind of "egoism" will get you into very little trouble!

CHAPTER 6

Some Definitions of Conditional Self-Esteem and Unconditional Self-Acceptance

Although I have largely defined conditional self-esteem (CSE), unconditional self-acceptance (USA), and related self-concepts in my previous chapters, let me be more precise and define them again, together with related concepts.

Almost all definitions of your *self* and how you appraise this *self* are slippery, because they overlap with other distinctions. But let us try to get a few of these definitions straight:

Self. Your total personality. It doesn't have to be appraised or rated, and actually cannot be if we think of it as consisting of all your thoughts, feelings, and behaviors—"good" or "helpful" to you and others, and "bad" or "unhelpful." Since it includes so many— and differing—aspects, you cannot give it an accurate global rating. But, alas, you often do. Be careful!

Conditional self-esteem. A global rating of your you-ness on the basis of your partial rating of your current or past traits. You rate *you*, your *self*, as "good" when you do "good," socially approved things, and as "bad" when you do "bad" things. This rating never is total and final, since your thoughts, feelings, and behaviors are *temporarily* "good" and "bad" and keep changing. But you frequently inaccurately *see* you as "proper" or "improper" when you act "well." You really *can't* do this; but you do!

You can also see your *self* as "mainly good" or "mainly bad." But you frequently don't do so and easily see your *self* as wholly "good" or "bad"—inconsistently! Where does that get you? Confused!

Must you rate your total *self* or *being* at all? No. But just try not to!

Are you what you *do*? No, you are too complex and changing. But you often *think* you are—yes, are—"good" and/or "bad." Why? Because, as Korzybski (1933) and others have pointed out, you often make your generalizations ("I often do bad things") into *overgeneralizations* ("I am a bad person"). And you are *sure* of this. But although you are *a person*, you cannot be (*steadily* be) good or bad.

Nevertheless, when you do a distinctly "bad" act, you often see yourself as a *bad person* and when you do a "good" act, you see yourself as a *good person*. Odd—but you *view* your *behaviors* and your *self* that prejudiced way. And when you pride yourself on having self-esteem, you almost always mean "good, conditional self-esteem." Odd—but that is your usual custom.

Unconditional self-acceptance. You *always, under all conditions*, evaluate your self (your being or your personality) as a *valuable, good person*. (1) Because you are you (and no one else); (2) because you are alive; (3) because you simply *decide* to do so; (4) because you acknowledge your "bad" traits and dislike them but *still* accept yourself *with* these; (5) because you refuse to give any global rating to your you-ness but *only* rate your thoughts, feelings, and actions as "good"—meaning, leading to effective individual and social results; (6) because you believe in some God, who always accepts you with all your failings and has the power to make you a *good person*; (7) because you use some other unconditional form of *total*, persistent *acceptance* of you with all your "good" and "bad" characteristics and performances.

Unconditional self-acceptance is arbitrary, definitional, and yours for the choosing (or nonchoosing). You can have it because you merely decide to have it. Or you can decide to have it for pragmatic reasons, because you think it will probably help you (and others) to have it. You cannot prove empirically that your having it will always and inevitably help you be more effective and happier; but you can prove that *in all probability* it will work better than conditional self-esteem and unconditional self-disesteem (USD).

Unconditional self-disesteem or self-downing. You can choose to believe in original and continuing sin and in your being eternally damned for having it and suffering the torments of hell, but it is not clear why you choose to create it—unless you see it as a temporary state that leads to the ultimate heavenly, glorious redemption. Even then, you can choose to live by this not-so-kind fate—or you can choose to disbelieve in and refuse to live by it. If you really believe that having USD is a choice, I doubt whether you will for any length of time select it. But if you believe that, as a fallible human, you are doomed to choose it but still have a *chance* for redemption, you may—or may not—temporarily choose to believe in it. Probably not—when you have other "better" choices.

If you devoutly believe that self-downing (Hell) is inevitable and will *not* lead to redemption, you can (1) believe it and suffer (accept what you can't change) and make yourself *less* depressed; or (2) you can *give up* that self-sabotaging belief and make yourself *much* less depressed and—what do you know!—even happy. Choose, I suggest, acceptance or nonacceptance of misery. At the very worst, you will die miserably. But you still can have *some* choice.

To believe or not to believe—that is the question! Believing in eternal sin and punishment will lead you to a hellistic existence—unless you fortunately surrender that belief.

Unconditional other-acceptance. Along with USA, you can always choose UOA—unconditional other acceptance. Though all humans are fallible, you can undamningly accept them with their failings and rate them as "good"—just because they are human; or as having "good" and "bad" traits but not being totally good or bad *persons*; or as being *generally* nonratable. Rating *them* as well as their *behaviors* will get you into trouble (deifying or devil-ifying); make you *passively* communicate with them; or make you enraged at them. Rotten choices! UOA allows you to democratically progress from USA to other-acceptance.

Unconditional life-acceptance. Life, as the Buddhists said twenty-four hundred years ago, *isn't* but *includes* suffering. See it as it is, accept the good with the bad, and thereby *enjoy* much of it. Deifying it may well lead to disillusionment; damning it will magnify its hassles. Accept it and enjoy its virtues. You can choose to *only* see its blessings—or to *only* magnify its indubitable pains. You can make it "awful" instead of an intermittent pain in the ass. With UOA, you use your antiawfulizing as well as your awfulizing talents!

Self-efficacy. Albert Bandura and his followers have specialized in investigating self-efficacy which is an important aspect of rating yourself. I could say that I anticipated them by calling it self-mastery or achievement confidence in *Reason and Emotion in Psychotherapy* in 1962 and in clearly differentiating it from self-confidence (as Bandura sometimes does not).

For you to have self-efficacy or achievement confidence means that you know you are able to succeed at important tasks (e.g., school, work, relating) when you try to master them. You feel good about that but you also unfortunately rate your success into self-confidence or conditional self-esteem. You correctly say, "*It* is good that I am able to achieve" and overgeneralize, "Therefore, I am a *good person.*" As Korzybski would have said, this is a mistake. You are a *person who* succeeded in one respect, while a *good person* would practically always have to succeed in all (or certainly most) respects.

Self-efficacy means that you acknowledge the goodness of your achievements. Self-confidence or self-esteem means that you like yourself, your being, because of your mastering certain skills. As Alfred Adler noted, you recognize your superior skill—good!—and see yourself as a *superior person*—not so good!

So in REBT, we congratulate you on your skill and your efficiency, but refrain from designating *you* as "superior." Similarly, when you act inefficaciously, we have you acknowledge that, but never denigrate you for your inefficacy. Quite a difference! Then you can perhaps correct your skill and become more efficacious—but still not a noble person!

CHAPTER 7

The Advantages and Disadvantages of Self-Esteem or Conditional Self-Acceptance

I f, as I am claiming in this book, your achieving self-esteem (SE) or conditional self-acceptance (CSA) has distinct disadvantages, we can expect and predict that it also has many benefits. It has lasted throughout human history and is still prevalent among most of the peoples of the world today. According to evolutionary theory, therefore, it has survival value; and those of us who live "successfully" with it will tend to have progeny who also reap its benefits, thus encouraging its continuation.

The same thing can be said for the survival of unconditional self-acceptance (USA), which has weathered many storms and is still (consciously and unconsciously) alive in the hearts and actions of many of us. Although difficult to define and design, we often crave it—and sometimes partially achieve it—because we figure out that it works. At least, partially! We see real advantages when we adopt it—such as liking our imperfect selves *with* our flaws and thereby making ourselves *less* flawed.

Let us first accept the definitions of self-esteem or conditional self-esteem (CSE) and of unconditional self-acceptance that we described in the previous chapter and then look at many of their "real" benefits and hazards.

In spite of its (later to be described) disadvantages, SE and CSE frequently lead to these gains:

Achievement and productivity. SE says that in order to like yourself, you had better significantly produce and achieve materially (money, success, land, possessions, art, music, literature, and science) and spiritually (religion, purposes, honors, and nonmaterial goals and values). You also must convince other people of your material and spiritual success and thereby enable them to recognize and honor you.

Especially under capitalism, but also under collectivism, achievement and product goals have led to vast material gains over the centuries, and are still doing so. Sometimes these two goals conflict, but often they don't. The Soviet Union was very spiritual (e.g., nationalistic and rabidly atheistic) and *also* very materialistically productive (munitions, steel, factories).

Efforts to control and plan. CSE encourages people to control and plan—in order to rate themselves as "good" or "efficient" individuals (Wittlict, Cudway, and Vanderlaan 2000), again, in both capitalist and collectivist setups. It may be monopolistically at times, but it still pushes production.

Emphasis on physical and mental health. CSA encourages people to admirably succeed in building their physical health (sports) and mental health (purposiveness) and thereby be acclaimed by others.

Self-actualization. Perhaps for the wrong reasons, CSA and its competitiveness urges people to actualize themselves and thereby to be "better people" than nonactualized persons (Cosken 2000).

Educational drive. CSA makes educational goals of parents and children outstanding—to "prove" that they are "superior" people.

Relationship goals. To gain conditional esteem, many couples and families work hard to relate better to each other—and to best other families (Cordura, Jacobson, and Christensen 1998).

Work for present and future. Competitiveness and CSE encourage people to work hard in the present, to not waste time—and to focus on building an approvable future (Zimring 2000).

Appreciation of one's own uniqueness. CSE-induced competitiveness encourages people to appreciate their own uniqueness—in order to be "more unique" than others!

Emphasis on own personal experiences. Conditional self-esteem sometimes overemphasizes self-fulfillment and unique personal experiences and loses sight of group and social involvements and *their* unique satisfactions. It also may encourage personal involvement that leads to contempt for the world (Siegel 2000).

Encouraging altruism. In order to do the "right" things and win approval, people may do altruistic and "good" deeds, and make themselves "holier than thou" (Ellis 2004a, 2004b).

Overfocusing on one's good traits. To make themselves into "good" persons with CSE, people may overemphasize their "outstanding" traits (moneymaking, artistry, sexual competence) and get themselves to lead one-sided lives (Ellis 1962, 2003).

Although I just did my best to list some of the advantages you can get by focusing on conditional self-esteem, I see that I have also included some of its disadvantages. Quite appropriately!—for anything that benefits you and others may also at times harm you and them. Why? Because nothing seems to be *all* good or *all* bad. For you—or anyone.

Now for some of the other side. Conditional self-esteem—liking *you* as a whole when you do some "estimable" deeds—may easily have more dubious than "good" advantages. To name a few:

Increased stress, aggression, and substance abuse. In order to excel at work, school, art, or almost anything, you had better—*even* when you succeed—put yourself under extra stress, anxiety, aggression, substance abuse, and the like. This has good points—it makes life more interesting. But whoa! How much can you and your body—not to mention your soul and your spirit—take? Mental and physical abuse—self-abuse—often follow (Crocker 2002; Ellis 2003a, 2003b).

Pessimism and hopelessness. The more you insist on doing, supposedly to win others' (and your own) approval, the less time and energy you may have for doing *normal* things (Dweck 1994). And since you *have to* produce, to be a "good person," you will often rate yourself "subnormal." Pressure may sometimes help. But *too much* pressure won't!

Conditional self-esteem may lead you to desperately seek social approval to "prove" you are a "good person." Actually, it mainly proves that you are desperate!

CSE may help you and your children to get better grades at school, but not to educate themselves (FitzMaurice 1997; Stout 2000).

CSE leads to awfulizing and self-discontent when you are not outstanding (FitzMaurice 1997).

CSE is not permanent but has to be continually rebuilt (Kruk 1996; Mills 2000).

CSE can easily turn into grandiosity by making you a "better person" (FitzMaurice 1997).

CSE leads to anger, rage, war, and so forth when people do not treat you the way they *should* (FitzMaurice 1997).

CSE encourages you to ignore or excuse your "bad" acts that will make you a "worm" if you admit them (Hauck 1991; Ellis 2003, 2004a).

CSE leads you to ignore how to solve some of your serious problems (Ellis 2004a).

CSE leads you to be very competitive in order to surpass others and be a "good person" (Ellis 2001a, 2001b).

CSE encourages you to be self-centered and narcissistic (Baumeister 1995).

CSA may easily lead you to behave psychopathically (Baumeister 1995).

CSA needs constant propping up (Baumeister 1995).

CSA helps you to present a false front to the world.

CSA helps you panic and panic about your panic (Hayes 1994).

CSA overstresses the "fact" that early childhood criticism makes you self-downing (Ellis 2001a, 2001b).

CSA encourages your procrastination and low frustration tolerance by "showing" that doing something badly is "awful" (Jacobson 1982).

CHAPTER 8
The Proverbs of Solomon and Self-Esteem

A mong the earliest writings on human conduct that include God-given and secular wisdom are the proverbs of Solomon. Some of these proverbs involve conditional self-esteem (CSE) and unconditional self-acceptance (USA), mainly the former. Let us now review the relevant ones, using the Revised Standard Version.

Proverbs 3:5: "Trust in the Lord with all your heart and do not rely on your own insight." The basis of all proverbs is faith in God *and* human wisdom. But, of course, you can choose secular rather than Godly wisdom if you are a nonbeliever in God.

3:29: "Do not plan evil against your neighbor, who dwells trustingly beside you." Social interest is brought in early in the game, and perhaps unconditional other-acceptance (UOA).

3:30: "Do not envy a man of violence and do not

choose any of his ways." Again: "Keep the peace" and implied UOA.

3:35: "The wise shall inherit honor, but fools get disgrace." Conditional self-esteem, not unconditional! *If* you act wisely, you can accept yourself and others will accept you. If not, you will damn yourself and rightly be damned by others—and perhaps by God.

6:3: "For jealousy makes a man furious, and he will not spare if he takes revenge." If you are jealous or envious you will hate others and may kill others. They *shouldn't* have more than you!—and you are right about being vengeful. Obviously, conditional other-acceptance. And others, of whom you are jealous, are not merely wrong, but are to be justly damned for being wrong.

9:7: "He who corrects a scoffer gets himself abuse and he who approves a wicked man incurs injury." This implies UOA: You hate what scoffers do but don't hate *them* and thereby encourage them to hate *you.*

10:22: "Hatred stirs up strife but love covers all offenses." Clear-cut UOA—you hate the sin but not the sinner.

10:27: "The fear of the Lord prolongs life but the years of the wicked will be short." Anti-UOA. You *deserve* to be damned for your sins and the Lord will be sure to roast you in hell. Contradicts Proverb 10:22.

11:2: "When pride comes, then comes disgrace." Very conditional self-esteem! If you are

proud of your accomplishments, you will
hate yourself when you fail to accomplish.

12:15: "The way of a fool is right in his own eyes."
Because he denigrates *himself* for his *errors*
and therefore defensively pretends that they
were not errors.

12:16: "The prudent man ignores an insult."
Because (1) he sees that *words* can't usually
hurt him; (2) he has USA, meaning that he
doesn't blame himself, but only his *behavior*;
and (3) not affecting himself too much by
others' insults, he realizes that insulting them
back would probably get him in trouble.
Mainly, he has USA—which Solomon may
have realized.

14:14: "A perverse man will be filled with the fruit
of his ways and a good man with the fruit of
his deeds." Possibly so; but hardly inevitably.
Justice will often prevail. But Hitler, Stalin,
and Saddam Hussein ruled for many years
before it got going!

14:29: "He who has a hasty temper exalts folly."
Good practical advice. But perhaps Solomon
also saw that if you have a hasty temper, you
quickly globally condemn *all* of a perpe-
trator, not merely her act, and foolishly overgeneralize.

14:134: "Righteousness exalts a nation but sin is a
reproach to any people." Overgeneralization!
Many people actually loved Hitler, Stalin,
and Hussein.

16:5: "Everyone who is arrogant is an abomination

to the Lord; be assured, he will not go unpunished." Clearly, this is conditional other-esteem and damnation for even some small offenses. The Lord is *too easily* offended!

16:22: "Folly is the chastisement of fools." Here Solomon hints at secondary disturbance. You worry about doing well—"I *absolutely must* always do well"—then you make yourself anxious. Then you worry about being anxious. Then you perform badly—because of your double anxiety. Then you blame yourself for doing badly. Worry and blame, blame and worry! Three musts: (1) "I must perform well!" (2) "I must not be anxious about performing well!" (3) "I must not perform badly because of my anxiety about performing!" On and on!

17:1: "Better is a dry morsel with quiet than a houseful of feasting with strife." Good UOA! But this rule mainly sees that strife is bad and does not clearly see that strife follows from damning *people* for not giving you what you want.

18:2: "A fool takes no pleasure in understanding but only in expressing his opinion." Good observation, but it fails to point out that a person who keeps acting foolishly is not a total fool.

From the proverbs just quoted and my comments on them, what can we conclude? First, that Solomon (or his ghostwriters) were accurate observers of people's self-downing and other-downing tendencies, and often recommended practical methods of helping themselves stay out of trouble by keeping their mouths shut and being tactful in criticizing these others. Solomon was something of a conciliator and seemed to realize how deadly honest criticism could be. So he often recommended *seeing* others' faults and flaws but not expressing, to them or to third parties, your observations. This is good social conduct, especially if you realize that many people who act badly, defensively do not admit that they do, and are hostile and vindictive to their detractors.

It is therefore best that you often see others' "wicked" or "wrong" behavior—but shut up about it. A more thoroughgoing tack to take, as the author of Proverbs *sometimes* realized, is to see the profound advantages of the philosophy of unconditional other-acceptance and thoroughly accept others' bad deeds but not their *badness*. You accept the *sinner* but not the *sin*—as Solomon's God, Jehovah, frequently did not do. I don't think that He merely penalized serious culprits to help them change (as we sometimes do in behavior therapy). He also vindictively damned them and gave up on them. He at times did not follow the Christian view of accepting the sinner but not the sin.

Solomon's God—and perhaps Solomon himself—mostly seemed to follow the principle of conditional self-esteem—that is, you act unwisely and you "deservedly" put yourself down, and then may act *more* unwisely. He at times, as I show above, sensed that unconditional self-acceptance had clear-cut advantages over CSE; but he kept slipping back to CSE. Now you see it, and now you don't.

For its day, Solomon's Proverbs made several good points regarding conditional self-esteem, unconditional self-acceptance, and unconditional other-acceptance—but too vaguely and inconsistently! Still pretty good for 1000 BCE!

CHAPTER 9

Lao Tsu and the Philosophy of Humility, Moderation, and Unconditional Acceptance

Over two thousand years ago Lao Tsu saw through the frantic competitive striving of the majority of Chinese people of his day and wrote *Tao Teh Ching: The Choice of the Way and Its Virtue*. He invented an ideal sage or ruler, who consistently followed virtue or nature; and advocated that if people were to model themselves after him, follow the Tao (or way of all things) and realize their true nature, they would embody the virtues of humility, lack of frantic striving, and compassion for others. Lao Tsu's teachings were remarkable in his day and even more unusual considering China's—and the world's—warring history and its contemporary capitalist about-face. Over the years, *Tao Teh Ching* has probably had a greater influence on Asian thought than any other single book, and today is also solidly influencing millions of people in other countries.

The main and consistent theme of Lao Tsu's philosophy seems to be the teaching of peace, open-mindedness, and compassion for other people, even when they behave obnoxiously and warringly.

Thus, we find these endorsements of unconditional other-acceptance (UOA):

"In dealing with others, know how to be gentle and kind" (p. 17).*

"Only he who can do it with love is worthy of being the steward of the world" (p. 27).

"He who knows how to guide a rule in the path of Tao/Does not override the world with force of arms." "You must never think of conquering others by force" (p. 61).

"The peaceful and serene is the norm of the world" (p. 93).

"If only the ruler and his people would refrain from harming each other, all the benefits of the world would accumulate in the kingdom" (p. 123).

"The best way of conquering the enemy/Is to win over him by not antagonizing him" (p. 139).

"The more the Sage lives for others, the fuller is his life" (p. 165).

UOA, then, is quite clearly espoused by Lao Tsu. Because of his poetic language, his endorsing unconditional self-acceptance (USA) is not quite as clear. However, he is consistently opposed to striving for superiority. He abhors boasting of your successes. He says that "racing and hunting madden the mind" (p. 25). He writes, "Abandon cleverness, and the people will be benefited a hundredfold" (p. 39). He says, "The Sage does not make a show of himself" (p. 45). He states, "What you want is efficiently to protect your own stake/But not to aim at self-aggrandizement" (p. 61).

---

*Page numbers refer to *Tao Teh Ching*, trans. John C. H. Wu (Boston: Shambhla, 1961).

Lao Tsu and the Philosophy of Humility, Moderation, and UA

Lao Tsu opposes desire but really seems to mean *need* and *greed*. Thus, "The Sage desires to be desireless" (p. 121). However, he seems to mean, "Don't strive *too hard* to succeed, but strive moderately." Again, he lists among his main treasures, "Not daring to be first in the world" (p. 117). Still again, the Sage "does not exalt himself" (p. 147).

It seems reasonably clear that Lao Tsu sees that conditional self-esteem (CSE), or rating yourself as a *good person* for your *good deeds*, is a distinct human weakness and that unconditional self-acceptance may be a more legitimate approach. However, he does emphasize that being virtuous and following nature's "rightful" path is the way to go—and at times he hints that only this will lead you to accept yourself. This is conditional.

Lao Tsu advocates high frustration tolerance (HFT) in life and says, "The Sage avoids all extremes, excesses, and extravagances" (p. 59). Also, "The full-grown man . . . prefers what is within to what is without" (p. 77). He also opposes low frustration tolerance (LFT) by pointing out, "He who thinks everything easy will end by finding everything difficult" (p. 129). And he advises facing your own disturbability and doing something about it: "The Sage is not sick, being sick of sickness:/This is the secret of health" (p. 145).

Lao Tsu does not quite get to unconditional life-acceptance (ULA) but hints at it by urging his readers to refuse to needlessly stress and strain to make their lives perfect. Life and nature, he keeps insisting, have their own peaceful, spontaneous way. So you'd better accept what you can get and stop whining about your unmet desires. Go with the flow and reap what you can. There is so much out there that you can naturally enjoy that you don't have to frantically push yourself and beat other people to lead a happy existence. With this philosophy, Lao Tsu does a reasonably good job of advocating USA and ULA; and he was remarkably good at advocating UOA. Quite good thinking for two thousand years ago!

CHAPTER 10
Jesus of Nazareth and Self-Esteem

Perhaps the most confusing and contradictory philosophy of conditional self-esteem (CSE) and unconditional self-acceptance (USA) is found in the sayings of Jesus, in the New Testament. This also holds true for the philosophy of damning wrong-doers and severely punishing them—which we can call conditional damnation of others (CDO)—and the opposing philosophy of unconditional other-acceptance (UOA). Back and forth, the pronouncements of Jesus go, so that it is difficult to tell what he *really* believed.

Let me illustrate with the gospel of Jesus according to Matthew, which takes up twenty pages of the New Testament in my 1953 Revised Standard Version and is largely repeated in the Gospels of Mark, Luke, and John.

At the beginning of Matthew, Jesus resists the temptation of the devil, and "from that time Jesus began to preach, saying 'Repent, for the kingdom of heaven is at hand.'" Obviously, those who did not follow God's commandments would, to say the least, suffer (Matt. 4:10; 5:3–10).

Who are righteous, have faith in God, will not suffer, and will enter the kingdom of heaven? Jesus answers: "The poor in spirit," "those who mourn," "the meek, for they shall inherit the earth," "those who hunger and thirst for righteousness," "the merciful," "the pure at heart," "the peacemakers," "those who are persecuted for their righteousness sake," and so forth.

Obviously, according to Jesus, God demands good behavior of people, rewards you greatly when you follow His rules, and gives you clear-cut penalties (banishment from heaven) when you are poor in spirit, unmeek, unrighteous, unmerciful, impure in heart, and unpeaceful. This is distinctly conditional other-acceptance (COA). God and Jesus say that you get what you deserve. It is also, presumably, CSE—you become a "good person" when you follow God's "righteous" rules and you become a "bad person" (who deserves punishment) when you don't. Quite clear!

This double denial of your personhood (by God and by yourself) is continually repeated in Matthew's gospel. Here are some typical instances of Jesus' conditional other-acceptance:

5:19: "Whoever relaxes one of the least of these commandments shall be called least in the kingdom of heaven."

5:22: "But I say to you that anyone who is angry at his brother shall be liable to judgment . . . and whoever says, 'You fool!' shall be liable to the hell of fire."

5:28: "Everyone who looks at a woman lustfully has already committed adultery with her in his heart. If your right eye causes you to sin, pluck it out and throw it away; it is better that you lose one of your members than that your whole body be thrown into hell."

6:52: "All who take the sword shall perish by the sword."

10:34: "Do not think that I have come to bring peace on earth. I have not come to bring peace but a sword."

12:32: "Whoever speaks against the Holy Spirit will not be forgiven, either in this age or in the age to come."

18:8: "If your hand or your foot causes you to sin, cut it off and throw it from you; for it is better for you to enter life maimed or lame than with two hands or two feet to be thrown into the eternal fire."

12:11: When a man came to a wedding without a wedding garment: "The King said to the attendants, 'Bind him hand and foot, and cast him into the outer darkness. There men will weep and gnash their teeth.'"

And so on and so forth. If you sin or even think of sinning—such as thinking of committing adultery—you are to be severely punished. An eye for an eye, and two teeth for a tooth. Now the odd part is that in his day, when practically all Jewish and Gentile law was extremely punitive, Jesus was also at times remarkably tolerant and forgiving. Not only did he fully accept Mary Magdalene, a prostitute, and insure her devotedly coming to his resurrection, but he also advocated and displayed unconditional other-acceptance on many other occasions. Witness these examples:

5:38: "If anyone strikes you on the right cheek, turn to him the other also; and if anyone will sue you and take your coat, let him have your cloak as well."

7:1: "Judge not that you be not judged."

7:12: "So whatever you wish that men should do to you, do so to them."

19:18: "You shall love your neighbor as yourself."

How do we resolve the contradiction that on the one hand Jesus was unjudgmental and forgiving and, on the other hand, so punishing and damning? I really don't know. I suspect that his God,

Jehovah, was the Old Testament God who commanded an eye for an eye, a tooth for a tooth, and that Jesus followed this rule to appeal to those who believed in Jehovah; and/or he lived surrounded by judgmental and terroristic Gentiles and felt that he often had to threaten them with return terror. Be that as it may, he gives us a *choice* of peace or the sword. Liberal Christians today take the choice of accepting and forgiving, while many fanatical conservatives take that of judging and condemning. Jesus' threats and predictions, we could say, were frequently judgmental but his actual way of life was peaceful in a world of stress. Something like the Dalai Lama's today.

Was Jesus also contradictory in his discussion of conditional self-esteem and unconditional self-acceptance? Yes, as far as I can see, he was. To begin with, he explicitly tells you that if you perform "well" and "rightly," you will be rewarded on earth and in heaven; and that, as I pointed out in the first paragraphs of this chapter, if you act badly, God, Jesus, and others will penalize and damn you—because, presumably, you can *choose* to act properly and actually select improper behaviors. Therefore, you absolutely should be punished and desecrated by God, Jesus, and humans.

This is clearly conditional self-esteem and conditional self-damnation (CSD), backed up by conditional other-acceptance. Here are some examples of conditional self-acceptance:

5:48:   "You therefore must be perfect, as your heavenly Father is perfect."

6:24:   "You cannot serve God and mammon."

7:6:   "Blessed is he who takes no offense at me."

9:8:   "Truly I say to you, whatever you bind on earth shall be bound in heaven, and whatever you lose on earth shall be lost in heaven."

Here, on the other hand, is Jesus giving people conditional self-damnation:

7:26: "A foolish man built his house upon the sand; and the rain fell, and the flood came, and the winds blew against the house, and it fell and great was the fall of it."

10:33: "Whoever denies me before men, I also will deny before my Father who is in heaven."

10:38: "He who does not take his cross and follow me is not worthy of me."

13:49: "The angels will come out and separate the evil from the righteous and throw them into the furnace of fire; there men will weep and gnash their teeth."

15:4: "For God commanded, 'Honor your father and your mother,' and 'He who speaks evil of father or mother, let him surely die.'"

26:24: "But woe to that man by whom the son of man is betrayed. It should have been better if he had not been born."

26:32: "Put your sword back into its place; for all who take the sword will perish by the sword."

Throughout the Gospels, we find these contradictory teachings: (1) Be righteous and have faith in Jesus and God and you will definitely reap good rewards. (2) Be unrighteous and have no faith in God and Jesus, and you will be damned on earth and in hell. (3) Be righteous and act properly on earth and you can thereby earn conditional self-esteem. (4) Be unrighteous and act immorally and you will feel deservedly worthless as a person. (5) Others will approve of you for your righteousness and good behavior and will disapprove of you for your unrighteous and improper behavior—conditional other-damning. (6) At times, others may accept you in spite of your poor behavior (UOA). (7) It is not clear that you can always choose to accept yourself even when you behave poorly and when others reject you.

Jesus, then, mainly endorsed conditional self-acceptance and conditional other-acceptance. But at times he gave people unconditional other-acceptance. This was partial acceptance of people in an era when almost everyone else was giving very conditional self-esteem to themselves and to others who acted immorally. But Jesus didn't thoroughly endorse USA and UOA.

In regard to helping people achieve unconditional life-acceptance or high frustration tolerance, Jesus had little to say. Unlike Job, God did not afflict him sorely, test his faith, and finally reward him. He led a good life; and even though he was cruelly crucified, he rightly predicted that he would be resurrected. Just before his death, he cried out, "My God, my God, why hast thou forsaken me?" This may seem to say that unlike Job, he finally lost his faith in the Lord. But not exactly! After his resurrection, he told his disciples: "All authority in heaven and earth has been given to me. Go therefore and make disciples of all nations, baptizing them in the name of the Father and of the Son and of the Holy Spirit."

In the case of Jesus, as with Job, faith in the Lord won out and all was well that ended well. This was a form of high frustration tolerance (HFT) or unconditional life-acceptance (ULA), since Jesus, Job, and other people could bear with the worst kind of troubles knowing that God, if they have devout faith in Him, will miraculously back them up and save them from the devil and everything else.

Marvelous. The catch is that there has to be an all-powerful God, he has to demand absolute faith from you, and then he has to come through with his miraculous support. Slightly unlikely—especially if you are an agnostic or an atheist.

On the contrary, ULA or HFT more practically assumes: (1) Your life, as the Buddhists have said for centuries, has and will most likely continue to have many Adversities. (2) There may be a Higher Power that, if you have great faith in Him, will help you manage and minimize these Adversities. (3) Your having faith in a Higher Power itself may help you minimize and cope with Adversities. (4) If you have no belief in a Higher Power, you still have a *choice* of *disliking* troubles but still *accepting* them and dealing as best you can with them—and this choice will create sorrow and disappointment, which are healthy feelings, about them. (5) Or, instead, you have a *choice* of demanding that serious Adversities *absolutely must not* exist, that they are *awful*, that you *can't stand them*. These views will usually lead to unhealthy feelings of depression, severe anxiety, and rage. (6) With or without your belief in a helpful Higher Power, you can have high frustration tolerance and unconditional life-acceptance. (7) Take your choice!

Although Jesus did not directly address the problem of unconditional life-acceptance (ULA), other religious leaders, such as Solomon and Paul Tillich, do manage to do so—to trust in God and keep their powder dry!

CHAPTER 11
Spinoza and Nietzsche and Self-Esteem

Among the classic philosophers who wrote influentially on self-esteem were Benedict de Spinoza and Friedrich Nietzsche. Both are not easy to interpret clearly, since Spinoza was a near-atheist who took refuge in pantheism, to ward off being persecuted by true believers; and Nietzsche was a poet, rabble rouser, and humorous attacker of his own views, so it is hard to say exactly what his diatribes meant. But let us try!

First, let me quote from *A Spinoza Reader*, which contains Spinoza's *Ethics* and all his other important writings (Spinoza 1994).

"This sting to do something (and also to omit doing something) solely to please men is called ambition" (p. 168).

Here Spinoza seems to say that self-efficacy is good; but when you use it solely in your own interest and against others, you take it to illegitimate, reputation-seeking extremes. Its virtue then becomes an obsessive hazard.

"When the mind considers itself and its power of acting, it rejoices, and does so more, the more distinctly it imagines itself and its power of acting" (p. 182).

Self-efficacy is good and leads to greater power—if it is *honestly* appraised.

"Joy arising from considering ourselves is called self-love or self-esteem" (p. 182).

This is okay when self-esteem is objective appraisal of your ability but not okay when you push it too far and it leads to conflict with others. Spinoza seems to be saying that "normal" self-efficacy *rightly* leads to self-esteem but he fails to point out that honest self-inefficacy leads to self-disesteem and hence to anxiety. No matter how honest your self-efficacy is, you are still saying, "It makes me a *better person*, so I *have to be* efficacious."

"Pride is an affect or property of self-love. Therefore, it can also be defined as *love of oneself*, or *self-esteem—in so far as it* affects a man that he thinks more highly of himself than is just." (p. 192).

Spinoza may mean here that if you love your *self*, you love *all* of *you* legitimately when only a *part* of you is efficacious. He then points out that if you imagine that you are *not* efficacious, "as long as he imagines that he cannot do this or that, he is not determined to do it and consequently it is impossible for him to do it." He beautifully sees that your prophecy—"I can't play tennis well"—becomes self-fulfilling and *makes you* unable to play well. He could have also predicted that your not playing well, when you think that you *have* to do so, will make you deprecate about your total self as well as your tennis ability. Your *self*-esteem when you succeed at something *implies* self-deprecation when you fail. Spinoza almost, but not quite, sees this—that self-esteem *includes* self-deprecation.

"Love and desire can be excessive" (p. 223).

Spinoza seems to say that love and desire are good (if "normal") but if you love winning *too much* you include (1) "I have to win!" and (2) "I have to win to be a *good person.*" Excessive, necessitous desire then leads to your rating your success *too* highly and your rating your *performance* and your *self* too lowly. Spinoza seems to have turned your *desire* for success into a dire (excessive) *need* for it. Your *neediness* then leads you to rate your desire as *necessary* and potentially *self*-downing. If you *only* desired and never needed success and approval, you could never *be worthless* for failing. But you easily *need* love and can hate *yourself* as well as your performance when you fail to get it.

"Shame contributes to harm only in those things which cannot be hidden" (p. 242).

If you are *honestly* ashamed of your acts, you are *sad* about them but not ashamed or self-damning. Because you are presumably telling yourself, "I did the wrong thing and am sad that I did it (which REBT calls a *healthy* negative feeling) but you are not telling yourself (excessively) "I did the wrong thing, which I *absolutely should not have done*, and I am therefore *no good* for doing it." Your willingness to *admit* your mistake defines *it* as bad but not *you* as a bad person who *absolutely must not* err. You *accept* your error but not your *self* as bad by sticking to the *desire* not to err but surrendering your *demand* to be perfect. Again, merely *desiring* to do well and not *insisting* on doing so does not absolve you or your "crime" but does absolve you of your *self*-loathing.

"Blessedness is not the reward of virtue, but virtue itself, nor do we enjoy it because we restrain our lusts; on the contrary, because we enjoy it, we are able to restrain them" (p. 204).

Here Spinoza *defines* enjoying and virtue as *being* virtuous—as a sort of thing-in-itself. But we are taught, socially, what is "virtuous" and then, if we follow that teaching, we (1) like our actions (or inactions) and (2) overgeneralizedly like *ourselves* for acting virtuously.

From the foregoing statements, we can surmise that Spinoza made some pioneering observations about self-efficacy, self-esteem, and self-acceptance and seemed to see real disadvantages in your excessively and generally liking your effectiveness and raising your joy in *it* to joy in your *self*. He was by no means opposed to "normal" self-esteem and self-downing as long as you did not take it to "unreasonable" extremes. But I doubt whether he clearly saw all the harm, and especially the anxiety, that results from almost any degree of your global self-rating.

In regard to your achieving unconditional other-acceptance (UOA), Spinoza was somewhat clearer. Witness these statements in *A Spinoza Reader*.

"The striving to do evil to him [another person] is called anger; and the striving to return an evil done is *called* vengeance" (p. 176).

"Hatred is increased by being returned, but can be destroyed by love" (p. 177).

Both anger and vengeance are your *choices* when someone harms you. You can choose to *accept* this harm gracefully and to replace it with love. You have some *control* over your feelings of hatred.

"We are a part of Nature, which cannot be conceived adequately through itself without other individuals" (p. 239).

Presumably, our nature is to exist in the world and to exist *with* other people. So we'd better take both our personal being *and* our social being into our living.

"Nothing can agree more with anything than other individuals of the same species" (p. 240).

You use your reason to get along with other humans—and maybe other animals.

"Though men generally direct everything according to their own lust, nevertheless more advantages than disadvantages follow from their forming a common society" (p. 241).

Spinoza obviously saw the practical advantages of unconditional other-acceptance. Just as I saw them three centuries later!

"We do not have an absolute power to adapt things outside of us to our use. Nevertheless, we shall bear calmly those things which happen to us contrary to what the principles of our advantage demands" (p. 244).

Here we see that Spinoza not only adopted UOA but also ULA—unconditional life acceptance.

All told, he figured out—using reason—the basic principles, if not the precise details, of USA, UOA, and ULA. Pretty good for the seventeenth century!

Nietzsche, in the late nineteenth century, did fairly well, too, with some aspects of USA, UOA, and ULA. But what he *really* meant by his poetic exclamations is often not clear. Let us try some of them selected from *The Portable Nietzsche* (1959) and translated by Walter Kaufmann.

"Do I recommend love of the neighbor to you? Sooner I should even recommend flight from the neighbor and love of the farthest" (p. 173).

Not very chummy, that time!

"Dead are all gods now that we want the overman to live!" (p. 191).

Certainly unconventional and courageous. But the overman concept pushes superiority to the hilt and is most undemocratic.

"Has he unlearned the spirit of revenge and all gnashing of teeth?" (p. 253).

Ah—against anger and presumably for unconditional other-acceptance.

"The lust to rule: The scoulding scourge of the hardest among the hard-headed" (p. 300).

Presumably against extreme self-esteem brought on by conquest.

"Indeed I committed adultery and broke my wedlock, but first my wedlock broke me" (p. 322).

Marriage is *too* restricting; it *deserves* adultery; why compromise? Not exactly UOA!

"O will, cessation of all need, my own necessity" (p. 326).

Perhaps—I am not sure—Nietzsche is saying that you'd better want without needing. Then you have strong will but can still be free. Strong *desire* is okay but *need* is a weakness leading to anxiety.

"What is bad? But I have said this already: all that is born of weakness, of envy, of revenge" (p. 646).

Strength and power are good and so, presumably, are achievement and self-esteem for having achievement. Conditional self-esteem once more seems to win out.

All told, Nietzsche presents a mixed bag. He is courageously rebellious in spite of much opposition and he will fight for what he thinks is right. But he often seems to condemn himself and other *people* for their weak *performances*; and though he is against anger and vindictiveness, he is for scorn, for putting people down. He favors self-efficacy but strongly implies it makes you a good *person*. Unconditional acceptance of himself and others he never quite sees. They are annihilated by power struggles. His translator and backer, Walter Kaufmann, pictures him as a would-be empiricist but still very much of a romanticist. Often, his realism and his romanticism conflict, so that he tries to be thoroughly enlightened but doesn't quite make it. Or half makes it.

It is interesting that Carl Rogers, like Nietzsche, was a romanticist, believed in honesty, and thought that people in the long run might have honest justice. But Nietzsche and Rogers partly ignored the powerful human urges to deflect honest appraisal of oneself and others into the *need* for others' approval and for accepting themselves *because* their leader or therapist loved them. They didn't quite see that you could accept yourself even when significant others did *not* fully accept you. That neat—and *totally* honest—trick was not in their vocabulary!

CHAPTER 12

Søren Kierkegaard and Self-Esteem

Søren Kierkegaard was something of a genius at making himself anxious. He revealed his problems, but only "solved" them by falling back on complete faith in God and Christianity. This I would say is a distinctly inelegant solution—particularly for atheists like myself. However, his brilliant thinking about anxiety resulted in several pioneering existentialist views. He also led an exemplary life; and though he hardly achieved unconditional self-acceptance (USA), he largely did espouse and achieve unconditional other-acceptance (UOA).

If we investigate his two semiclinical masterpieces, *Fear and Trembling* (1843) and *The Sickness Unto Death* (1848), we find the following statements about anxiety and despair that are relevant for our discussion of USA and UOA.

"Only in the infinite resignation do I become clear to myself with respect to my eternal validity; and only then can there be any question of grasping existence by virtue of faith" (p. 59).*

In *Fear and Trembling*, Kierkegaard talks about Abraham's most difficult dilemma of obeying God's command to sacrifice his son, Isaac, or to dishonor God's command by saving his beloved son, whom God has miraculously given him after fifty years of Sarah's bearing him only daughters. Kierkegaard also presents his great personal problem of totally resigning his love for Regina, who married another man, when she was betrothed to him.

In both cases, Kierkegaard "solves" the dilemma by having Abraham and himself have absolute faith in God, to become resigned to this faith, and to give up Regina—as well as give up guilt in case God is displeased. This seems to me to be a cop-out. If Søren Kierkegaard truly achieved unconditional self-acceptance, he could tell himself, "God exists and I have absolute faith in Him and think He will make everything turn out fine no matter what I do. So even if I thoroughly displease God, I can always accept my wrong *choice* of doing so and feel that my *act* is wrong but I am never a damnable person for committing it. So, unlike Abraham, I'll choose saving Isaac and displeasing God and *still* totally accept myself with this wrong act; and as myself, I'll give up Regina, perhaps foolishly, but again accept myself with this foolish 'good' behavior."

Kierkegaard—and Abraham—could thereby do practically *anything* and still be guilty of doing the "wrong" thing but still not damning themselves. Kierkegaard does this trickily by having complete faith in the Christian God who somehow is *always* "right" and "forgiving"—yes, even when He sadistically asks Abraham to sacrifice Isaac and when Kierkegaard foolishly favors giving up Regina instead of trying once again to win her.

---

*Page numbers refer to *Fear and Trembling*, trans. Walter Lowrie (New York: Doubleday Anchor Books, 1954).

The elegant existential choice here is to do the "wrong" thing (if it turns out to be so) but *never* damn yourself—which is USA. Faith in God and Christianity *assumes* that God *can* do no real wrong, that He himself will accept a sinner but not Abraham's or Kierkegaard's sin, and almost miraculously, God will make things turn out "all right" even when foolish and "wrong" choices are made by humans.

Pure or elegant USA accepts the *human* at all costs because it—or the human—*decides* to do so. Faith-inspired USA, like Kierkegaard's—accepts the human's acceptance of God at all costs, even when He is possibly wrong and sadistic. Kierkegaard's "solution" is inelegant because it gratuitously assumes that there *is* an all-knowing God and that He can make mistakes, but never be damnable. So it has two gratuitous assumptions, while more human-inspired USA doesn't require them.

"The ethical as such is the universal, and as the universal applies to everyone. It applies every instant" (p. 64).

Here is where Kierkegaard, with his absolutist faith, gets into trouble. If ethics is universal, and applies to everyone every instant, we humans have no choice of being right or wrong. Once an ethical rule is established, we have to be right or wrong by its dictates. We can *choose* to follow or not follow these dictates, but cannot argue with them. So we are always right or wrong. This, as Alfred Korzybski said, is a ridiculous overgeneralization. In our *human* lives, we do thousands of deeds under many different conditions. Therefore, there *can* be no absolute ethics—except for angels and God. If Abraham kills Isaac at *God's request*, he is *always* right and ethical *under this condition*. So he has no ethical problem. But under *another* condition—say, he kills Isaac because he doesn't like his looks—he might be said to be quite wrong. Ethics have to be set up according to conditions which *make them* right or wrong. But conditions always, like all things, change. They are *not* universal, and obviously cannot be. So under God's conditions—which he *on faith* accepts—Abraham had better do what God says and sacrifice Isaac. How the hell is he going to make different conditions? No way! Solution—sacrifice Isaac and be done with it!

The condition that Abraham *dearly loves* Isaac is a profound one, but is not a universal condition. It is a *particular* (chosen) one. So, according to this ethical rule, it is *desirable* but not *universal*. Okay, then, pity poor Isaac and poor Abraham for Abraham's having this *personal* choice. But as long as it is personal and not universal, down with Isaac!

Of course, we could establish another "universal" rule: "No father under any condition should kill his own son."

Now we—certainly Abraham—would be in real trouble. For the two "universal" rules conflict: (1) "God's commands must always be obeyed." (2) "Abraham must never kill his own son." No resolution here!

This tends to prove that universal rules of ethics absolutely must be always followed; and that these rules must never conflict with other universal rules of ethics. Now where the hell are we? Nowhere.

Obviously, we had better have ethical rules—and sometimes strict ones. But we set them up because we believe that they will do more good than harm; and as time and conditions go by, we had better modify and sometimes eliminate them. Otherwise, as in Kierkegaard's case, we create many problems—and few resolutions. The beauty of our devising and following USA, UOA, and ULA is that they make ethical problems minimal—as they preferably should be—and their solutions much easier. Kierkegaard gets himself into almost interminable ethical problems by not really following the notion of unconditional acceptance.

"Abraham acts by virtue of the absurd, for it is precisely absurd that he as the particular is higher than the universal" (p. 67).

Actually, the universal is absurd, practically never exists, and cannot be rigidly followed. Let us change it to something like: "Under many conditions, some general moral rules can be set and followed and they often do more good than harm. But not *rigidly* and *universally* followed. *Tentatively* set and carefully followed to determine under what conditions at what times they seem to lead to more good than harm."

If we examine *The Sickness Unto Death*, we see another religious "solution" to Kierkegaard's problem of anxiety and despair. Here are some of his observations and my comments.

"There lives no one outside of Christendom who is not in despair, and no one in Christendom, unless he be a true Christian, and if he is not quite that, he is somewhat in despair after all" (p. 155).*

Despair seems to be universal and only true Christendom can remove it—maybe! This seems to be circular thinking. The power behind us all is faith in Christianity—and without that we have despair. Only pure Christian faith, which is rare, saves us. But the nature of humans is to doubt—and to doubt one's doubt. No wonder we have despair!

"Despair . . . is quite universal" (p. 159).

But Kierkegaard forgets to add: "if you believe it is, and if you *demand* that you must get what you want and that you *absolutely*

---

*Page numbers refer to *The Sickness Unto Death*, trans. Walter Lowrie (New York: Doubleday Anchor Books, 1954).

must not experience despair." He forgets to note that *you create* despair with absolute musts, shoulds, and oughts. You probably can live without it if you *stick to* preferences.

> "Sin is, after having been informed by a revelation from God what sin is, then before God in despair not to will to be oneself, or before God in despair to will to be oneself" (p. 227).

You can't win! When God tells you what to do and what not to do, and you choose (will) to not be yourself, or to be yourself, you suffer. God asks you to be yourself—whatever, exactly, that is—and won't accept you if you say yes or no for this demand. But somehow, if you have absolute faith in Him, you win. How, I am not sure!

> "By relating itself to its own self and by willing to be itself, the self is grounded in the Power which constituted it. And this formula, again, as has often been noted, is the definition of faith" (p. 262).

Let's see if we can unravel this. (1) God is the supreme power that lets you have (or not have) faith. (2) He wants you to have total faith in Him and His power. (3) If you choose to have faith in Him, your faith gives you the power—Godly power—to *be* yourself. (4) Then, your faith somehow lets you get by without despair. So you *are* yourself (with God's permission) and your faith in Him lets you (a) be yourself, right or wrong, and (b) makes you regardless free from despair. (5) Everything finally turns out all right—presumably because you took a great risk—a leap into faith—which allows you to be you and to have a great ally—God.

I think—but am not sure how—you can at one and the same time be fallible you and also be Godly. But if you have enough faith that you can be, you damned well can accomplish this miracle. Catch-22: Yes, you made it but only with miraculous faith. Your *choice* of faith provides you with this miracle. Otherwise, you are in profound contradiction with you, God, and the universe.

Now, using REBT, and forsaking all miracles, you could solve your problem as follows: (1) knowing that you (and possibly God) have contradictory goals and values, you choose one set of values that seems to be the greater good or the lesser evil. (2) You know your choice may be wrong—have great disadvantages—but you still make it. (3) You decide that even if there is a God, He accepts your good and bad choices (and His own) because even God is contradictory and fallible. (4) So you *and* God accept your limitations, and you *both* decide on unconditional self-acceptance with these limitations. (5) Why? Because your goal *is* USA and consequent lack of damnation—for you and for your possible God. And the only way you can get it is to *stop* damning anyone. (6) So you pick what you *think* is the greater good or lesser evil and you live with it. You *decide* to suffer with it but you never damn yourself (or God) for your stupidly flipping the coin wrongly and thereby suffering. You *accept* you, God, and the universe *with* your mistaken choices. You dislike your mistakes but never damn anyone for them.

With the foregoing steps, you choose USA, UOA, and ULA. You thereby surrender certainty and infallibility. And you lead a *reasonably* happy life. Imperfectly!

If you want to retain some kind of God, you can do so—but of course don't *have to* do so—by redefining Him (or Her) as *somewhat* fallible. I think that does it. If you want to dispense with God, you can keep a good deal of faith in imperfection, fallibility, and uncertainty—and therefore in *you*.

In the story of Genesis, Abraham can choose to follow God's command and kill his son, Isaac, or to save Isaac and antagonize

God. He decides to kill Isaac; and because God really wanted to test his faith and because he has now shown remarkable faith in God, God considers Abraham's *intention* to constitute great faith, and because of this "proven" faith lets Abraham off the hook.

According to Abraham's perception of God and the cruel dilemma God has placed him in, he rationally decides to kill Isaac because: (1) He knows God is powerful and could punish or kill him if he doesn't sacrifice Isaac. He has *faith* in God's command. (2) He dearly loves Isaac but also loves his own life perhaps a little more. (3) He fully accepts God with His cruelty. (4) If he decides to save Isaac, God may naturally kill Abraham, but—quite likely!—Isaac, too. So Abraham acts quite sensibly by choosing what he thinks is the lesser evil. By luck it turns out to be good!

God, however, has serious emotional problems: (1) He not only desires Abraham's faith, he *absolutely needs it*. He's insecure! (2) If Abraham doesn't provide him with the faith he needs, God well may sadistically kill him. (3) God really doesn't intend to knock off Abraham but to test his faith. So He lies to him and—ironically—has bad faith. (4) The dilemma God presents to Abraham will, to say the least, help him become exceptionally anxious. (5) God is *not* unconditionally accepting Abraham but proves that he is largely a God of vengeance.

If Abraham used REBT philosophy some five thousand years before it was invented, he could have acted unusually sensibly by: (1) hating God's edict but unconditionally accepting Him with His fiendish cruelty. (2) Perhaps choosing the lesser evil by realizing his days were going to end soon, and Isaac might live a long time more, and therefore choosing to save Isaac and not himself. (3) See that God's edict was indeed highly unjust and annoying, but not define it as *awful* and *terrible*. (4) Kill himself rather than kill Isaac. (5) Figure out some other possible "good" solutions.

The point is: By unconditionally accepting himself, God, and grim conditions, Abraham—and Søren Kierkegaard—would still have a serious problem, but make himself much better able to cope with it—without his making himself panicked!

Following through with several of Kierkegaard's statements in Walter Lowrie's translation of *The Sickness Unto Death*, we find these questionable views:

"Consciousness is the decisive characteristic of despair" (p. 134).

No, it is consciousness *plus* the dogmatic *beliefs* that life *must* not be as difficult and as contradictory as it often is; that you *absolutely should* have certain *good* solutions for the problems it presents; and that faith in God will offer great solutions to its dilemmas.

"All Christian knowledge, however strict its form, ought to be anxiously concerned; but this concern is the note of the edifying. Concern emphasizes relationship to life" (p. 142).

Yes, but Kierkegaard didn't quite see that anxiety and the sickness unto death result from *over*concern and the demand for certainty and safety of which it consists.

"'Either Caesar or nothing.' . . . Precisely because he did not become Caesar he now cannot endure to be himself" (p. 152).

No, he is convinced that he *must* be outstanding and that since he absolutely *must be*, and obviously is not, he only has *conditional* self-esteem (CSE), which is always very shaky.

"There lives not a single man who after all is not to some extent in despair" (p. 154).

Yes, because we all *to some extent* must have *guaranteed, continual* success. Or else . . . !

"The opposite of sin is faith" (p. 213).

Pretty good for 1849! Today we have considerable evidence that if you have profound faith in God or the devil, it can give you a sense of self-efficacy, even when it is false. Your *belief* in God or the devil can temporarily help you. But look out for disillusionment!

"The lowest form of offense declares that Christianity was a falsehood and a lie. It denies Christ. . . . In this denial of Christ as the paradox there is naturally implied the denial of everything Christian: sin, the forgiveness of sin" (p. 262).

Here Kierkegaard, who is often tolerant of dissenting views, becomes absolutely intolerant. He keeps talking about sin and forgiveness, but doesn't really forgive those who honestly disbelieve in Christ and Christianity. Although at times he has unconditional other-acceptance, in regard to faith in God, Christ, and Christianity he loses it. To not pass any judgment on Christ—to not care whether or not he existed, to let all about Christ to passively remain in doubt, or to deny everything Christian—all these views are sin; since thou *shalt* follow the ten commandments, none of them are truly forgiven. Damnation still impends; and if you don't *really* have Christian faith, you will end up with despair. Kierkegaard goes so far with unconditional other-acceptance. Then he stops.

CHAPTER 13

Martin Buber and Self- and Other-Acceptance

O f all the theories of unconditional acceptance, Martin Buber's seems to particularly emphasize the *I-Thou* relationship and thereby favors your gaining "true" or "spiritual" self-acceptance *through* "true" other-acceptance. But does it? Like Nietzsche, Buber was a poet and something of a mystic—so we never can be sure of some of his goals, purposes, and meanings. But let us try.

Let us take Buber at his own words:

"The primary word *I-Thou* can only be spoken with the whole being. The primary word *I-It* can never be spoken with the whole being" (p. 3).*

This looks like romantic perfectionism—which is native to poets and idealists. When you think, feel, and act *I-Thou*, you are convinced that you *totally* do so. That is, you *entirely* acknowledge

---

*Page numbers refer to *I and Thou*, trans. Ronald Gregor Smith (New York: Scribners, 1958).

the personhood of others and only *secondarily* acknowledge your trying to master it, the world, and yourself. This is probably an illusion, since you, the acknowledged person, cannot (as I shall show later) be separated from *your* acknowledgment and feeling. So *I-Thou* is what you *also* but not *only* think and feel. *I-It* (being in and reacting to the outside world—and to your *own* feelings) seems to *always* and *also* be there. You may *like* to only and completely acknowledge *I-Thou*, since you recognize the one-sided dangers of being too self-centered. But can you *really* totally split your *I-Thou* from your *I-It*? I—and soon Buber—say no.

"The man who experiences has not part in the world. For it is 'in him' and not between him and the world that the experiences arise" (p. 5).

As I said in the previous paragraph, you, the acknowledged person, feel and cannot be separated from your thoughts and feelings about the world. Buber then says, "As *experience*, the world belongs to the primary word *I-It*. The primary word *I-Thou* establishes the world of relation." Both/and, as my friend Alfred Korzybski would say; not either/or.

"In each *Thou* we address the eternal *Thou*" (p. 6).

Yes, when we are *conscious*. When we are not conscious—in a stupor, for instance, or even a dreamless sleep—our awareness of the *Thou* is hardly eternal. It returns to consciousness—but not (in all probability) when we are dead.

"Let no attempt be made to separate the strength from the meaning [of my relation with a tree]. Relation is mutual" (p. 8).

Like hell it is! The tree doesn't give a shit for me! I-It is related to my meanings, because I give it meaning. But it doesn't relate actively to me.

"The *Thou* meets me through grace—it is not found by seeking" (p. 11).

No, I am *with* other people but I don't really *accept* them except by *deciding* to do so and working very hard to implement my decision. No one and nothing *give* me *Thou*. I *manufacture* it.

"The present arises only in virtue of the fact that the *Thou* becomes present" (p. 12).

No—even alone on a desert island I have a present with *I-It*—water, trees, stones, food, and so forth.

"Love is responsibility of an *I* for a *Thou*" (p. 14).

Or for objects, events, consciousness, and the like.

"All who love . . . venture to bring [themselves] to the doubtful point—to love *all men!*" (p. 14).

Some trick! You can *accept* all people, even those you dislike. But *love* them? Hardly!

"So long as love is 'blind,' that is, so long as it does not see a *whole* being, it is not truly under the sway of the primary word of relation" (p. 16).

Here Buber seems to espouse unconditional other-acceptance

(UOA). You accept the *whole* person—yes, but not some of her thoughts, feelings, and actions. Again, this is clearly UOA.

> "Whenever the sentence, 'I see the tree' is so uttered that it no longer tells of the relation between the man—*I*—and the tree—*Thou*—but establishes the perception of the tree as object by the human consciousness, the barrier between the object and object has been set up. The primary word *I-It*, the word of separation, has been spoken" (p. 23).

Here Buber becomes tricky. You can see a tree as an *object*, and not relate to it—but *how*, I am not sure. Seeing it *is* (a) partly creating it and (b) therefore having *some* relationship to it. You never quite see it purely objectively. Even on a desert island, you evaluate it in relation to your own goals—for example, climbing it or trying to get fruit from it. Seeing it as a *pure* object seems most unlikely!

> "Only when things, from being our *Thou*, become our *It*, can they be coordinated. The *Thou* knows no system of coordination" (p. 31).

Why not? We order and relate to people we encounter—some love us and some don't. This may be more complicated than ordering trees, but we still do it. *Thou* is not *pure* relating—it is *varied* and *changing* relating.

> "The particular *Thou*, after the relational event has run its course, is *bound* to become an *It*. The particular *It*, by entering the relational event, may become a *Thou*" (p. 33).

Confusing! Does the *Thou* ever truly become nonrelational—or, perhaps, less relational? Does the particular *It*, though related to the individual, ever *itself* relate to the individual?

Martin Buber and Self- and Other-Acceptance

"Without *It* man cannot live. But he who lives with *It* alone is not a man" (p. 34).

He is not a *full* man or human, but he still lives—as shown by the existence of several feral children.

"Man lives in the spirit, if he is able to respond to his *Thou*. He is able to if he enters into a relation with his whole being. Only in virtue of his power to enter into a relation is he able to live in the spirit" (p. 34).

A prejudiced view that equates your spirit with your *Thou*. But again, on a desert island you could *spiritedly* relate to food, animals, and trees. Without other humans, you could *still* have a vital absorbing interest in animals and things. Maybe, not easily; but you could!

"True marriage always arises [out of] the revealing by two people of the *Thou* to one another" (p. 45).

Prejudice again! As I said in my first book, *The Folklore of Sex*, in 1951, all love is really "true" love—because it exists. It may well be "better" love when two people reveal their *thou* to one another. But passionate unrequited love, or even intense love of nature, can be *true* and *real*.

"The man to whom freedom is assured . . . knows that his mortal life swings by nature between *I* and *Thou*" (p. 52).

Normally, yes. He is born and reared with tendencies toward *I*-ness and *Thou*-ness and almost invariably lives in a social group. He can obsess about *I*-ness or *Thou*-ness—to some extent—but rarely survives well if he does.

"To be free from belief that there is no freedom is indeed to be free" (p. 58).

Good point! ULA, unconditional life-acceptance, means that you accept the fact that you are never really free from Adversities. Otherwise, they will strike you and your *belief* that they must not exist will make you miserable. They *will* exist—*accept* that.

If you give your pupil an *I-Thou* relation, you must practice inclusion; but you must also awaken in him "the *I-Thou* relationship as well." But by your special relationship with him if he also practiced inclusion, "It is plain that the specific educative relation as such is denied full mutuality" (pp. 132–33).

This seems to say that perfect, mutually practiced *I-Thou* is not possible. Further, if you are a therapist, you cannot have the client include you. "Healing, like educating, is only possible to one who lives over against the other, and yet is detached." So *mutual I-Thou* is limited. I think Buber is saying that the very best *I-Thou* had better be *accepted* as partially one-sided; and that *mutual* UOA is ideal but not exactly realizable. Buber says again: "Every *I-Thou* relationship, within a relation, which is specified as a purposive working of one part upon the other, persists in virtual of a mutuality which is forbidden to be full" (pp. 133–34). You can *give I-Thou* but don't expect to fully receive it. This seems to be a realistic observation.

Buber consistently appeals to and relies on God—who he assumes is contradictorily a Person to be encountered and "the absolute Person, i.e., The Person who cannot be limited" (p. 156). He says, "As a Person, God gives personal life, he makes us as persons become capable of meeting with him and with one another" (p. 136).

In other words, God gives us the capability of achieving *I-Thou* relationships. Whether we have to *work* at activating this capability is not at all clear. Sometimes Buber seems to be saying that we do have to work at differentiating *I-It* from *I-Thou* relationships; and sometimes the two processes seem to merge together. All told, *I-Thou* and *I-It* stem from God. This is quite an assumption. As Buber notes in his final paragraph (p. 137), "The existence of mutuality between God and man cannot be proved; just as God's existence cannot be proved." Correct! We are not realistic, if we just *assume* it—and then use this *assumption* to explain our *I-Thou* and *I-It* relating.

If we omit God and rely only on empirical evidence and on how we can pragmatically use Buber's *I-Thou* and *I-It* concepts to help you and the human race survive and be happier, I think we can say something like this:

1. You have Being and Being-There. You are born and reared in a world of other people and of things.
2. You relate intimately to both—have *I-It* relationships—and to other people—have *I-Thou* relationships. With few exceptions, you do both. Your *I-Thou* relationships are usually more intense and involving than your *I-It* relationships. But not always.
3. Your *I-Thou* relationships are often more purposive and inclusive than your *I-It* relationships and can (if you wish) therefore be termed more "spiritual." But, again, not always. You have some degree of *choice* about which of the two to make more involving—if you consciously *see* and *predict* what will probably happen from both choices. Also: if you *work* with your thinking, feeling, and action to favor either or both choices.
4. Since your *I-Thou* relationships are usually more involving, you may choose to concentrate on creating and maintaining your *I-Thou* rather than your *I-It* relationships. But you also

had better give some time and practice to your *I-It* relations, which are inevitable and not to be neglected.

5. You had better not try to achieve ego satisfactions or conditional self-esteem (CSE) for you then become too self-centered and may neglect *I-Thou* or other-acceptance relations.

6. You had better experiment to some extent with both *I-It* and *I-Thou* relating, to see which leads you to a better life without neglecting the other.

7. You had better accept without liking all kinds of *I-It* and *I-Thou* Adversities after first trying to improve them. You are emotionally free when you know and fully accept the fact that your life naturally swings between *I-It* and *I-Thou* relationships. That's life!

I am not sure that Martin Buber would endorse these aspects of unconditional self-acceptance that REBT espouses, but I think that they realistically and logically follow from his *I-It* and *I-Thou* teachings. He doesn't specifically favor showing people the disadvantages and dangers of conditional self-esteem—as described in the chapters of this book. But specifically adding them to his teachings would be making clear what he often implies.

CHAPTER 14
Martin Heidegger and Self-Esteem

Martin Heidegger is one of the main founders of the theories of self, of self-rating, of existential choice, of Dasein, and of many other concepts that underlie self-theory. But I have difficulty fitting him into this book on self-esteem for several reasons:

1. I don't quite understand some of his main definitions, because they are overgeneralizations that apply to almost everything about human existence.
2. He rarely specifically tackles some of the main points of this book and differentiates conditional self-esteem (CSE) from self-efficacy (SE), and from unconditional self-acceptance (USA).
3. He personally led a contradictory life—sometimes favoring and protecting himself too much when he was a professor in Hitler's Third Reich and sometimes being remarkably "objective" and open to impersonal analysis of important self and social issues.

4. While seeming to grasp (and even invent) the concept of unconditional self-acceptance, he missed that of unconditional other-acceptance (UOA).

5. He enormously considered the ontological possibilities of Dasein and Being-there but kept refuting the practical and a posteriori (and more likely) aspects of Existence.

6. He tended to be absolutistic in his thinking, tautologically defined his premises about Being and existing and used circular thinking in "proving" that certain "facts" followed from his tautologies.

7. He seems to have missed the point that anxiety and self-rating do not merely stem from human existence in a world of probability but in people's insistence that they have certainty and perfect safety which they cannot have in a non-absolutistic, uncertain, and futuristic world.

As you can see from my prejudiced views of Heidegger and his philosophy, he is often a mystery to me; and some of the things I am about to say about him may easily be wrong and do him an injustice. But let me see what comes of my prejudices. Here are some statements from Heidegger's *Being and Time*.

"Essentially, the person exists only in the performance of intentional acts, and is therefore *not* an object" (p. 73).*

If I only exist when I *intend* to do something, then when I am in a coma, do I *not* exist? No, I then exist *less* but I still exist. I *actively* exist when I have intentions, but I can *passively* exist. When I intend, I most probably also exist, but when I exist I don't have to intend. I could be in a coma for years. "Existence" is a bad

---

*Page numbers refer to *Being and Time*, trans. John Macquarrie and Edward Robinson (San Francisco: HarperSanFrancisco, 1962).

word if linked with intention. The two are *partly* but not entirely the same. I may not exist for others when I am in a coma. But—unless others are completely deluded, I *do* exist. Even if they have no intentions about me, my body, in a coma, exists. So isn't that *part* of me? What about when I am in a coma for awhile and then come *out* of it and *intend*? Do I, again, exist *more*?

"The question of Being is the spur for all scientific thinking" (p. 77).

If I think, scientifically or not, I am *in all probability* alive, because thinking is one aspect of aliveness. But, again, thinking is *part* of being alive. In a coma, I am *still* alive. But can I be alive and not think (be in a coma)? Yes, but not *as* alive as when I think. Can I not feel, be numb, or in a deep sleep, and be alive? Yes, but not *as* alive as if I feel. There seem to be *degrees* of thinking, feeling, and acting that make me *more* or *less* alive. Existing or being seems to vary in *degree* of aliveness.

"'Being-in-the-world' stands for a unitary phenomenon. This primary datum must be seen as a whole" (p. 79).

Why? Why can't Being exist in heaven or hell? Or even *in itself*? If my ghost or soul exists, *must* it have a world to exist in? Since it is disembodied, why does it *need* a world? If it exists in heaven, that is *its* world, but is it truly *a* world? Why can't my soul exist and then later, not *exist*? If my soul exists today, why *must* it exist eternally? We can *define* my soul as something that exists eternally. But does that prove that I have a soul or that it must—*except* by definition— be eternal? If my soul must exist *somewhere* and there is nowhere— not even purgatory—for it to exist in, does this prove that since it does not have a being-there (Dasein) it really cannot exist?!

143

"That which enduringly remains, is" (p. 128).

An apparition or an illusion may enduringly remain. *Is* it? Suppose the person who has it dies? Does it still remain? Can he convince others that they still have it? If we enduringly convince ourselves that God exists, does that prove that he does? Or the devil?

"Being-in-the-world itself is that in the face of which anxiety is anxious" (p. 232).

No, anxiety seems to stem from a *need* (certainty) that things turn out well, that you get what you want, that you not be anxious, and so forth. *Desire* says, "If I don't get what I want or do get what I don't want, too bad! I don't *need* it." It ends with, "I am *concerned* about it but not anxious—and not anxious about my anxiety."

"Only because Dasein is anxious in the very depth of its Being, it becomes possible for anxiety to be elicited physiologically" (p. 234).

No, *strong* anxiety will probably affect you physiologically, but *weak* anxiety may not. Even existential anxiety may be *weak*.

"Existentially is eventually determined by facticity" (p. 236).

But Dasein or being-there is also determined by ontology. Is ontology *also* determined by facticity?

"Being-in-the-world is essentially care" (p. 237).

Care about people? Or care about anything? And care can be light or heavy. Again, if you are in a coma for a period of time, do

144

you *still* care? Do you have Being-in-the-world? Or just plain existence, plain Being?

"Selfhood is to be discerned . . . in the authenticity of Dasein's Being as care" (p. 369).

If you are nonauthentic in your Being as care, or authentically *don't* care, do you have *no* Self? Or a *limited* Self? Suppose you *only* care for your personal Self? Is that okay?

"Anxiety, however, springs from Dasein itself" (p. 345).

From *only* being there? Suppose you're *just* there and don't have to be there completely, perfectly, or in the future?

"Whatever may happen to Dasein, it experiences it as happening 'in time'" (p. 429).

More or less! You can be more aware or less aware of time. You *mostly* experience time awarely. But always? You may *have* time and space. But *are* you in time? Sometimes you *barely* perceive time passing. When in a coma, you may never do so.

"The Being of Dasein has been defined as care" (p. 434).

Ah! Now we are—perhaps—getting somewhere. If we forget about ontology and merely accept that, first, we have Being-there or Dasein and that, second, this Being includes care, we may get to a practical and existential importance of care and of REBT's placing it almost inevitably with unconditional other-acceptance. For REBT holds that thinking, feeling, and behaving *include* each other, though they may not be entirely the same. Why, then, couldn't Being-There (Dasein) also not *include* Being-There for *others* and why couldn't Being-There-for-others *include* Being-There (Dasein)? You fairly obviously have Being and *at the same time* have Being-There, Being-in-the-world, *and* Being *caring.* Aren't they all *integrated?*

If we say that they *most probably* are, then Heidegger's existentialism *philosophy,* if not exactly his *living* that philosophy, may be one of the first advocacies of unconditional other-acceptance.

As you can see—if you let yourself *see*—from my skepticism about some of Heidegger's maxims, they seem evident and ontological (unquestionable)—but *are* they? Let us assume that it is our innate (intrinsic) nature to have Dasein just because you (and other humans) have it. How can you be *certain* that this is *so?* How can you *for all time, under all conditions,* know and follow Heidegger's rules? They could all be "true" and you can *strongly tend* to follow them. But *must* you? Will you not exist—have Being-in-the-world and *still* be alive? *Still* exist until you are dead?

To be safer, why don't we say, "It *appears that under nearly all conditions,* I think, feel, and behave in the world, and therefore I can *know* that I exist and have Dasein in-the-world that I can also see exists. Now since this *seems* to be so, how can I get on with my life, continue my existence, and *mainly* enjoy myself?"

Back to the main issues of self, self-esteem, and unconditional self-acceptance in this book. We can fairly safely—not absolutely for all time—say:

1. I believe I think, desire, and act in the world and therefore *most likely* I do.
2. I especially have some *intentions* of thinking, feeling, and behaving like most humans most of the time do.
3. The world exists and although it can exist without me, I exist, have my Being, *in* this world and not nowhere.
4. To live better in the world, I'll assume that it exists and I have my Dasein, my Being in it.

5. I'll assume that I most probably have aliveness only for an indefinite period of time and one of these years I will be unalive, unexistent.
6. I therefore will do my best to prolong my existence and find personal ways of enjoying it and of avoiding pain, hassles, accidents, and diseases.
7. To help me live this way, I shall strive for self-efficacy, rate and evaluate what I do and not do, but accept myself unconditionally with my errors and dysfunctional feelings and behaviors so that I can get more of what I want and less of what I do not want. Period.
8. Although my plan of living may not be practical and may have flaws, let me try it experimentally to see if it works. While I am still alive, I can always revise and change it. Let me experiment and see.
9. I want to live peacefully with other people, so in addition to unconditional self-acceptance (USA), I will work to achieve unconditional other-acceptance (UOA), and unconditional life-acceptance (ULA). This plan may work and if it doesn't, I'll again revise it. Let me experimentally see!

CHAPTER 15

Jean-Paul Sartre and Self-Esteem

J ean-Paul Sartre was one of the greatest and clearest philoso- phers and existentialists of the twentieth century, and his views of conditional self-esteem (CSE) and conditional self-accept- ance (CSA) are well worth discussing. Following his teacher, Hei- degger, but also being avoidant of the ontological and religious traps of the other leading existentialists, he got closer to USA and UOA than the other thinkers. Remarkable.

Let me make some of his main points of *Being and Nothingness* and show why I often favor them.

"I am aware that I doubt, therefore I really am" (p. xi).*

Most probably, my awareness of my doubting shows that I exist. But not certainly. I could be deluded that I doubt and think I doubt when I really don't. And I could deludedly think I doubt but really not doubt. But if I am aware that I may be deluded about my

---

*Page numbers refer to *Being and Nothingness*, trans. Hazel E. Barnes (New York: Philosoph- ical Library, 1951).

doubting, then I most probably exist. On one level or another, my delusion about my awareness of doubting and being deluded most likely shows that I exist. So let me assume that in all probability I do.

"The final appeal, the standard of judgment, is reason" (p. xiii).

The standard of *good* judgment may be reason. But what if I have bad judgment and *think* it's good? What if I'm alive—like an amoeba—and barely judge but randomly take the "right" path and (statistically) still survive? What if I *feel* I'm doing "right" things with minimal reasoning and judging?

"To know is to know one knows" (p. 12).

Yes, it would be difficult to know one knows without knowing that one knows one knows. But impossible? With certain kinds of brain injury, one could possibly *sense* one knows, and avoid fatal accidents without fully knowing that one knows.

"Being is itself. It is neither passivity nor activity" (p. 27).

If it is *only* itself, could we then be *conscious* of our being? To be conscious, we'd better be more than *just* alive.

"Kierkegaard considers anguish instead of the apprehension of nothingness" (p. 65).

I think he is saying, "I *must* have life, or somethingness, else it is *terrible*," and *then* he makes himself feel anguish.

"All knowing is the consciousness of knowing" (p. 93).

This is true if you *define* knowing as consciousness. You could also say that all feeling, even the slightest, is *some degree* of consciousness. Because whenever you feel, you have *some* consciousness of your feeling. Otherwise, could you really *feel*?

"I am never any one of my attitudes, any one of my actions" (p. 103).

Sartre seems to have made this statement in 1943; but Alfred Korzybski clearly made it in 1933. I *am many* of my feelings and actions, not any *one* of them.

"Bad faith attempts also to constitute myself as being what I am not" (p. 111).

I *pretend* to be what I am not and to some extent *know* that I pretend. If I lie about having money, that is a lie but is *not* bad faith. If I say that I *am* a *rich person*, when I only know that I have *some money* that is identifying *me* as wealthy, that is bad faith. As Korzybski would say, I cannot *be* rich at all times when I have *some* money some of the time.

"The nature of consciousness is to be what it is not and not to be what it is" (p. 116).

Not necessarily! I can *sometimes* be conscious that I like you and sometimes not realize that I do. I am not *always* conscious or unconscious. Can't I have different *degrees* of consciousness?

"Shame is shame of oneself before the other. These two strictures are inseparable" (p. 303).

No, Sartre seems to see that there are two *kinds* of shame: (1) shame about your act—say cheating someone—which includes (a) the person you cheated and (b) your whole *self* for being *a cheat*; and (2) shame only about your act (cheating the other) but *not* about you as a *total* person.

Sartre sees these two kinds of shame as intrinsically the same. If so, he misses a very important point. You can be quite ashamed of any thought, feeling, or behavior, and note that *it* is "bad" and "shameful" without being ashamed of having or doing it. Then you could say, "It is wrong and ineffective, but since *it*, my act, is bad and I am responsible for it, I am *not* it, but *a person who did* it and who can change and act better next time." Then you would not feel *un*healthily ashamed of *you* but only of what you *did*.

Sartre sees that most people who acknowledge their "bad" acts to others and are deprecated by others for doing misdeeds think they have no choice but to blame themselves *and* their deeds. But they *do*—especially if they follow REBT principles—have such a choice and can healthfully exert it. They *are* not their misdeeds, even when they indubitably effect them. Using REBT, they *act* badly but are never bad *persons*. Sartre almost, but not quite, sees this. So he almost, but not quite, achieves unconditional *self*-acceptance (USA).

> "It is *probable* that this object is, is man. It is possible that he is dreaming of some project . . . that he is idiotic" (p. 342).

Yes, he could be dreaming, in a daze, or confused. *Usually* and *probably* if he "sees" a man, it is a man. But not certainly. He may be blind or dreaming.

> "To love is to be wished to be loved, hence to wish that the other wish that I love him" (p. 481).

Not always! I could love Hitler, even compulsively love him, and dote on my love for him without wishing that he love me. Usually, if I love him, I *want* him to love me back. But not always! I can love someone unrequitedly and still get satisfaction from my love and not *need* his return love.

"I preserve the past with me and I *decide* its meaning" (p. 640).

Yes, I can give it good, bad, or indifferent meaning. And I can *keep* giving it the same meaning or can *change* its meaning. For years I can think my father neglected me, then see that he was very busy, had to neglect me, and think that he did the best he could and really loved me.

"The psychoanalytic explanation of his case is a probable hypothesis" (p. 733).

Yes, psychoanalytic "explanations" always *could* be "true" but most of them are guesses that could easily be false. I *decide* that my analyst's interpretations are or are not valid. Today, I may think his interpretation is "true" and tomorrow decide that the same explanation is "false."

All told, Sartre has many good points, especially in regard to shame. But he doesn't quite see that:

- You never *have to* feel ashamed of *yourself* even when you acknowledge your immoral acts and see that they needlessly harm others.
- By the standards of your community, you sometimes *act* immorally, but never have to view yourself as an *immoral person.*

153

- You live in a social community and therefore *had better* treat other people fairly and help preserve them and yourself. So you had better have unconditional other-acceptance (UOA) as well as unconditional self-acceptance (USA) but you obviously don't *have* to have these philosophies.
- Your choosing to fail to have USA and UOA will *probably* bring "bad" results to you and your social group, but you still can risk getting poor results by having, as most people have, conditional self-esteem (CSE) and conditional other-acceptance (COA). If so, you'd better unwhiningly accept these penalties and work at improving your and other people's lives in the future.

CHAPTER 16

Paul Tillich and Unconditional Self-Acceptance and Unconditional Other-Acceptance

Although Heidegger and Sartre were pioneering existential-ists, the most thoroughgoing discussion of the ideas of unconditional self- and other-acceptance was presented by Paul Tillich in 1952, in *The Courage to Be*. I mainly took and developed these ideas when I read Tillich's brilliant book in 1953 and there-fore incorporated them as fundamental philosophies in REBT, which I was creating at that time.

Unfortunately, Tillich was a little too brilliant for his and my good, since he described many different kinds of USA and UOA, but failed to see the forest for the trees. The kinds of *The Courage to Be* and how to achieve these major forms of acceptance some-times got lost in the shuffle. Ultimate concern, faith in God, and the ontology of being-there—which he mainly recommended—are *not* acceptable to "pure" self- and other-acceptance and don't ring bells for me, as I shall try to explain in this chapter. They are indeed different from conditional self-esteem. But they are not "truly" unconditional.

Tillich tried hard, however. For instance: Courage "is the readiness to take on the acceptance of want, toil, insecurity, pain, possible destruction" (p. 78).

"He who has the courage to be as a part has the courage to confirm himself as a part of the community in which he participates" (p. 91).

The man with the courage to be "reacts with the courage of despair, the courage to take his despair upon himself, and to resist the radical threat of nonbeing by the courage to be as oneself" (p. 140).

Pretty good! *Un*conditional—for the most part. But finally dependent upon the courageous man or woman's absolute faith in God. Therefore, not as courageous as it could be.

Tillich gives several reasons why your having the courage to *be*—which I take to mean courage to exist *no matter what*—won't exactly work. But he never convinces me that they fail. He therefore adds "surefire" reasons which presumably make it elegantly work. These mainly are:

1. Ontological reasons. Your being is actually being-there, your being-in-the-world. Why? Because it *is*. You can't exist entirely by yourself; you have to be *there*—as Heidegger and Sartre agreed. That presumably proves that you are *given* being (and nonbeing), merely have to have the courage to accept it, and have this courage ontologically because you have it. If you merely have the courage to accept what is— being-there—you tautologically have it.

Well and good—almost! For to have courage—or anything else—tautologically, only proves that you *say* you have it. You agree with *yourself*, by *definition*, that you have it. So what? It is quite *likely*, most *probable*, that you do. But where is the *evidence* that you are not wrong or deluded, that courage, your self, being-there, or anything else exists? It *may*—or it may not. Your tautologies—"I exist. I exist *there*. I have courage. I have the courage to exist"—all could be factual, and probably are. But *certainties*? *Except* by definition? No—only high degrees of probability. You could be mistaken, deluded, psychotic, and so forth, in *thinking* you exist.

Even Descartes was possibly mistaken. He said, "I think." Well, maybe. "I think I exist." Quite possibly, but possibly not. "Therefore my thinking proves that I think." *Does* it? "And my thinking I exist proves that I really do exist." Again: *does* it?

Tautologies prove very little. Only if you add, "I *probably* think." That *probably* shows I, the thinker, exist. But it *could* show that I *merely* think I exist and that merely shows that I *probably* do. But there's no *certainty* that I exist. So I'd better *assume* that I do, act as if I do, and get by. Nothing may be certain—*including* my thought that nothing may be certain. Too bad! I'll live as best I can with probability, and no certainty. I have the courage to *accept*, even if I don't *like*, uncertainty.

By using the ontological argument to "prove" he, and all of us, have being-there, Tillich cops out with *lack* of courage to be. To have this courage, he'd better *accept* uncertainty—which his ontological argument does *not* accept.

2. Tillich brings in "ultimate concern" as a "proof" of the courage to be. But ultimate concern means that you care—for yourself, for others, for the world, and for anything—totally, 100 percent, under *all* conditions. But is that possible? Even if you decide that you have ultimate concern, or if others think that you have it, do you really have it perfectly, all the time, *ultimately*? Is anything ultimate? Will it always remain so? Maybe. But I doubt it.

3. If you depend on and believe in God *ultimately*, can you actually do so? For all time, totally, ultimately? If you could do so, how do you know your ultimate concern for God would last forever? Do you? Many God-lovers become thoroughgoing atheists or partial God-lovers.

In sum, if your having the courage to be means ultimately, totally, at all times, or anything like that, you can only prove that *in all probability* you will have it completely, under *all* conditions—but you just can't prove that you *always* have it—especially, always *ultimately* have it. How can you be sure that you *ultimately* have it now, let alone will guarantee having it in the future?

All this seems to add up to: you cannot prove *any* all-time ultimates—as Tillich's ultimate concern seems to posit. *Maybe*, if you reach it, you'll do so forever. Maybe!

Even ontology is limited. We can say being-there exists today. But does it *have to* exist tomorrow? *There* can fairly easily exist with and without a being to interact with it. Being does not *now* exist without a *there*, but could in the future possibly do so. Maybe somewhere in the universe a being exists without a *there*—or could exist in the future. *Probably* not. But it could independently exist—for example, a pure soul.

Whenever we say *being* includes being-there, we probably overgeneralize. We more accurately could say, "Being *now* ontologically means being-there." It also *in all probability* now means being there *forever*. But how can we prove *forever*?

Also, assuming that our planet and our universe was lifeless (both before and after the big bang occurred) and *later* gave rise to living entities, wasn't there first a *there* without a *being*?

Once life (a being) did exist, we could guess that it *created a there*. But, even so, did it *have to* do so? Couldn't it possibly create an (immortal) soul without a *there*? Most improbable—but possible.

If we carefully add *in all probability* instead of *intrinsically* and *certainly* to being-there, we would lose little and (probably!) gain much. We then could say, "*In all probability* being-there exists and *in all probability* it will continue to exist for humans (and other living creatures). But sometime in the future *being* or *there* could independently exist. Now for the time being, let's *assume* that they invariably go together." If we believed that, how would it change our lives?

Let me start off with this probability (and not ontological) statement and see if I (and Tillich) can still derive unconditional self- and other-acceptance. I can say that in all probability, and by much empirical observation, we are fallible, limited humans who think, feel, and behave for about one hundred years in this world and desire to keep living and be reasonably healthy and satisfied. But we can live and be fairly unhealthy and dissatisfied. Nonbeing (death) exists but let's try to avoid it. This includes, as Tillich said, "our readiness to take on the acceptance of want, toil, insecurity, pain, possible destruction." Acceptance means tolerate, bear, and live with many possible displeasures when we try to change but cannot change them. But it also means to unwhiningly and uncomplainingly accept them even though we don't *like* them.

We could stop right there and have a good measure of unrebellious acceptance. And we could do so without depending upon any God or miraculous predestined kind fate. We could unconditionally accept whatever "good" and "bad" fate occurs in our lives for pragmatic reasons: Because nonacceptance or refusing to accept them *in all probability* leads to worse results—to horrifiedly complaining about them, often making them worse, not improving them, and making ourselves needlessly depressed about them. Whining rarely leads to winning.

What more do we need for unconditional self- and other-acceptance? Little or nothing. We have kept empirical and pragmatic reasons for acceptance—and dispensed with Tillich's redundant ontological and God-hypothesized arguments. Good riddance!

I could give many allied elements for unconditional acceptance and the courage to have it and I will give them later. Briefly, unconditional acceptance means liking yourself, others, and the world when you are not getting what you want and in spite of your getting what you don't want.

More specifically, unconditional acceptance means:

- Trying but not necessarily succeeding to minimize frustrations, hassles, pain, disgust, and depression.
- Trying but not necessarily succeeding to be approved, loved, being accepted by, not being resented or hated by others.
- Trying but not necessarily succeeding to be competent and achieving.
- Trying for fair treatment by others and not feeling desperately hurt when you don't get it.
- Trying but not necessarily succeeding to be undisturbed, unanxious, and unpanicked.
- Trying but not always succeeding in controlling your own life and not being tyrannized.
- Trying to but not always succeeding in having meaning and purpose in life.
- Trying but not always succeeding in accepting your mortality, and your living less long than you would like to live.
- Accepting the fact that there well may be no magical solutions to your own and others' problems and there may well be no deities that will help you and others with their problems.

More details on USA, UOA, and ULA in later chapters. Meanwhile, go back to Reinhold Niebuhr's serenity statement of the early twentieth century: Give me the courage to change what I can change, to accept what I cannot change, and the wisdom to know the difference.

Now that I think about it again, this includes at least three important points: (1) your courage to try a new path when the old paths are not working; (2) your acceptance that some hassles, whether you like it or not, won't (right now) disappear or be removed; and (3) your figuring out whether it is probably better for you to try a new path if you surmise that the old one will continue to bring poor results.

This means that you have *acceptance* that your present path is not likely to work, *acceptance* that hassles will still exist, *acceptance* that you had better try a different path, and *acceptance* that the new path (or any new paths) may still not work. At least four forms of acceptance!—which is probably why *graceful* acceptance is so hard to take and to keep taking. But what better choices do you have?

CHAPTER 17

Self-Esteem and the Practice of Tibetan Buddhism by the Dalai Lama, Howard Cutler, and H. Gunaratana Manhathera

Tibetan Buddhism follows some of the main principles of Gautama Buddha but with some significant differences from Zen Buddhism. In this chapter I shall review some of its important aspects, as described in the book *The Art of Happiness* by the Fourteenth Dalai Lama and the American psychiatrist Howard C. Cutler (New York: Riverhead Books, 1998) and in their second book, *The Art of Happiness at Work* (New York: Riverhead Books, 2003).

Both these books present the Dalai Lama's views on happiness in such detail that my summary will have to be very brief. By all means read the books themselves, preferably several times, since they are exceptionally meaty and authoritative. Here is what I find about unconditional self-acceptance (USA), unconditional other-acceptance (UOA), and unconditional life-acceptance (ULA) from *The Art of Happiness*.

The Dalai Lama opposes the Western endorsement of conditional self-esteem (CSE) based on striving for success:

"The Dalai Lama seeks to build determination and enthusiasm in more wholesome behavior and to eliminate negative mental traits, rather than emphasizing the achievement
of worldly success, money, or power. . . . The Dalai Lama's
primary interest in motivation lies in *reshaping* and
changing one's underlying motivation to one of compassion
and kindness" (p. 273).

"Within the Buddhist practice, the cultivation of certain
specific positive mental qualities, such as patience, tolerance, kindness, and so on can act as specific antidotes to
negative states of mind, such as anxiety, hatred, and attachment" (p. 239).

"Low self-confidence inhibits our efforts to move ahead, to
meet challenges and take some risks, in the pursuit of our
objectives. Inflated self-confidence can be equally haz-
ardous. Those who suffer from an exaggerated sense of
their own ability and accomplishment are continually subject to frustration, disappointment, and rage when reality
intrudes and the world doesn't validate their idealized view
of themselves" (p. 275).

"For those engaged in Buddhist practice, the antidote to
self-hatred would be to reflect upon the fact that all beings,
including oneself, have Buddha nature, the seed or the
potential for perfection, full Enlightenment—no matter how
weak or poor or deprived one's present situation may be"
(p. 287).

In regard to people's achieving unconditional other-acceptance,
The Art of Happiness includes almost innumerable advocacies of

the Dalai Lama. Read the book and see for yourself. Here are a few of its many passages:

"Reaching out to help others may be as fundamental to our nature as communication" (p. 59).

"I believe that the proper utilization of time is this: If you can serve other people, other sentient beings. If not, at least refrain from harming them. I think that is the whole basis of my philosophy" (p. 64).

"The Dalai Lama's model of intimacy is based on a willingness to open ourselves to many others, to family, friends, and even strangers, forming genuine and deep bonds based on our common humanity" (p. 84).

"Compassion can be roughly defined in terms of a state of mind that is nonviolent, non-harming, and non-aggressive. It is a mental attitude based on the wish for others to be free from their suffering and associated with a sense of commitment, responsibility, and respect for others" (p. 114).

"I truly believe that compassion provides the basis of human survival, the real value of life, and without that there is a basic piece missing" (p. 119).

"I think we should make our ultimate goal very clear. The whole world should be demilitarized" (p. 190).

"We need to actively cultivate the antidotes to hatred: patience and tolerance" (p. 249).

Of the three major forms of acceptance that REBT advocates and that I am describing in this book, the Dalai Lama clearly advocates unconditional life-acceptance. Although driven (with many other Buddhists) out of Tibet and forced to live in a remote city in India for many years, he managed to survive and create much happiness for himself and his followers by his serene philosophy of life. Witness these acceptance teachings in *The Art of Happiness*:

> A reliable way to gain happiness, "is not to have what we want but rather to want and appreciate what we have" (p. 29).

> "Since all things are subject to change, nothing exists in a permanent position, nothing is able to remain the same under its own independent power" (p. 163).

> "If you can make comparisons, view your [awful] situation from a different perspective, something happens. . . . If you look at the same problem from a distance, then it appears smaller and less overwhelming" (p. 174).

> "A balanced and skillful approach to life, taking care to avoid extremes, becomes a very important factor in conducting one's everyday existence" (p. 193).

> "The Dalai Lama has repeatedly emphasized that inner discipline is the basis of a spiritual life" (p. 311).

The Dalai Lama and Howard Cutler continue their examination of the good life in *The Art of Happiness at Work* and get even closer to the mark of seeing that conditional self-esteem is dangerous and endorsing unconditional acceptance. In regard to self-esteem, here are some of their recommendations:

Self-Esteem and the Practice of Tibetan Buddhism

"If individuals are confident in recognizing their own positive inner qualities, they don't need to rely so heavily on others' praise to supply that feeling of accomplishment" (p. 131).

The Dalai Lama: "If your life becomes only a medium of production, then many of the good human values and characteristics will be lost—then you will not, you cannot, become a complete person" (p. 146).

When he met some of Washington's elite people at a reception in his honor at the Capitol Building, the Dalai Lama "was relating to them just as one human being to another, with a complete lack of pretense." A security agent in charge of his security said: "He likes to talk with the drivers, the janitors and waiters, the service staff wherever he goes. And he treats everybody just the same" (pp. 202–203).

"The trouble with pursuing money just for the sake of money is that it makes us a victim of greed. Never-ending greed. Then we are never satisfied" (p. 32).

It is difficult to find, in *The Art of Happiness at Work*, an unequivocal statement of unconditional self-acceptance because the Dalai Lama, as will be shown below, thoroughly focuses on unconditional other-acceptance and keeps bringing the topic back to that. He does keep on pointing out, however, that most of what we call misery is self-caused and self-perpetrated. Therefore, he says, self-centeredness and rating one's ego as good or bad are destructive.

"The core of Buddhist practice," the Dalai Lama says, "is to bring about inner transformation" (p. 152). Then you can train your mind to give up its protective chatter and its status seeking and can focus on what you really choose to work at for your own enjoyment. He keeps stressing that you pick your vocation not to make loads of money and to win favor from others but to find your own main goals, interests, and purposes and to devote a good part of your life to actualizing them.

In this way, although he does not clearly endorse USA, the Dalai Lama favors the essence of self-actualization—that is, you discover what you chiefly want to do in work and in life and you do it regardless of how much acclaim you get. You then really become your own person.

The be-all and end-all of the Dalai Lama's existence, as Howard Cutler well expresses it, is "his sincere wish to be of service to others" (p. 4). He almost obsessively-compulsively tries to get all the rest of the human race to become devoted to UOA, too. Here are some full endorsements of unconditional love of humanity in *The Art of Happiness at Work*:

"Think about the world, the global economy. Think about the environment. Look at the various forms of social injustice. Perhaps you could even make a small contribution to improve things in some way" (p. 32).

"In all human activities, whether it is work or some other activity, the main purpose should be to benefit human beings" (p. 37).

"The foundation of what I consider to be basic human values is a sense of concern for others" (p. 54).

"The essence of one's job might be to assure survival, of course, but it may also involve making a meaningful contribution to others in some way" (p. 155).

Self-Esteem and the Practice of Tibetan Buddhism

"If you can, serve others. If not, at least refrain from harming them" (p. 173).

"We must also consider the results of our labor, the effect it will have on ourselves, our family, society, and the world" (p. 183).

It is exceptionally clear from the conversations the Dalai Lama had with Howard Cutler that compassion for others is the watchword of Tibetan Buddhist philosophy—and that, with unusual consistency, the Dalai Lama practices what he preaches. Considering the great trials and tribulations foisted on Tibet by the Chinese government for decades, his and other Buddhist monks' skill in accepting their enemies is quite remarkable. They go far out of their way to deal with the Chinese in a nonblaming, unhostile manner. Which tends to back up one of their main philosophies: It is not injustice and unfairness by themselves that cause your rage, but your damning *view* of such "horrors." The ideas of REBT and Tibetan Buddhism are considerably supported by the thoughts, feelings, and actions of the Dalai Lama and his followers.

What about the Tibetan Buddhist philosophy of unconditional life-acceptance? Once again, this is ably supported by the Dalai Lama's views and behaviors. Here are some prime examples from *The Art of Happiness at Work*:

If your job situation is far from desirable, "You begin by realizing that no situation is one hundred percent good or one hundred percent bad" (p. 26).

"If you can't change the work environment or the wider forces that contribute to the work environment, then you may need to change or adjust your outlook. Otherwise, you will remain unhappy at work and in your life" (p. 53).

The Dalai Lama doesn't mean by karma (fate) that "one's current circumstances are the result of one's past actions, either in this life or a previous life. . . . Just as one's past actions may have contributed to one's current circumstances, one's present actions can change one's future" (p. 144).

Therefore, you are never stuck with your karma if you take *action* in the present to change.

"In seeking to gain a sense of fulfillment for one's work, I think one's attitude is the most important thing. Yes, attitude toward one's work is the most important thing" (p. 98).

Howard Cutler: "The Dalai Lama . . . is someone who has completely fused his self with his work. His personal life and his work life were perfectly integrated—so fully integrated that there was no separation between his 'personal' life, 'spiritual' life, or 'home' life" (p. 200).

All told, the Dalai Lama and Tibetan Buddhism make a fine showing. Although they are not exceptionally clear about advocating the philosophy of unconditional self-acceptance, they are unusually precise about espousing unconditional other-acceptance and unconditional life-acceptance. The Dalai Lama not only is happily involved in his work as a spiritual leader, teacher, scholar, and diplomat, but he also shows many other people how to lead a peaceful, kind, and compassionate existence in spite of the many problems they may encounter. He works consistently at forgiving himself, forgiving others, and tolerating his often harsh world. By his personal example and his Buddhist teaching, he helps others conquer their own self-hatred, their rage at their detractors, and their whining about the world. What more could we ask?

Self-Esteem and the Practice of Tibetan Buddhism

As I was about to conclude this chapter, Shawn Blau gave me a copy of an unusual book on Vipassana meditation by H. Gunaratana Manhathera, *Mindfulness in Plain English*. It discusses some Tibetan Buddhist traditions that seem a little different than the Dalai Lama's views, so let me briefly consider them.

The Vipassana style of meditation, as practiced in South and Southeast Asia, is "insight meditation" whose purpose is to give the meditator "insight into the nature of reality and the accurate understanding of how everything works." Fine. But we'd better watch the term "everything." "Its intention is to pick apart the screen of lies and delusions through which we normally view the world, and thus to reveal the face of ultimate reality." Quite a goal!

Samatha is tranquility and *Vipassana* is insight meditation. Vipassana focuses mainly on breathing. You, like all humans, are afflicted with constant tension—especially jealousy, suffering, discontent, and stress. This comes from the conditions of your own mind. But you are on a perpetual treadmill to nowhere, bounding after pleasure, fleeing from pain, endlessly ignoring 90 percent of your experience. But you can experience happiness and peace and "the prime issues in human experience," even though you can't control everything completely and can't get everything you want. You can give up your obsessive-compulsive driveness (OCD) of your desires and learn to not want what you want and to recognize your desires but not be controlled by them.

To get peace and happiness "you've got to see who you are and how you are without illusion, judgment, or resistance of any kind." You've got to see your duties and your responsibilities to your fellow humans, and above all your responsibility to yourself as an individual living with other individuals. Vipassana meditation cleanses your mind of greed, hatred, and jealousy. "When you have learned compassion for yourself, compassion for others is automatic."

So far, so good! Insight meditation focuses on your breathing but really watches *how* you think—in both a sensible and muddled way. It separates your constructive from your destructive thoughts—especially destructive greed, hatred, and jealousy—and lets you clearly see the results you get, peace and happiness. It *recognizes* your obsessive-compulsive *centering* on your desires and helps you also *focus* simultaneously on *others'* goals and values. It obviously, like REBT, includes *both* USA and UOA. Marvelous!

What's wrong, then? Several important *assumptions*: (1) Seeing that USA and UOA are quite *different* than obsessive-compulsive desires, you *automatically also* see that they are *better* procedures and that you damned well *had better* adopt them. (2) Despite your *innate* and *learned* tendencies to give into your OCD urges, you *somehow* keep fighting like hell to give them up. (3) You almost invariably *win* this fight.

These are all very questionable assumptions! Practically everyone today *sees* (has insight into) the great harm of smoking, but how many *keep* inhaling unto death? Insight *plus* a strong cost-benefit attitude toward smoking and its harm *sometimes* persuades people to stop. But insight *alone*?

REBT strongly agrees with Vipassana insight meditation that insight into your greed, jealousy, and tensions are very helpful. But automatically effective? Hardly! REBT also quite honestly holds that *if* greed, jealousy, and stress are *viewed* as relatively harmful, *seeing* that you experience them will often—not always—help you fight them, while Vipassana meditation insight never quite acknowledges their harm and only *hints* at it. It therefore had better be fully acknowledged: "*When* you see greed, jealousy, and stress as distinctly harmful, *and* you *oppose* harming yourself with these feelings, *then* your insight may truly help you fight to give them up." Wouldn't that be more honest than the Vipassana equation, insight = prophylactic action? Manhathera states "an accomplished meditator has achieved a profound understanding of life and he inevitably relates to the world with a deep and uncritical love." Yes—perhaps!

Suppose that you profoundly meditate and have a deep understanding of life (or even, at least, of your own thinking). How and why *must* you relate to the world with a deep and uncritical love? You may choose several possibilities besides this one: (1) You may deeply and critically relate to others. (2) You may choose *not* to relate to others, despite your "profound understanding of life." (3) You may deeply relate to animals, science, art, sports, and the like. You may *probably* and more *often* relate to the world with a "deep and uncritical love." But inevitably?

Manhathera, and perhaps Vipassana philosophy in general, consistently takes a romantic attitude toward people and their relationships. When you have insight or understanding of the way things "actually are"—which is multifaceted and, as Manhathera keeps pointing out, difficult to truly *see*, you can still, being human, *choose* to react in various "favorable" and "unfavorable" ways. But you don't *have* to pick the "good" ways. So Vipassana insight *may* be helpful. But does it *have* to be?

Vipassana meditation gets you to "come to a direct knowledge of things as they really are without prejudice and without illusion." Does it? A couple of centuries ago, Immanuel Kant showed that "things as they really are" may exist, but we have no certain ways of knowing "things in themselves." Postmodern philosophers of the last century have been equally skeptical. Manhathera, again, presumably *knows* how things really *are* (and will always be). *How* do he and the Vipassana devotees really know?

"There are three integral factors in Buddhist meditation—morality, concentration, and wisdom." This sounds okay, but I would guess that you largely *bring* these three factors to Vipassana meditation. If you bring other factors—such as immorality—the meditation most probably won't work. If I am correct, your bringing immorality to insight meditation definitely won't get you unconditional other-acceptance and perhaps not even unconditional self-acceptance. UOA and USA work *because* they are, in common terms, moral. *Moral* even means, essentially, roles that work in a social group. Therefore, you bring your morality in to create UOA and USA. You *start* there; and Manhathera omits acknowledging this point.

You have "to see the entire situation from an objective point of view, giving equal weight to [your] own needs and those of others." Some trick! What point of view is completely objective? Every person's view is his or her own.

However, Manhathera has a very important point here. All points of view, he rightly says, are self-centered and biased; and they cannot be *totally* unbiased but can be much *less* biased and *more* objective. And *preferably* should be. But he confuses the *preferable* with the *absolutely should and ought.*

It would be *preferable* if you favored—reasonably favored—your own desires over others but did not obsessively-compulsively *only* do so and failed to see that others have *their* legitimate preferences. So you try to see your desires as "good" but not *uniquely* "good" and "legitimate." Otherwise, you would become a hermit!

But *preferable* means preferable *to you* and not to all others as well. That would be "objective"—and impossible! So you don't give *equal* weight to your and others' desires. But you "objectively" give *some* weight to both. This, as I have been pointing out in this book, has many advantages—especially peaceful living. So you lean over backward to achieve some measure of it—as Vipassana meditation instructs you to do. But you still *often* favor your desires even when you clearly *see* that they are prejudiced. However, you don't always *choose* to fulfill them. You thereby achieve a good—not a *perfect*—degree of unconditional other-acceptance UOA.

In the main, you solve many of your problems in this respect, by *seeing*—having *insight* into—REBT's theory of *desire* and *need*. You *desire* what you want, but don't *need* it. Even if it is food and you are starving, you *need* the food to stop from starving—but you don't *need* it to live! What you *want* is a desideratum—never, really, a necessity. So you'll be *uncomfortable* and *inconvenienced* if you lack food. Tough!

Now if you really *saw* this and also *accepted* it, you would have little trouble leading an unmiserable life. No, you wouldn't necessarily be *happy*, but you would be quite *peaceful*. Then you could *decide* to have USA and ULA—and I doubt whether you would often bother to meditate.

"Compassion means that you automatically restrain yourself from any thought, word, or deed that might harm yourself or others." Yes, after you *consciously* choose to be compassionate for quite a period of time—as the Dalai Lama has apparently done. But so have many people who *don't* meditate. This kind of USA and UOA is a main goal of REBT—with or without meditation—as I show in all my recent books. Several philosophical systems of achieving USA and UOA exist, such as Enright and Fitzgibbon's (2000) forgiveness method. Which of these systems produce better results with and without meditation remains to be investigated.

"Accept everything that arises. Accept your feelings, even the ones you wish you did not have." Now we're getting back to *real* acceptance. If only its devotees would actually do this, Vipassana meditation would be remarkably good. But do they truly accept its limitations and *dis*advantages? Especially some of its compulsive pollyannaism?

Vipassana insight—as perhaps you can see from my questions—*assumes* fundamental *truths* which cannot be validated and, to say the least, are questionable. They *look* pretty good—but only constant experimenting will tell whether they *"really"* are; and *if* they are "good," only more experiments and more time will tell if they *still* work.

I am not objecting, in all of this, to the goals of Vipassana meditation. In fact, I endorse them. I am merely questioning the essential *truth* of its goals. Indeed, I am questioning the *essential truth* of any goals. Goals may be *better*—more effective for a chosen purpose—than present ("deluded") goals. But are they once and for all (and for all *time*) *true*? Hmmm!

Manhathera seems to tackle the disadvantages of conditional self-esteem which lead to pride, envy, and jealousy. This "unskillful habit," he holds, causes "estrangement, barriers between people, and ill feeling." Correct. But instead of coming to a full UOA philosophy, as REBT recommends, he tells the meditator "to center his attention on those factors that are universal to all life, things that will move him closer to others."

However, this will work only if you center your attention on all those *good* factors that are universal to life—such as love, friendship, and unconditional acceptance. This is what the Dalai Lama does. For—aha!—several "bad" factors are also universal—especially competitions, envy, hatred, fighting for *your* gain, and so forth. So the meditator has to *select* the universal *socializing* factors from the universal *antagonizing* factors. I agree, of course, that this can—with distinct trouble and reflection—be done. But it is a definite—and crucial—*choice*. As usual, Manhathera *goes to* meditation with these "good" goals and *directs* it to achieving them. Lovely! But it still is a decision. Meditation *alone* again will not achieve these goals. But, *if* directed "properly," it can distinctly help.

"Mindful meditators manage three or four hours of practice a day." *Forever*? Isn't that *much*? Doesn't meditation consume considerable time that could be better spent in other pursuits? Where is the evidence that *that much* steady meditation is worth it? *Some* degree of it may be quite beneficial. But, again, *how much*?

"No matter what the source of your fears, mindfulness is the cure." Not exactly! Fears of falling from heights and of terrorism may be real—and you'd better keep them and act against them if you can. Fear of fear, however, stems from, "I *absolutely must not be afraid!*" and can be removed by, "I hate being afraid of terrorists, but I'd better be cautious and live with this fear."

"Thoughts to which we are attached are poison." The *attachment* is poison, not the thought. Attachment—or *over*attachment—is compulsive. It stems from, "Since success and love are good, I *absolutely must always* succeed and be loved." *Desire*, again, foolishly leads to *need*—which Vipassana meditation *sees* and *Disputes*. Therein lies its great strength.

"Positive attachments hold you in the mud just as assuredly as negative attachments." Yes, if they often are *necessities* and compulsions. Compulsiveness changes your entire view of life. More perfectionism. When you achieve mindfulness, a good cigar is a cigar and a good fuck is a fuck.

I have presented some of my main agreements and disagreements with H. Gunaratana Manhathera's Vipassana meditation, as he clearly presents it in *Mindfulness in Plain English*. I have other points I could make but enough (for the present) is enough! He especially favors and describes some important ways of achieving USA and UOA. I hope he will consider my relatively mild objections to some of his views. These views are sometimes not quite thoroughly accepting, because unconditional acceptance means, in my view, just that, unconditional. Yes, hardheadedly questioning, skeptical, and realistic. No perfectionism!

CHAPTER 18

D. T. Suzuki's Zen Buddhism and the Philosophy of Acceptance

Although all forms of Buddhism basically include Gautama Buddha's four noble truths that lead to enlightenment, many different forms exist and some are quite unique. Thus, Zen Buddhism and Tibetan Buddhism stress different views on and ways of achieving unconditional self-acceptance, other-acceptance, and life-acceptance. I consider some Tibetan Buddhism views in chapter 17; and I shall consider some Zen Buddhist views in this chapter.

D. T. Suzuki is known as the leading authority in the West. So I shall quote from his book *Zen Buddhism and Psychoanalysis*, which he wrote with Erich Fromm and Richard DeMartino (New York: Grove Press, 1960).

Suzuki's description of Zen Buddhism includes several semi-mystical positions of self, oneness, absolute subjectivity, inner creativity, the deification of personal feeling, and extreme opposition to logic and intellectualization. But his presentation also includes some clear Zen positions on USA, UOA, and ULA. Let us look at these philosophies.

THE MYTH OF SELF-ESTEEM

In regard to unconditional self-acceptance, the Zen follower is not concerned with proving how "good" he is to others; on the contrary, he "is never obtrusive, but always self-effacing and unassuming" (p. 66).

Zen "proposes . . . to seek Enlightenment for oneself and to help others attain it" (p. 75).

A Zen prayer is "However inexhaustible my passions may be, I pray that they may all be eradicated" (p. 76).

The main Zen goal seems to be to rid oneself of self-centeredness and craving for success and love. This agrees with REBT. Some Zen sects, however, seem to oppose all desire, and not just craving, and to achieve desirelessness. The famous Zen scholar Rinzai, for example, says, "The aristocrat is he who is not burdened with anything, remaining in a state of nondoing." From a mental health standpoint, this would be an extreme reaction against healthy living.

Regarding the achievement of unconditional other-acceptance and compassion, Zen is more concrete:

"The will is . . . wisdom plus love" (p. 58).

"He may not turn the right cheek when the left one is already hurt, but he works silently for the welfare of others" (p. 68).

"His whole existence is devoted to doing good for others" (p. 69).

"However numberless all beings be, I pray that they all be saved" (p. 75).

D. T. Suzuki's Zen Buddhism and the Philosophy of Acceptance

"In the *Lotus Sutra*, we have this: 'As long as there is one single solitary soul to be saved, I am coming back to this world to save him'" (p. 70).

Among the six cardinal virtues of Buddhisattva or Zen-man is "(1) charity, or giving, is to give away for the benefit or welfare of all beings (*Savassattva*) anything and everything one is capable of giving" (p. 72).

Like Tibetan Buddhism, as you can see, Zen is full of compassion. No nonsense about it!

High frustration tolerance or unconditional life-acceptance is also an important part of Zen:

Zen Buddhists "would go on patiently under all unfavorable conditions" (p. 72).

"*Dhyana* is retaining one's tranquil state of mind in any circumstance, unfavorable as well as favorable, and not being disturbed or frustrated even when adverse conditions present themselves one after another. This requires a great deal of training" (p. 72).

This, again, is quite clear. Several forms of Buddhism, including Zen, specialize in teaching patience and fortitude and the philosophy of unconditional life-acceptance.

All told, Zen does reasonably well in promoting USA, notably in encouraging its practitioners to accept themselves *without* desperately striving for material success and love. It does even better with promoting UOA and ULA. It's 2,500-year-old philosophies still nicely hold their ground!

CHAPTER 19

Windy Dryden, Michael Neenan, and Paul Hauck on Unconditional Acceptance

Following my forceful espousal of unconditional self-acceptance (USA) and unconditional other-acceptance (UOA) soon after I created REBT in 1955 (Ellis 1957, 1958, 1962), other REBTers started to make acceptance a crucial goal in psychotherapy. Leading the field in this respect were Michael Bernard, Raymond DiGiuseppe, Russell Grieger, William Knaus, Sue Walen, Janet Wolfe, and Paul Woods. And many others!

Exceptional clear espousals of unconditional acceptance were published by Windy Dryden (1994, 1997, 2002; Dryden and DiGiuseppe 2004; Dryden and Gordon 1991; Dryden and Neenan 2003; and Neenan and Dryden 1992). In addition to promoting USA and UOA with his regular clients, Windy Dryden has also successfully used it in REBT coaching and in special classes with people who are not in therapy.

Typically, Dryden tells his readers, under the heading of self-acceptance, in his book *Life Coaching*, with Michael Neenan, "We have discussed this concept repeatedly in this book because we

183

think it is vitally important in developing and maintaining emotional stability in life. Internalizing the philosophy of self-acceptance helps you to avoid putting yourself down and keeps your focus on your actions, traits and experiences (e.g., 'I made a mess of this situation, which I want to learn from, but I'm not useless because of it.') Self-acceptance greatly reduces the frequency and intensity of your troubled emotions because you refrain from attacking yourself which is often at the heart of such emotions" (Neenan and Dryden 2002, pp. 159–60).

This, of course, is clear-cut USA. Again: "You are neither inferior or superior as a person for having or not having problems. So what are you then? As we have argued throughout this book, you are a fallible (imperfect) who refuses to rate yourself on the basis of your actions or characteristics but does rate those aspects of yourself which you wish to change or improve (e.g., 'I can accept myself for having panic attacks, but I really wish I didn't have them. So I will be seeking professional help to overcome them')" (Neenan and Dryden 2002, p. 146).

Again, a fine urging of clients and readers to refuse to denigrate themselves when they bring on disturbed symptoms. In this same volume, Neenan and Dryden at first neglect making unconditional other-acceptance very important, but finally say, under the heading of "Learn Tolerance": "tolerance means you are willing to allow the existence of other opinions and behaviors but without accepting or liking them; if you find someone's opinion or behavior objectionable, then argue against it. But without condemning the other person for it. Tolerance allows you and others the right to be wrong and thereby reduces the potential for emotional upset" (Neenan and Dryden 2002, p. 167).

This is fairly close to the REBT philosophy of UOA, but could emphasize it still stronger. Dryden consistently teaches his clients and his readers that rating their total self is mistaken and harmful. Here is a typical interchange with a client.

WD: You said that a part can never define the whole. That's a very good reason not to rate yourself at all because *yourself* is too complex to be given a single rating.

Client: So it's okay to rate parts of yourself but not the whole?

WD: Right and the alternative is to accept yourself as an unratable, fallible human being with good and bad aspects. (Dryden and DiGiuseppe 1990).

Dryden (1999) wrote a whole book for the public, *How to Accept Yourself*, which includes a chapter, "The Importance of Unconditional Self-Acceptance," that thoroughly explains conditional self-esteem (CSE) and its dangers. Among other things, he says, "Can you give yourself a rating or evaluation that can give full justice to it, given though as we have already seen, the self is exceedingly complex, and constantly changing? Thus, if you have low self-esteem you are consistently giving your exceptionally complex and changing self a global rating, which is what you would have to do if you wanted high self-esteem. . . . The answer is unconditional self-acceptance" (pp. 17–18). In the same chapter, Dryden shows that self-deprecation stems from a *demand* that people perform well, while USA "is closely linked with a flexible, preferential philosophy." He also espouses unconditional other-acceptance and encourages his readers to challenge their self-centered demands that others *absolutely must* treat them fairly (p. 20).

In his *Fundamentals of Rational Emotive Behaviour Therapy*, a manual for REBT practitioners, Dryden (2002) gives empirical, logical, and pragmatic arguments for self-acceptance and other-acceptance (p. 132).

In their handbook for REBT therapists, Dryden and Neenan (2003) advocate the use of USA quite consistently: "Help your clients to accept themselves for their tendencies to disturb themselves" (p. 66). "Take care that you make clear to clients that

REBT's principle of emotional responsibility does not involve *blaming* them for largely creating their own emotional problems. They are *responsible* but not *damnable* for being responsible" (p. 81). "Try, as far as possible, to keep your ego out of your work as an REBT therapist. Evaluate what you do, but not *yourself* for doing it" (p. 231).

Dryden and Neenan, in their *REBT Therapist's Pocket Companion* (2003), also strongly endorse the REBT theory and practice of unconditional life-acceptance (ULA), as follows: "Help your clients to see that adversities are not the end of the world—they are part of the world" (p. 131).

All told, Windy Dryden and Michael Neenan are solidly behind USA and UOA; and in many other writings they show clients and readers how to surrender their low frustration tolerance (LFT) and how to acquire unconditional life-acceptance (Dryden 1994, 2002; Neenan and Dryden 2002, 2003). Down the REBT line they go!

Paul A. Hauck has practiced Rational Emotive Behavior Therapy since the 1960s and has written a number of popular self-help books on it that have consistently advocated USA, UOA, and ULA. One of his early books was *Overcoming Depression* (1973), in which he noted, "Just blame yourself and you have a depression coming on" (p. 23). Yes, "and what does it mean to feel guilt? It means that you have *labeled* yourself by your behavior" (p. 27).

Throughout his many books on REBT, Hauck shows how conditional self-esteem is harmful and how unconditional self-acceptance is exceptionally helpful. His masterpiece in this respect is *Overcoming the Rating Game: Beyond Self-Love—Beyond Self-Esteem* (1991), to which we refer many people at the Albert Ellis Institute psychological clinic.

As Hauck clearly says at the beginning of chapter 3 of his book, "There is only one technique you need to help you if you wish to avoid feelings of inferiority, low self-respect, low self-esteem, and low worth. To cure yourself of these conditions, do one thing: *never rate yourself or others*" (p. 32). Then he goes on to show "Why you cannot logically rate yourself" and gives many REBT reasons for *il*logically doing so. Then he describes emotional disturbances such as depression, jealousy, and rage that accompany self-rating and other-rating.

Hauck goes on to say, "Accept yourself with your shortcomings if you cannot alter them" (p. 47). And fully accept others, too, in spite of their failings!

Hauck concludes his excellent book with: "Work on this problem until you learn to go beyond self-esteem and beyond self-love. Instead, strive for self-acceptance" (p. 101). A good summary of the REBT position!

In his various other self-help books, Paul Hauck (1974, 1976) consistently shows how people who procrastinate and who are addicted to alcohol and other harmful substances are telling themselves, "It's too hard to stop! I can't stop!" when they could use unconditional life-acceptance to minimize their low frustration tolerance.

As can be seen by the material in this chapter, Windy Dryden, Michael Neenan, and Paul Hauck, all of whom are leading REBT practitioners, ably carry on the Rational Emotive Behavior Therapy traditions of USA and UOA. They also include much advice to professionals and lay people on how to cope with lack of discipline and low frustration tolerance by working at achieving unconditional life-acceptance, so they cover the major REBT psychotherapeutic philosophies.

CHAPTER 20

Self-Esteem and Self-Acceptance in the Writings of Aaron Beck, David Burns, and William Glasser

Aaron Beck became an authority on depression and its treatment by his form of Cognitive Therapy by doing many studies of the dysfunctional schemes of people with mild and serious depression (Beck 1961, 1963, 1967, 1976; Beck, Rush, Shaw, and Emery 1979). In a seminal work, *Anxiety Disorders and Phobias: A Cognitive Perspective*, he also showed how self-esteem and disesteem are crucial elements in creating anxiety and panic states (Beck, Emery, and Greenberg 1985).

In a section on Acceptance in *Anxiety Disorders*, he and his coauthors point out that "the core belief of a person concerned with acceptance is that he may be flawed in some way and thus be unacceptable to others. . . . He *overgeneralizes* and *homogenizes*, that is, he sees acceptance as essential and equally important. . . . Because other people's opinions directly affect his self-esteem, he is highly dependent on feedback from others. . . . In other words, his self-acceptance is based on sand" (pp. 302–303).

In his book *Depression*, Beck (1967) shows that in severe cases, the person's "self-evaluations are at the lowest point. . . . He regards himself as completely inept, and a total failure" (p. 21).

In his main book, *Cognitive Therapy and the Emotional Disorders*, Beck (1976) points out that "Low self-esteem and self-criticism are fundamental in patients with depression and anxiety," and he says that self-deprecation often stems from dysfunctional thinking which includes overgeneralization, all-or-nothing thinking, disqualifying the positive, magnification and minimization, and, from Karen Horney (1950), tyranny of the shoulds. It is remarkable that Beck's formulations in this respect clearly overlap with my own discoveries (Ellis 1958, 1957a, 1957b, 1962), even though they were independently arrived at.

However, although Beck includes the teaching of high frustration tolerance and what I call unconditional life-acceptance to patients with depression and anxiety, he never seems to thoroughly advocate ULA. On the contrary, when patients have low self-esteem because they exceptionally put themselves as well as their behavior down, he shows them their good traits and actions in order to stop their self-deprecation. But in REBT terms, he merely is showing them that if they have enough competent traits, they can accept themselves *conditionally*—have conditional self-esteem. The concept of *un*conditional self-acceptance, even if people have many inadequate behaviors, seems foreign to Beck—as I think is shown in his (Padesky and Beck 2004) and my paper (Ellis 2004) on the similarities and differences between Beck's Cognitive Therapy and REBT.

David Burns, a psychiatrist who authored the famous book *Feeling Good, The New Mood Therapy* (1980/1999a) studied with Aaron Beck at the University of Pennsylvania and learned Cognitive Therapy. Consequently, in *Feeling Good*, he first endorses conditional self-esteem and recommends that depressed individuals who denigrate themselves be shown that they mistakenly overgeneralize and that they have some distinctly good traits and perform-ances for which they can esteem themselves.

Fortunately, Burns doesn't stop there, but has a remarkably good chapter 13, "Your Work Is Not Your Worth," which clearly espouses unconditional self-acceptance. Thus, he states that what he calls *real* self-esteem "is the capacity to experience maximum self-love and joy whether or not you are successful at any point in your life" (p. 262). This is exactly the REBT definition of USA; and because he gives credit to my books, *Reason and Emotion in Psychotherapy* (Ellis 1962) and *A Guide to Rational Living* (Ellis and Harper 1961/1975), he may well have learned this definition from my writings.

Throughout *Feeling Good*, Burns shows how conventional self-esteem is harmful and will frequently lead to depression and anxiety. He gives some excellent role-playing and other exercises for readers to combat it and construct USA. He has a special section, "Escape from the Achievement Trap," that shows his readers how to refuse to be a victim of CSE.

In his book *Ten Days to Self-Esteem* (1993), and the revised *Feeling Good Handbook* (1999b), Burns expertly continues his thoroughgoing assault against conditional self-esteem and his advocacy of unconditional self-acceptance. He still endorses "self-esteem" but redefines this term to mean "self-acceptance." He has a section in *Ten Days to Self-Esteem*, "Conditional vs. Unconditional Self-Esteem," that clearly makes the distinction I have been making in this book. This section includes eight benefits of USA, including "I will always feel equal to other people—never superior or inferior. This will make my personal relationships more rewarding" (p. 186).

Burns also shows the difference between healthy sorrow and grief and unhealthy depression when someone you love dies; and the difference between healthy anger at someone's unjust acts and unhealthy rage at the person performing these acts. This is quite similar to REBT's distinction between healthy and unhealthy negative emotions (Ellis 2001a, 2001b, 2002, 2003, 2004).

In his *Feeling Good Handbook*, Burns (1999b) continues to endorse unconditional self-acceptance and recommends, as some of the main techniques to help people fully accept themselves with their incompetent behavior, my shame-attacking exercise which I describe in chapter 25 of this book. In doing this exercise, people deliberately act foolishly, risk social criticism in doing so, and work on feeling healthfully sorry but not unhealthfully self-hating or depressed about the disapproval they receive.

Burns covers anger quite thoroughly in chapter 7 of *Feeling Good* and though he does not come out clearly for unconditional other-acceptance, he especially shows how anger results from the *shoulds* of self-centered entitlement: "I am entitled to people treating me exactly the way I want them to do, and when they treat me unfairly, as they *absolutely should not*, they are no damned good!" He shows that you can never be certain about others' unfairness—since there is no way of absolutely defining unfair behavior; and that your entitlement to it is mythical and irrational. In several ways he comes close to specifically teaching UOA and he implicitly endorses it. In his discussion of empathy and stroking in the *Feeling Good Handbook*, he points out that even when people treat you badly and unfairly, "Don't criticize or condemn them as a person. . . . Attacking them personally is very different from commenting negatively on something they are doing or thinking" (p. 409). Here he gets to the essence of UOA; and in his constant reminding his readers of the cost-benefit considerations of their whining about changing their horror of work, relationships, and other stresses, he keeps advocating unconditional life-acceptance along with unconditional self-acceptance. So David Burns gets an A for his consistent acceptance of acceptance! Unlike Aaron Beck, he goes out of his way to teach the *philosophy* of USA, UOA, and ULA—as, of course, does REBT.

William Glasser emphasizes the great importance of love and relationships throughout his writings, particularly in *Choice Therapy* (1998) and *Reality Therapy in Action* (2002). Unfortunately, he keeps stating that people *need* to relate to others instead of their strongly *desiring* compassion for their happiness. Therefore, the *choice* that he gives them is not the REBT choice of desiring and feeling healthfully sorry when you are loveless instead of needing and feeling unhealthily depressed when you fail to make good relationships.

Nonetheless, he clearly shows the value of acquiring unconditional other-acceptance in *Choice Therapy*. Thus:

> To maintain a good relationship with others, "we must stop choosing to coerce, force, compel, punish, reward, manipulate, bias, motivate, blame, complain, nag, badger, rant, rate, and withdraw. We must replace these destructive behaviors with choosing to care, listen, support, negotiate, encourage, love, befriend, trust, accept, welcome, and esteem" (p. 21).

> "Marriage has the best chance when both partners have a low need for power" over the other (p. 101).

> "The only person we can control is ourselves" (p. 97).

> "The relationship takes precedence over always being right" in a good marriage (p. 210).

In regard to unconditional self-acceptance Glasser is not as clear or as forceful as he could be. He definitely sees that you *choose* to insist you are more powerful than and superior to other people and says, "Driven by power, we have created a pecking order in almost everything we do. . . . Trying to get ahead even to the point of pushing others down is a way of life" (p. 211).

Glasser keeps pointing out that if you refuse to strive for power over others and desist from making your status with others a pecking order, you can focus on the much better choice—working on your own self-centeredness, and considering others as your *equals*, and enjoying cooperative and enjoyable relations with them. His main solution for your achieving unconditional self-acceptance is for you to focus on achieving unconditional other-acceptance. Somewhat like the Tibetan Zen Buddhists, he uses compassion as an antidote to the demand for one-upmanship and its concomitant foolish insistence on putting yourself down when you do not manage to be a "superior person." Glasser largely advises you to avoid self-downing by avoiding all other-downing. But he rarely tackles it in its own right.

Glasser approaches the philosophy of unconditional life-acceptance by saying at the beginning of *Choice Therapy* that you can only control your thoughts, feelings, and actions, not those of others. Therefore, you can't have everything you want—and you had darned well better *accept* frustration. Even preschoolers, he says, therefore "have to learn the process of not wanting too much" (p. 58).

Glasser also insists, when treating a woman with depression, "I shall start to teach her some choice theory—that no one can make her miserable, only she can do that to herself" (p. 132). Moreover, he says, "it is also crucial to teach clients that life is not fair"—and they had better accept that reality (pp. 132–33).

All told, Glasser clearly presents the philosophy of unconditional other-acceptance and makes it a cardinal point in his therapy. He more vaguely promotes unconditional self-acceptance and unconditional life-acceptance but shows his clients and readers how, using his Choice Theory, they can always *choose* to follow those ideals.

CHAPTER 21

Stephen Hayes and Other Cognitive Behavior Therapists Who Endorse Acceptance and Commitment Therapy

Steven Hayes was once a radical behaviorist but has now constructed a relational frame theory that stresses the behaviorist point that human disturbance always occurs in an environmental *context*; and that the main reason why people disturb themselves is that, unlike other animals, they have language. This is an enormous advantage to them in many ways, and of course we'd better not abandon it. But language and symbolic processes also are tricky and help you invent emotional "horrors" that do not really exist. Thus a depressed person who suffers real misfortunes—like disability, poverty, and rejection—will with language *imagine* a lovely future in heaven when he has no *experience* of death. He may then talk himself into a worse state of depression, may then tell himself that he *can't stand* his depressed feelings, may insist that he must not even *think about* his poor conditions and his dismal feelings, and may *invent* a peaceful afterlife that will save him from all his pain. He may thereby, without any realistic reason, commit suicide. An animal, in similar circumstances, would not commit suicide because it has no language and imaginations about the future to "help" it do so.

Following up his relation frame theory (RFT), Hayes has created an unusual form of therapy called Acceptance and Commitment Therapy (ACT) (Hayes, Stroshal, and Wilson 1999). ACT is allergic to disputing the content of disturbed language—for example, "I *absolutely must not* be in continual pain! I *can't bear* it. It's *awful!* My only way out is to kill myself, have real peace, and even enjoy my afterlife." Where REBT would show a suicidal client how to dispute her musts, her inflexible thinking, her philosophy of low frustration tolerance, her *awfulizing*, her hopelessness, and her refusal to accept life's troubles, ACT says that this kind of disputing the *content* of her thinking will frequently lead to more disturbance, to more avoidance of experiencing her pain, to more awfulizing, and to more disturbance.

Partially, Hayes is correct. Language, as REBT shows, often helps people overgeneralize and say, "I must not suffer from severe frustrations!" "I must not experience depression when I have a poor life." "I *can't stand* facing frustrations and feelings of depression. Therefore I can't be happy *at all* and I have to kill myself!" So language *sometimes* involves musts and musts about musts and "causes" people to have problems about problems. But REBT teaches that you can *choose*, by realistic, logical, and pragmatic disputation—by thinking about your thinking—to turn your musts to preferences and better solve your emotional problems about your unfortunate environment, and then also reduce your environmental and situational difficulties.

ACT does similar cognitive-behavioral therapy, but especially tries to untangle clients' verbal knots "by loosening the bonds of language itself" (p. 78). It does so by a variety of cognitive-emotive-behavioral methods, especially philosophical evaluation, cost-benefit analysis, mindfulness training, and an emphasis on metaphor instead of active-directive disputing of what REBT calls dysfunctional and irrational beliefs. I have recently taken the ACT and RFT formulations of Hayes (in press) and shown that they are quite compatible with REBT.

Ciarochi, Robb, and Goodsell (in press), who have taken ACT workshops and also practiced REBT, have done the same. We think that ACT and REBT can be integrated, but Hayes (in press) demurs.

The main point that I want to stress in this chapter is that ACT distinctly lives up to its name. It is an innovative form of cognitive behavior therapy that tries very hard to help clients have unconditional self-acceptance (USA). It fully endorses the Buddhist view that "suffering is a basic characteristic of human life" (p. 1). But humans can minimize their suffering if they *choose* to do so, if they analyze how they create their disturbances. With ACT techniques, they can understand their own destructive verbal processes "and work to alter them or better contain them" (p. 12).

As its name clearly implies, ACT is a *philosophy* that says that "truth is always local and pragmatic" (p. 19). "In ACT what is true is what works" (p. 20). ACT's three goals are "interpretation, prediction, and influence" (p. 24). It fights against clients' rigid rule-governed behavior, such as too much compliance to social rules. It urges both clients and their therapists to acquire unconditional self-acceptance (USA), unconditional other-acceptance (UOA), and unconditional life-acceptance (ULA) for pandemic human suffering. It is quite definite and pushy about the desirability of these three forms of acceptance; and that is why I think that it is in many ways compatible with REBT and can be integrated with it (Ellis, in press).

A good example of ACT's endorsement of UOA is this: "One of the most elegant forms of willingness is forgiveness. . . . However, the gift of forgiveness is not a gift to someone else. Giving what went before is most particularly not a gift to the wrongdoer. It is a gift to oneself." Bien!

ACT requires, as does REBT, unusual commitment by therapists and clients. Since it views human disturbance as biologically prone,

197

language oriented, and enmeshed in difficult environmental situations, it holds that dysfunctional behavior cannot be easily altered. Also, since ACT requires basic changes in people's values and philosophies, and ongoing efforts to keep looking at them and revising them, it requires the learning of functional new experiences to solidify workable change. Like REBT, again, it stresses active work and practice toward emotional health. No rest for the weary!

Hayes (Hayes, Follette, and Linehan 2004), in a new book, *Mindfulness, Acceptance, and Relationship: Expanding the Cognitive Behavioral Tradition*, acknowledges that quite a number of innovative cognitive behavior therapists are adopting and adapting various kinds of techniques that have important acceptance and commitment elements. These include several well-known therapists who are included in his anthology—such as Zindal Segal, John Teasdale, Robert Kohlenberg, T. B. Borkovec, G. Terence Wilson, and G. Alan Marlatt.

These authors and their colleagues all largely favor Hayes's ACT procedures and his RFT theory, but they also add some original concepts and therapeutic techniques. They and Hayes agree that their innovative methods can be integrated with ACT; and it seems strange that Hayes does not also agree that REBT, which is much closer to ACT than some of these other therapies, cannot also be integrated with ACT.

I have no space to show here how these and other innovative therapists have endorsed significant aspects of USA, UOA, and ULA in their chapters of *Mindfulness, Acceptance, and Relationship*. Read the book and see for yourself. But I am delighted to see that contemporary cognitive behavior therapy is nicely advancing in these respects. At this rate, its theory and practice may soon routinely include the therapeutic endorsement of unconditional self-acceptance, unconditional other-acceptance, and unconditional life-acceptance. Their time seems to be truly arriving!

CHAPTER 22

Existential Anxiety and How to Defeat It with the Courage to Be

According to Kierkegaard, Heidegger, Sartre, and other leading existentialists, people all have existential anxiety, often severely. Is this true; and if so, how can you minimize it, especially by having the courage to be?

Yes, *in all probability*, practically all of us have considerable existential anxiety—for a number of reasons which I will now try to clarify, since existentialists often do not do so. Here goes!

We all seem to be born and reared with major conflicting and contradictory tendencies.

1. As infants, we can't take care of ourselves, are innately passive in many ways, and perhaps neurologically train ourselves to be more passive.
2. As we develop, we retain a great deal of our passivity but we also enjoy activity and independence.
3. Our dependent and independent propensities often significantly conflict and battle with each other.

4. We often simultaneously strive for great (maybe perfect) dependency-passivity *and* great (maybe perfect) independency-autonomy. Real conflict, inconsistency, and no perfect solution!

5. We are born and reared with strong tendencies to raise our *preferences* into *musts, shoulds, oughts, and demands.* We then convince ourselves that we prefer *and* need (a) dependency, to be greatly cared for and (b) autonomy, self-direction, and caring for ourselves. More conflict!

6. Our contradictory and conflicting desires are bad enough, but when we (frequently) raise these to dire needs, we suffer great frustration, rebelliousness, anxiety, depression, and rage. Maybe all three!

7. We often have strong *perfectionistic* leanings (again, innate and socially learned). We demand, for example, *absolute* autonomy and *unmitigated* love. We demand *complete* gratification *and thoroughgoing* lack of frustration. When partially (or even mainly) satisfied, we demand and are anxious about not having *more.*

8. Another way of putting it, we often demand *guarantees* that we will not now (or sometime later) be deprived of what we want or inflicted with what we don't want. Yes, guarantees.

9. We *need* what we *want* easily, immediately, yesterday!

10. When we make ourselves anxious, depressed, or raging with our infantile, contradictory, and perfectionistic demands, we frequently horrify ourselves about these uncomfortable feelings; insist that they *absolutely must not* exist; and wind up anxious about our anxiety, depressed about our depression, and self-damning about our raging. Double whammy!

11. Because we *insist* that we must be competent and achieving

in dealing with our contradictory and unrealistic demands, not to mention the world's problems, and because we cannot solve all of them, we practically always doom ourselves to near-despair and to (perfect) nondespair. Even when we temporarily are at peace with ourselves and the world, we demand a (perfect) guarantee that we will *always* remain so. Lots of luck!

12. In these—and many other—ways, we keep asking for, and often demand, existences that don't humanly exist—perfection, guarantees, dire necessities, absolutes, unconflicting contradictions. Humbug!

Philosophers and religious prophets have faced these problems for centuries and have come up with several solutions, for example, magical or supernatural solutions. All we have to do is to invent a kindly God who will nicely solve our existential problems, and devoutly believe S/He will do so, and that will end that. This is an improbable "solution" but, if you devoutly believe it, it may work—for a while. You make yourself absolutely certain that your deity completely and perfectly will provide for you—and hope for the best. Since, alas, you cannot be sure that S/He will provide, you fervently hope so.

Another main "solution" that sages have provided is Nirvana. This means that you voluntarily give up all desire—let alone need—for satisfaction and you discipline yourself to consistently lead a "perfect" desireless life. Assuming that you could still survive—which I somehow doubt—you would then experience no pain or deprivation—and no pleasure. Sounds pretty boring.

A better solution to your frustrating and contradictory human existence is the more realistic one, which has been advocated by St. Francis, Paul Tillich, Reinhold Niebuhr, and others—what they and REBT call acceptance: (1) unconditional self-acceptance (USA),

(2) unconditional other-acceptance (UOA), and (3) unconditional life-acceptance (ULA).

Preliminary to or along with your achieving these major forms of unconditional acceptance, you had better accept ruthless realism, or what Karl Popper called critical realism. Instead of the *un*realistic "solutions" to existential anxiety listed above, try these substitutes:

1. Don't give in to your infantile behaviors when you are an adult and let yourself be quite dependent on your caretakers and to passively "exploit" their kindness. Choose your more active and less passive urges to largely—not perfectionistically!—take care of yourself.
2. Work at naturally and deliberately *enjoying* your activity and your independence.
3. See that your overdependent and your independent activities sometimes conflict and battle with each other, and that you can't always have exactly what you want when you want it.
4. When there is a real conflict between your overdependent and independent urges, accept that unideal conflict.
5. Recognize that you have a strong desire to escalate your *preferences* to be autonomous and dependent into dire conflicting *needs*.
6. Especially recognize that your *neediness* for anything easily makes you anxious, depressed, and raging.
7. Watch your *perfectionism*. Your strong desires for love, gratification, and success can be helpful. But your needs for absolute love, and complete and perfect gratification can maim you.
8. Wanting is fine, but demanding *guarantees* that you will get what you desire and never get what you abhor will lead to anxiety.
9. Watch it when you think that you *easily* and effortlessly must get what you want.

10. When you make yourself feel anxious, depressed, or raging don't whine about being so disturbed—as you presumably *must not* be.
11. Don't *insist* that you have to be competent and achieving. Do your best to be—which is all you can do.
12. Again *extreme* perfectionism, necessitizing, and absolutizing are light-years removed from trying to do well or even very well. Try forever—but you don't *have to* perfectly make it!

Once you *un*perfectionistically, *some* of the time, *strive* to do what you can do, you have laid the groundwork for unconditional acceptance of yourself, others, and the difficult world. To summarize some of the main things I have been saying:

Try, try, and try again for the success, the love, the artistic and material things you want and to minimize what you don't want. But—

- *Accept* the frustrations, hassles, pain, disgust, and depression you no longer want but can't reduce.
- *Accept* the disapproval, neglect, scorn, resentment, jealousy, and hostility of others. Don't hurt *yourself* by their names and gestures.
- *Accept* without *liking* your failing and incompetence. But try, try again!
- *Accept* unfair treatment from others. Forgiveness, not revenge, may change it in the future. But nothing *has to* work!
- *Accept* your self, your being, your aliveness but do your best to change some of your inept and immoral *behaviors*.
- *Accept* control of your own sabotaging ways. Accept help but not dependency on others. Be autonomous but not narcissistic.
- *Accept* meaning and purpose in life and make long-range, ongoing vital absorbing interests that *you* choose.

- *Accept* your mortality and don't forego the one life you definitely have for a promised afterlife.
- *Accept* that magic won't solve your problems but hard work and effort may alleviate them.
- *Accept* the fact that you are a social creature and can live without the goodwill and cooperation of others—but pretty badly. Unconditional other-acceptance (UOA) will help you preserve and enjoy others and ward off human extinction.
- *Accept* your (and others') human fallibility. Damning yourself for your inadequacies will hardly make you (or anyone) less fallible!
- *Accept* your proneness to good and bad feelings. You can, with hard work and reflection, improve your self- and other-destructive feelings. But achieving minimal feelings will achieve minimal aliveness. Reflect on and change your destructive feelings—but don't make yourself into a zombie!
- *Accept* the fact that you are a person who thinks, feels, and behaves. Interactionally! You feel the way you think and behave, behave the way you think and feel, and think the way you feel and behave. All three! You can change all three—with the help of the other two.
- *Accept* persistent thinking, feeling, and acting. You can start right now; but time and persistent practice are the great healers!
- *Accept* the fact that self-control is the most effective control that you have.
- *Accept* that acceptance is largely compassion—for you and *your* self, for others and *their* self, and for the troubled world and *its* self. Once again, all three.

Is that *all* you'd better accept? Maybe. I still may think of more!

CHAPTER 23
Taking the Road Less Traveled to Unconditional Self-Acceptance

I now have shown you what unconditional self-acceptance (USA) is and how it significantly differs from self-efficacy and, especially, conditional self-esteem (CSE). Let us assume that I have made some good points and that you see the disadvantages of acquiring CSE and the real advantages of acquiring USA. It took awhile, but supposedly we made it. Now what?

Now the simple question and the not-so-simple answer: Question: "How do I get unconditional self-acceptance?" Answer: "In many cognitive, emotive, and behavioral ways—but mainly in two ways: (1) By deciding and determining to get it, against all odds; and (2) By working your butt off to create the willpower that you have presumably already decided to get."

First, as to the deciding. According to the theory and practice of REBT, you are a choice-making person and have the innate and acquired ability to choose to get USA. You have had years—maybe decades—of not having it and suffering thereby. As this book has helped you see so far, you see the virtue of self-efficacy and would like to have a lot of it. But, like most people, you easily confuse it with conditional self-esteem and now see that that doesn't exactly work too well. You sometimes push yourself to do well and to be approved of by significant others; but even when that "works," it has its great limitations. You get some efficiency for a while in striving for success, but you are underlyingly or overtly anxious. You see that you can't guarantee it—and you put yourself down: which is exactly what CSE is. You don't do well *enough*, or do *temporarily* well, or first do well and then fall on your face. You soon realize this and see that you have very conditional self-esteem (not to mention conditional self-acceptance). You want more.

Seeing the perfidy—and trickery—of your ways, and having at least a notion that you can achieve USA, you seek it out. You start with one of the first REBT propositions or assumptions: whatever you think, feel, or do is interactional and transactional. You feel the way you think and act; you act the way you feel and think; and you think the way you feel and act. All three!

So you decide, somewhat reluctantly: "I guess I'll have to change some of my thinking, feeling, and acting. In fact, considerably!" Ah, a good start. But still merely deciding to change—not very much feeling it and doing it. You have the will; perhaps you have the determination; but still no willpower.

Okay, so you work for a while on the will and determination. You remind yourself of the many disadvantages of CSE and the potential advantages of USA. You perhaps go back and read chapter 7 of this book, which outlines many advantages (not so bad) of CSE, as well as many disadvantages of CSE, as well as many possible greater advantages of USA. You do a cost-benefit ratio in regard to them and figure out—several times!—that your goal, all right, is unconditional acceptance, but that it is very easy for you to confuse this with self-efficacy and with conditional self-esteem! Amazingly easy, because you naturally think and feel these other ways; and you have practiced doing this for a good many years.

So you keep willing and determining. You try to get some relevant information and see that even willing and determining take hard work and that you have to keep from sidetracking yourself in those respects.

Well, you got some relevant information from Korzybski and general semantics: globally rating yourself as a *good person* when you do a *good act* is false, for you are always a *person who* does well (or badly) and never a totally good or bad person. So when you slip back to CSE—for example, "I'm good for even deciding to work for USA"—you tell yourself, "Hogwash! *It* is good but *it* doesn't make *me* good." So you give up CSE about your deciding to change, and return to your decision and emphasize that *it* is good, but *you* are not good or bad. You're just *working* good.

Back to striving for USA, not CSE. And you keep *striving*, which means *acting*. So you try out USA again—"I *can* accept myself *unconditionally*, even though I'm slipping back! What do I do to *keep* choosing and determining to do so? Let me point out to myself the vast *difference* between accepting my *working* at this and accepting *me* for working at it."

You forge ahead—slowly but surely. You dislike your fallbacks, but resist disliking *you* for your fallbacks. Determinedly! Correctively!

Your pace is persistent and endless. Many little—and big—fallbacks to conditional self-acceptance. Many times seeing this and *stopping* this, until CSE gets much less and USA gets more frequent. On and on!

Always, as on you go, using three main interactive tools:

1. *Thinking, plotting, scheming, imagining.* "I *can* work for USA." "CSE, which I just returned to, sabotages me!" "I

stupidly slipped again but that never makes me a stupid person—that's *over*generalizing."

2. *Feeling, experiencing.* "It feels challenging and fine to work on myself." "Feeling noble for working at this challenge is great, but I am not a great person." "I *enjoy* changing, but it doesn't make me *a special person.*"

3. *Acting, behaving, moving.* "I can work hard at this changing but I can also relax, relax." "If I risk changing myself and fail, I still have *learned* some valuable things." "If I find it too hard to go on with my changing and people put me down for failing, it is too bad but never a disgrace."

With these three complex and interactive tools, you *keep* deciding, determining, getting new information, reflecting, experiencing, risk-taking, backsliding, unbacksliding, regrouping, and so forth. No rest for the weary! Your thinking prods you to feeling and action. Your feeling prods you to thinking and action. Your action prods you to thinking and feeling.

As an additional bonus—as well as additional practice—your conscious quest for USA can vaccinate you against the common secondary symptoms of disturbance of striving people. When you make yourself feel anxious and depressed because your search for USA is hardly marvelously effective and includes considerable pain and disappointment, you do not put yourself down for your setbacks and make yourself anxious about your anxiety, depressed about your depression, or intolerant of your great efforts. Too bad!—but not *awful* or *horrible.*

If all this sounds vague, let me in the next several chapters describe how you can use some of the main cognitive, emotive, and behavioral techniques of REBT and Cognitive Behavior Therapy and show you how to use them specifically to achieve USA rather than conditional self-esteem. Again, I shall explain how you can use them interactively.

CHAPTER 24

Specific Thinking, Plotting, Planning, and Scheming Techniques of Achieving Unconditional Self-Acceptance

Many cognitive methods have been used for centuries, in addition to emotive and behavioral methods, by philosophers, religious leaders, counselors, and therapists to help people interrupt their disturbances and gain greater happiness. Therapists have adopted and adapted many of these techniques—including Pierre Janet, Alfred Adler, and Paul Dubois. When these methods were beginning to fall into disuse in the 1950s, George Kelly and I independently revived them in 1955; and a little later Aaron Beck, Donald Meichenbaum, David Barlow, William Glasser, and others repeated this revival in the 1960s and 1970s in using many kinds of cognitive behavior therapy.

REBT was pioneering in that, starting in 1955, it integrated emotive and behavior with thinking methods; it particularly stressed the importance of thinking about thinking; and it uniquely zeroed in on the unusually important issues of unconditional self-acceptance (USA), unconditional other-acceptance (UOA), and unconditional life-acceptance (ULA). With these main thinking-feeling-behaving methods of REBT, you can particularly experiment to help you achieve USA.

Like Cognitive Behavior Therapy, REBT stresses the role of rational beliefs (RBs) and irrational beliefs (IBs) in individual and social disturbances. Its ABC theory hypothesizes that humans strongly desire approval and success in several areas and are commonly thwarted by Adversities (A) that lead to healthy Consequences (C)—such as disappointment, sorrow, and regret—or to unhealthy Consequences (C)—such as depression, rage, and severe anxiety. Rational Beliefs (RBs) take the form of preferences—for example, "I would like very much for you to love me, but obviously you don't have to. If you don't I will hardly kill myself." Irrational Beliefs (IBs) take the form of demands—for example, "You *absolutely must* love me, or else it is *awful*, I'll never win love, and maybe I'd better kill myself!"

To profoundly Dispute (D) your IBs about worthlessness, you choose several pathways, especially these:

Realistic Disputing: "Why *must* you absolutely love me? Why are you the *only* beloved for me?" *Answer*: "You obviously don't *have to* love me, though that would be *preferable*. Obviously, there can be other beloveds for me."

Logical Disputing: "If I can't win your love, does that make me an unlovable, worthless person?" *Answer:* "No, it merely makes me a person who failed to win you. I *am* not unlovable but a person *who is unloved* this time. Others may find me very lovable."

Pragmatic Disputing: "What makes it *awful*, as *bad* as it could be, if you don't love me, as you must?" *Answer:* "Nothing makes it *awful* or *terrible*, for all time—just highly *depriving and inconvenient*. For now!"

Using REBT, you Dispute and rip up absolutistic thinking, including *never, always, as awful as it could be*, and other overgen-

210

eralizations, and you keep *strongly* and *emotionally* doing this until, first, you accept *you* with your *failings* (USA). Second, you accept other *people* with their poor *behaviors* (UOA). Third, you accept *life* but do your best to reduce its *hassles* (ULA). You *persistently* do this until you unconsciously and automatically tend to achieve USA, UOA, and ULA.

While doing this—actively, vigorously Disputing your IBs— you tend to *work out* and *reflect* on rational coping statements for present and future use with possible or actual Adversities (As). Such as: "I never *need* what I definitely want." "*Too bad* but not *awful* when I am deprived." "*No one*, including me, is a worthless person." "Other people may treat me *unfairly* but are never *bad people*." "Life is *often* but not *always* miserable."

LOOK FOR POSSIBLE SECONDARY SYMPTOMS

Since it is common, suspect that you may have symptoms about your symptoms—these may create self-downing and then you down yourself for having it. Or you may defame other people and then defame yourself for defaming them. Or you may whine about life's Adversities and then beat yourself up for your childish whining. If you see that you are castigating yourself for your *lack* of acceptance, these symptoms will block you from making yourself more accepting. So see that you first *acknowledge* your nonacceptance; second, accept *it* as a failing but not *you* as a failure; third, work like hell at unblamefully remedying *it*.

KEEP ASSESSING YOUR COST-BENEFIT RATIO ABOUT USA, UOA, AND ULA

As I noted before, acknowledge the benefits and the costs of your various kinds of self-rating. Even the worst kind, conditional self-esteem (CSE), has its advantages; and the best kind, USA, has some disadvantages (such as possible narcissism and grandiosity). Keep assessing their benefits and disbenefits. Your steady question to yourself is: "Is this attitude *worth* it?" When it isn't, prove this to yourself. Show how sabotaging it is. Prove that it does you more harm than good.

Along these lines, you can make a list of, say, the advantages of conditional self-esteem *and* the disadvantages. Give all of these a personal-rating (to you) of from one to ten. Then add up the benefits and disbenefits and see if one side doesn't really outweigh the other. Use this knowledge!

USING DISTRACTION METHODS

When you have difficulty using some of the methods described here, especially if you are anxious about using them well, you can calm yourself down with various distraction techniques—such as meditation, yoga, and other relaxation techniques. These are often palliative and only work for a while—but meanwhile they enable you to figure out better solutions and come back to your problems afresh.

If you get confused, say, about whether you are really accepting yourself unconditionally or, instead, are giving yourself conditional self-esteem, you can take time out for relaxation techniques—such as Jacobson's progressive relaxation method—and work for a while relaxing the muscles of your body. This in itself may distract you from your worry and will help you. Or it will give you time to think things through and come to a reflective conclusion.

MODELING METHODS

Albert Bandura (1997) and other psychologists have used modeling to help children and adults to acquire learning skills, and REBT and cognitive behavior therapists have often taught their clients how to successfully use it (J. Beck 1995; Ellis 2001a, 2001b, 2003a, 2003b). If you want to use this technique to help yourself acquire better self-efficacy and unconditional self-acceptance, you can take several channels:

1. You can find people you personally know who exhibit unusual USA, talk to them, discover exactly how they do so, and use their relevant thoughts, feelings, and actions as models. Clarissa, for example, admired June's rare ability to accept herself in spite of the severe criticism of her boss; she spoke to June about this and discovered that whenever June was criticized at work she went out of her way to list a few reasons why her boss's suggestions were *correct* and *potentially helpful*, thanked him for his suggestions, and never put herself down. June made herself learn from her errors and was proud of her *ability* to do so but not proud of *herself* for correcting them. Clarissa, following June, forced herself to look for her supervisor's valid criticism, to use it, and to not berate herself for her defects. She then started to become more self-accepting.
2. You can find other people, especially some famous ones, who accept themselves very well, and use them as models. Norman was amazed when I told him the famous story of

how Epictetus, who was a Roman slave, warned his master not to tighten the ball and chain on his leg because he might break Epictetus's leg. The master ignored him, tightened the chain, and actually broke his leg. Whereupon, without feeling hurt and angry, Epictetus calmly said, "See, I was right. You broke my leg." His master was so impressed with Epictetus's self-acceptance and lack of anger that he freed him to become the leading Stoic philosopher of Rome. Norman followed Epictetus's unusual demeanor and made himself self-accepting and unangry.

3. You can find other models of USA to talk to and read about to help with all kinds of your nonacceptance and other emotional-behavioral problems and use them to your advantage.

USING BIBLIOTHERAPY
AND HOMEWORK MATERIALS

REBT and some of the other cognitive behavior therapies use various kinds of handouts, books, recordings, REBT self-help forms, and games to repetitively sink home the rational philosophies and practices that therapists recommend to clients. They especially encourage people with self-deprecation and conditional self-esteem to regularly fill out the REBT Self-Help Form.

Carol had a very difficult time seeing that although her school and work failings were forgivable, her savagely berating her teenage son, Henry, for his lies and excuses was wrong and harmful and unforgivable. Only after I practically forced her to fill out a score of REBT Self-Help Forms did her final example show that she really "got" and was consistently using some aspects of unconditional self-acceptance with excoriating Henry's delinquencies.

TEACHING USA TO FRIENDS AND RELATIVES

I have used REBT with considerable group therapy since I first experimented with it in 1959. I quickly found what I had suspected: When people talk out their problems with group members, they get all kinds of cathartic and educational help. But, more importantly, when they sensibly talk other group members out of their rigid irrationalities, they also talk themselves out of their own.

Jonathan, for example, kept convincing himself that when he solved difficult math problems—which he often did, being a math major—that proved how intelligent he was, won his professor's acclaim, and made him a "superior person." He wouldn't accept my and other members of his therapy group's logic that since he was *sometimes* superior at math, that never made him a superior—and practically "noble"—person. He fixated on the fact that he *always* did well at math, therefore he *was* superior.

In group, Jonathan encountered his cousin, Tom, who was almost his exact replica and who held that since he excelled in drawing, and *always* did so, that made him a superior artist—and, of course, a superior person. Tom rigidly held his ground—until he came in second in his art class and felt quite unsuperior and depressed. The group gave Jonathan the homework assignment of getting together for an evening with Tom and persisting at talking him out of his "superior person" feelings. He did so—but made at first only slight inroads with Tom—getting him (almost!) to see that his superiority at (some forms of) drawing couldn't make him (a) a totally superior artist nor (b) a wonderfully superior person. Jonathan lost with Tom—but largely gave up his own complex about being a "superior person" at math and *everything*.

MORE COGNITIVE-EMOTIVE TECHNIQUES

A number of REBT practitioners have devised specific cognitive-emotive exercises for achieving unconditional self-acceptance that you can find in *REBT Resource Book for Practitioners* (Bernard and Wolfe 2000). Here are some good suggestions you can put to use:

From Paul Hauck: The Psychology of Self-Rating

1. There are three ways to overcome inferiority feelings:
   a) never rate yourself;
   b) develop performance confidence;
   c) make people respect you.
2. Of these, the first is the best and only method that always works.
3. Self-rating can lead to one or both types of extremes:
   a) feelings of inferiority, guilt, low self-esteem, or depression;
   b) feelings of superiority, conceit, or vanity.
4. Inferiority feelings are at the heart of all feelings of guilt, self-consciousness, low "self-esteem," fear of people, and fear of failure.
5. The "self" is the sum of all the good and bad judgments that can be made about your traits and behaviors. These run into the millions. Therefore, you, as an entity, can never be rated; only the numerous things *about* you can be rated.
6. Always separate the rating of the *person* from the rating of the *behavior, possessions, titles,* or *character traits*.
7. Rating yourself causes four common disturbances:
   a) embarrassment;
   b) humiliation;
   c) shame; and
   d) insult.

8. If you refuse to judge yourself again, you will never feel those emotions again.
9. Embarrassment = falling mildly short of your expectations. (E.g., you arrive late at a wedding.)
10. Humiliation = falling moderately short of your expectations. (E.g., you were drunk at the wedding.)
11. Shame = feeling greatly short of your expectations. (E.g., you vomited on the bride.)
12. When you feel *insulted*, you are in effect admitting that the rude remark about you means you are undesirable. No one can insult you without your permission.
13. Give up the idea of "self-love" and "self-esteem." They are both derivatives of self-rating.
14 How should you rate yourself? Don't! Instead, *accept yourself*. That's your best bet.

For more help, read Paul Hauck's book, Overcoming the Rating Game.

From Bill Borcherdt, Thoughts to Help Increase Self-Acceptance

1. I'm not a bad person when I act badly; I am a person who has acted badly.
2. I'm not a *good person* when I act well and accomplish things; I am a person who has acted well and accomplished things.
3. I can accept myself whether I win, lose, or draw.
4. I would better not define myself entirely by my behavior, by others' opinions, or by anything else under the sun.
5. I can *be* myself without trying to *prove* myself.
6. I am not a fool for acting foolishly. If I were a fool, I could never learn from my mistakes.

7. I am not an ass for acting asininely.
8. I have many faults and can work on correcting them without blaming, condemning, or damning myself for having them.
9. Correction, yes! Condemnation, no!
10. I can neither prove myself to be a good nor a bad person. The wisest thing I can do is simply to accept myself.
11. I am not a worm for acting wormily.
12. I cannot "prove" human worth or worthlessness; it's better that I not try to do the impossible.
13. Accepting myself as being human is better than trying to prove myself superhuman or rating myself as subhuman.
14. I can itemize my weaknesses, disadvantages, and failures without judging or defining my*self* by them.
15. Seeking self-esteem or self-worth leads to self-judgments and eventually to self-blame. Self-*acceptance* avoids these self-ratings.
16. I am not stupid for acting stupidly. Rather, I am a nonstupid person who sometimes produces stupid behavior.
17. I can reprimand my behavior without reprimanding myself.
18. I can praise my behavior without praising myself.
19. Get after your behavior! Don't get after yourself!
20. I can acknowledge my mistakes and hold myself accountable for making them—but without berating myself for creating them.
21. It's silly to favorably judge myself by how well I'm able to impress others, gain their approval, perform, or achieve.
22. It's equally silly to *un*favorably judge myself by how well I'm able to impress others, gain their approval, perform, or achieve.
23. I am not an ignoramus for acting ignorantly.
24. When I foolishly put myself down, I don't have to put myself down for putting myself down.
25. I do not have to let my acceptance of others be at the mercy of my circumstances.

26. I am not the plaything of others' reviews, and can accept myself apart from others' evaluations of me.
27. I may at times need to depend on others to do practical things for me, but I don't have to emotionally depend on anyone in order to accept myself. *Practical* dependence is a fact! *Emotional* dependence is a fiction!
28. I am beholden to nothing or no one in order to accept myself.
29. It may be better to succeed, but success does not make me a better *person*.
30. It may be worse to fail, but failure does not make me a worse person.

From Janet Wolfe, Weekly Self-Acceptance Log

Ways in which I acted SELF-DEFEATINGLY this week (took *poor* care of myself and my life).

Include cognitive/emotive/behavioral ways you kept yourself stuck in bad feelings and *off*-track on your goals.

_____

_____

_____

_____

_____

Ways in which I took GOOD CARE of myself and my life this week.

Include cognitive/emotive/behavioral ways you got yourself unstuck from your bad feelings and on track with your goals.

What I'd like to work on in therapy this week: _____

_____

_____

_____

From Michael E. Bernard, Self-Acceptance Exercise

Instructions: This exercise is designed to help you challenge the belief that if you've failed at something, or if someone criticizes or rejects you, you are a totally hopeless failure.

To overcome your irrational thinking leading to low self-acceptance, complete the top half of a circle by filling in the appropriate spaces with pluses (+'s) for the things you do well at work or school and with minuses (-'s) for the things you don't do so well. Then complete the bottom half of the circle by writing in things you do well and things you like about yourself, as well as things you don't do well or don't like about yourself.

To counter the tendency to put your*self* down when things aren't going so well, ask yourself the following questions:

- Does this bad situation (mistake, failure, rejection, criticism) take away my good qualities?
- Does it make sense to conclude that "I am totally hopeless" because of one or more negative things that have happened?

CHAPTER 25

Emotive-Evocative and Experiential Exercises for Achieving Unconditional Self-Acceptance

Many emotive-evocative and experiential techniques for achieving unconditional self-acceptance have been created and used by several psychotherapies over the years, including by Rogerian, existential, Gestalt, and other therapists. REBT and cognitive behavior therapies have used these methods and also invented a number of their own experiential techniques. You have many exercises to choose from in this respect, and I shall now describe some that I have often used with my own clients over the years to help them reduce their anxiety and depression and to especially help them achieve USA. Here are some you can experimentally try:

USING RATIONAL EMOTIVE IMAGERY

I describe Rational Emotive Imagery (REI) in the revised edition of *Overcoming Resistance: An Integrated Rational Emotive Therapy Approach*, and adapt my description here:

221

As I have mentioned before, using imagery is largely a form of cognizing, but it also has a highly emotional and dramatic quality and has been advocated by a number of therapists (Lazarus 1997). Maxie Maultsby Jr. (1971), who studied with me in the late 1960s, originated rational emotive imagery, which I and many other REBT practitioners have been using ever since that time. It is a technique that uses cognizing, feeling, and behaving and combines them quite successfully. I frequently use it at my workshops, and many of the volunteers with whom I do therapy demonstrations report back to me that they have subsequently used the imagery, and that it helped them considerably to get in touch with—and change—their strong dysfunctional feelings.

Rational Emotive Imagery helps people vividly experience one of the fundamental concepts of REBT: that when people are faced with Adversity, negative emotions are almost always healthy and appropriate when they consist of feelings of sorrow, disappointment, frustration, annoyance, and displeasure. It would actually be aberrant for a person to feel happy or neutral when these events occurred. Having certain negative emotions is fundamental in helping people to deal with unpleasant reality and motivate themselves to try to change it. The problem is that practically the whole human race very often transmutes the healthy negative feelings of disappointment and regret into disturbed feelings like anxietizing, depressing, raging, and self-pitying. These are legitimate emotions in the sense that all emotions are legitimate; however, they usually sabotage rather than help people.

Therefore, it is preferable that in using Rational Emotive Imagery, you think of something that you see as very unpleasant and strongly feel the kinds of unhealthy negative feelings that you frequently experience. You then get in touch with these feelings, feel them strongly, and then work on changing them to healthy negative feelings about the same unfortunate situation. When you have changed your feeling to a healthy negative one, you are then to keep practicing, preferably at least once a day, for the next thirty days, until you train yourself to automatically or unconsciously experience the healthy negative feeling whenever you imagine this Adversity or when it actually happens. You usually can manage to bring on your healthy negative feelings within two or three minutes, and within a few weeks you are usually able to automatically bring them on.

I used Rational Emotive Imagery with a volunteer client with whom I demonstrated at a workshop in England before an audience of one hundred counselors and therapists. The volunteer had been angering himself at his mother for twenty years because she hadn't taken care of him as a child as she, of course, *should have* done, and because she criticized him severely all his life for little things which she, of course, *shouldn't have* done. She was nasty and mean to others, except to his younger sister, to whom she was consistently nice. People agreed with him, including his own father, that his mother had treated him badly, so he was sure that (1) she was definitely wrong, (2) his anger was justified at her, and (3) her wrongdoing directly created his anger and probably would for the rest of his life. On the other hand, he knew that his anger was disabling, especially since his physician had told him that it wasn't doing his nervous system and his cardiac functioning any good; and his wife kept complaining to him about his making himself so angry and said that he was neglecting her because of it. So he had some incentives to change.

I showed this client that he was in all probability creating his anger by demanding that his mother not be the way she now was and was probably going to continue to be until her dying day. He agreed with this lightly but argued that because he had such great evidence of how wrong his mother was, how much she harmed himself and others, he was justified in remaining enraged at her. Oddly enough, I pointed out, he seemed to believe that she *could* change her behavior, while he couldn't change his angering himself at her until she behaved differently.

So I used Rational Emotive Imagery with him, beginning with having him close his eyes. "Now imagine the worst—that you are going to meet your mother and father as you usually do for Christmas, and that she is going to act just as badly as she always does. She's going to accuse you of everything including, practically, murder and say that you are no good, and that if you don't change your ways, you're going to get in trouble forever. And she particularly picks some minor infringement of yours and harps and harps and harps on it very negatively. Can you vividly imagine that?"

My client immediately replied, "I certainly can! That's typically her." So I said, "All right. Now strongly keep focusing on her ranting and railing against you . . . stay with the experience. How do you feel?" When he responded, "Homicidal," I said, "Good. Get in touch with that and let yourself feel it, feel it strongly. Let yourself feel very angry, very horrified, very homicidal—as enraged as you can be. Really get in touch with it; really feel it."

My client said, "Oh, I do. I do." And I said, "But really thoroughly feel it. Make yourself feel as angry as you possibly can and stay in touch with your rage, feeling it in your gut and in your heart." And he said, "I'm feeling it quite strongly—as if she were in the room."

So I said, "Okay. Now that you really feel it, experience it, and know what it feels like once again, try to make yourself—right now—feel exceptionally sorry and regretful that your mother acts this way, but not feel enraged against her. Sorry, disappointed, and regretful, but not, not, not enraged." He said, "I'm having a very hard time doing this." And I said, "Understandably so, since you practiced so many years feeling enraged when you think of this kind of thing or when it actually happens. But now make yourself feel very sorry, disappointed, regretful—which you are able to do."

My client was silent for a couple of minutes. As with other of my demonstrates, I hadn't met him previously and we had no unusual rapport. But as with others, before I gave him the rational emotive imagery to do, I had told him that he creates his own anger, and that he can definitely change it if he changes the musts, shoulds, and oughts that create and maintain it.

So my client finally said, "Well I am still feeling pretty sorry and regretful, but right now I'm feeling a lot less anger." So I said, "Fine. How did you get there? What did you do to change your feeling from the unhealthy feeling of rage to the healthy feeling of disappointment and regret?"

Maxie Maultsby, who invented this technique, usually asks the client at this point what Rational Beliefs he used to change his feelings until he solidly does so. But since I want the client to be able to see on his own how he reduced his rage, I never ask him, "What did you say to yourself?"—because that would give the solutions to his problem away; or he might give me the "right answer" that he really didn't believe. My goal is to enable him to change his unhealthy negative emotion by himself, to see that he is really in charge of his feelings. Rather than tell him what to say to produce healthy negative feelings, I merely say, "What did you do to change?" This particular client said, "Well, I told myself that she's really a very disturbed person, she's always been that way, and that although it's very sad and very disappointing, there's no reason why she *shouldn't* be that way—and in fact, there are many reasons why she should be."

I said, "That was very good, and I think you'll be able to use this process effectively: To strengthen your skill, I want you to do exactly what we just did for the next thirty days. That is, vividly imagine that your mother is going after you and beating you over the head verbally. Let yourself feel your feelings—including the rageful ones—and then change your extreme anger the way you just did, using the coping statements that worked for you."

The client asked, "What kind of coping statements?" I replied, "You have a choice of several: 'Isn't it too bad that she behaves that way, but alas she does and it seems to be her nature.' Or, 'I'll never like her putting me down and calling me all kinds of names, but I definitely can stand it—it won't kill me. I can still lead a happy life in spite of it. I just don't like it, but I have the power to feel only sorry and regretful, rather than horrified and terrified.'" The client said, "Oh, I see." And I said, "Fine. Will you commit to doing this once a day? Just now, it took you only a couple of minutes, and after a while it will even take you less time."

He agreed to this thirty-day plan. I said, "Okay. Just to make sure—or to make almost sure—that you do it, let's give you a reinforcement for doing it." "What do you mean?" "Well, what do you like to do that you do almost every single day of the year—some pleasure?" He said, "Golfing." So I said, "Fine. That's very good. Only allow yourself to play golf *after* you've done the rational emotive imagery and changed your feeling. Make your golfing contingent on it; then, once you do it, you can golf all day if you want to, especially if it's a weekend. Now what do you hate to do that you normally avoid because it's such a pain in the ass?"

The client gave the same response as many clients: "Cleaning and straightening up the house."

I then counseled him, "If bedtime arrives on any one of the next thirty days and you haven't done the Rational Emotive Imagery, you are to stay up for an hour cleaning the house. And if your house gets too clean, you can put your neighbor's house in order."

"Fine."

"Now will you really do that?"

"Yes."

The client actually wrote me a letter from England two months later and said that he had been practicing Rational Emotive Imagery, and after about fifteen days he had begun to almost automatically feel disappointed and sorry about his mother's behavior, but not enraged at her.

Rational Emotive Imagery can be done in various ways, but I usually do it this way because I want to emphasize its emotive-evocative-experiential elements. I also want my clients to continue to be able to do it on their own, and not because I instructed them to change their feelings by revising the self-statements they use to create their unhealthy feelings.

Usually Rational Emotive Imagery is done together with several other REBT techniques, so there are only a couple of studies where the researchers specifically did it to see if it was effective. But I have clinically observed that many people who strongly use it to de-anger themselves or de-depress themselves tend to get excellent results. They still may fall back—especially if they have a severe personality disorder. But it does help them to significantly decrease their dysfunctional feelings of rage, depression, guilt, or anxiety.

In regard to achieving USA, you can use Rational Emotive Imagery to vividly imagine your making some "terrible" act—such as "shamefully" betraying a friend who has gone out of her way to help you, being found out by this friend and several other people, and being scathingly put down by those who discover your perfidy. Really vividly imagine this "shameful" incident and let yourself feel—feel, feel, feel—low-down, excruciatingly embarrassed, and self-damning. Feel that not merely your betrayal, your act, but *you* as a person, are worthless. Feel it, thoroughly feel it! Then—don't let go of your image!—change your shame and embarrassment to the healthy negative feelings of real sorrow and regret but not—no, not—self-immolation.

When you have changed your feeling—which usually takes only a few minutes if you work at it—see what you did to change it: how you changed your Irrational Beliefs (IBs)—"I shouldn't have betrayed my friend! I'm no damned good for doing so!"—to a set of Rational Beliefs (RBs)—"My betrayal was vile, but I am a *person who* acted vilely, never a rotten person!"

If you do REI for thirty days in a row, you will strongly, emotionally, make yourself still liable for your betrayal but fully *self-accepting*. Moreover, you will—says REBT—train yourself to automatically and unconsciously become more USA-ing in the future. And also, probably, less betraying!

USING SHAME-ATTACKING EXERCISES

The one emotive-evocative, as well as behavioral, exercise that REBT is famous for is my popular shame-attacking exercise. I was ashamed of many things I did in my teens and twenties and easily put myself down if I acted "disgracefully" in front of my friends. If I were weak, or stupid, or foolish, I quickly saw myself as a weak, foolish, or stupid *person*—as did virtually all my friends and associates in my middle-class Bronx neighborhood. We took on low self-esteem and *no* self-esteem following our social errors.

It was worse in my own case because from my nineteenth year onward I was a political radical and an atheist and prided myself enormously on my independent thinking. So when I realized I was in some ways a social conformist who simultaneously *had to* be independent and not need people's approval, I knew that I was foolishly contradicting my own views. So I felt terribly ashamed of my arrant conformity, of my being a very weak "rebel," and of my shame itself. I had a neurotic symptom and I put myself down—greatly *dis*esteemed myself—for having this symptom. Both!

I worked on accepting myself with my shame and only partly succeeded. At that time, I didn't have the REBT concept of USA—only saw it very lightly. So I did my best to work on relieving my feelings of shame—which I partly knew were silly—but I still definitely had them.

Then and there, at the age of twenty-four, I invented my shame-attacking exercise. I would do a series of "shameful" acts—such as get a glass of water and nothing else in a cafeteria and turn in my check with nothing on it as I left—and took the risk of being yelled at by the cashier.

I merrily did that for several months—as well as wore unsuitable clothes to school and to parties, and did other shame-attacking exercises—and I found that they worked beautifully. Few people actually noticed or criticized me; and when they did, I soon didn't give a damn. In fact, I often enjoyed "upsetting" my blamers.

A decade later, when I became a therapist and had scores of clients—in fact nearly all of them—with problems of conditional self-esteem, I began to see that giving them my shame-attacking exercise was one of the best experiential homework assignments while teaching them the philosophy of unconditional self-acceptance. I and my REBT trainees have now used it with thousands of people all over the world—often with dramatic results.

To help conquer your own self-deprecation and lack of unconditional self-acceptance, you can use any or all of the philosophies described in the previous chapter and can emotionally and actively-directively back them up with a number of shame-attacking exercises. I recommend in my book *Anger: How to Live with It and without It*, "Think of something you and most other people would think foolish for you to do in public and deliberately do this 'shameful' or 'embarrassing' thing. Like singing at the top of your lungs in the street. Or walking a banana, as if walking a dog or a cat on a leash. Or wearing a headband with a large yellow feather stuck in it. Or stopping a little old lady and asking if she would help you cross the street."

These shame-attacking exercises can help! At the Albert Ellis

Institute's psychological clinic in New York, two of the best that work to aid people to get USA are: yelling out the stops in the subway or on a bus; and stopping a stranger on the street or in a hotel lobby and saying, "I just got out of the mental hospital. What month is it?" Try these. Shamelessly work on your USA!

USING STRONG COPING STATEMENTS

I showed in the previous chapter how you could Dispute your Irrational Beliefs (IBs) and arrive at rational coping statements. Good cognizing! You can make these statements strong, emotional, and powerful, so that they forcefully grip you. Thus, to make them sink into your head and heart, you can repetitively convince yourself:

- I *never, never* have to perform well and win others' approval to unconditionally accept myself! That will make me more effective, but *not* a better person.
- Succeeding at work, school, and sports will give me joy—but not personal worth. Never!
- All I have to do to unconditionally accept myself is to choose, choose, choose to do so!
- Money makes me *do* better and live better but not to enter the kingdom of heaven!
- I can easily fail, but there's no way I can be a total *failure*!
- Living by itself can be exceptionally enjoyable and worthy.
- I can always forgive myself and other fallible humans!
- Nothing is *awful*—only damned inconvenient!

ROLE-PLAYING "DANGEROUSLY"

Using friends, relatives, and group therapy members to role-play with you, you can take on "dangerous" assignments: For example, you can have a "risky" job interview, try for a talented team, and apply to graduate school. Have the role-player give you a hard time with your interview and do your best to succeed at it. Let others critique your interview. Try it over again. If you feel anxious during it, have you and your interviewer look for the Irrational Beliefs—*shoulds, oughts, and musts*—you are telling yourself to make yourself anxious and insecure. Dispute them and make yourself healthfully concerned but not unhealthily anxious. Strive in the role-play for an effective pursuit of your goal when you have no guarantee you will reach it.

MAKE STRONG DISPUTING TAPES

Tape-record some of your Irrational Beliefs (IBs), such as "I must always show others how effective I am and prove to them and myself that I am a worthwhile person!" Dispute it on the same tape realistically, logically, and pragmatically. Make your Disputing as forceful and emotive as you can. Listen to your Disputing tape with critical friends, who note how forceful it is. Do it over until you make it truly *convincing*. Don't give up!

DISPUTING YOUR RATIONAL BELIEFS

When, in doing your Disputing of your Irrational Beliefs (IBs) about your conditional self-esteem (CSE), you only convince yourself of them *lightly* and *unforcefully*. Now go back and Dispute them—yes, your Rational Beliefs!—again. Try using Windy Dryden's (Dryden and Neenan 2004) technique of Disputing some of your Rational Beliefs until you solidly and emotionally convince yourself of their validity.

ACTIVELY AND STRONGLY DISPUTING YOUR ANGER-CREATING BELIEFS

Several REBT therapists have articles in the *REBT Resource Book for Practitioners* (Bernard and Wolfe 2000) describing how you can fight like hell against your other-damning beliefs and minimizing your feelings of anger. Michael Bernard, Michael Broder, Paul Hauck, Jeff Hughes, Joan Miller, and Ray DiGiuseppe include these relevant suggestions:

- Don't blame others for making you angry. You greatly *add* to their contributions.
- *Like* but don't *expect* others to return your favors.
- Accept others' enormous fallibility.
- No one can *guarantee* to love you.
- You can *stand* rejection and refusal.
- You're not annoying me—I am. I'm choosing to take you too seriously.
- Your depriving me is not *awful*—only inconvenient.
- You can easily frustrate me—but only I can whine about your doing so.
- I never *need* you to fulfill myself—though that would be nice!
- People who frustrate me act badly but are never bad people!
- Anger toward others will frequently stop me from getting what I want.

- I really wish others would treat me better, but they obviously do not have to do so.
- My *demand* that you treat me nicely is not exactly a *preference*!
- Where did I get the quaint idea that people absolutely must be on time?
- You *are not* your poor behavior—not all of the time!
- I really *wish* you would act better but my wish is hardly your command.
- If you *absolutely should* be fair to me, you would always have to be. Lots of luck!
- Nothing blocks problem solving like anger!
- Anger makes me obsess about the behavior of people I find distasteful. Thoroughly wasteful!
- Nothing wrecks relationships like rage.
- Anger is hardly an aphrodisiac.
- Is this really going to matter that much tomorrow, next week, or even two years from now?
- What can I tell myself to get rid of my anger?
- What are the advantages of holding on to my anger? What are the advantages of letting it go?

CHAPTER 26

Behavioral Exercises for Achieving Unconditional Self-Acceptance

Let me repeat again so we do not lose track of it: REBT pioneeringly said in 1955 that human thinking, feeling, and behaving are integrated and always seem to include important aspects of each other. Why? Because that is the nature of people's reacting to important stimuli: they think, feel, *and* actively respond to them. Just try to separate these aspects of reacting!

The cognitive and emotive techniques you can use to achieve unconditional self-acceptance (USA) overlap with each other. In REBT's famous shame-attacking exercise, for example, you strive to achieve the philosophy of unconditional self-acceptance. You explore any Irrational Beliefs (IBs) that interfere with you achieving this unusual outlook. You realistically, logically, and pragmatically Dispute these IBs. You come up with strong, persistent Rational Coping Statements that attain and maintain USA. You solidly show yourself in several cognitive ways how and why USA works for you.

At the same time that you keep using these thinking methods, you emotionally and persistently put yourself in forceful action. You disrupt your regular routines to do several shame-attacking exercises. You vividly and dramatically do several unusual things. You determinedly follow your attacks on your conventionality. You persist at making your shame-attacks courageously suitable. You resist any of your cop-out tendencies, fight against your excuses and your defensiveness, and give yourself in several ways a rough time. No running away! Preferably act more outrageously than you originally planned. Shame yourself!

So your shame-attacks *combine* thinking, feeling, and acting endeavors. And almost anything else you can devise and enact. Obviously, they are behavioral. And to make them highly active-directive, you can use various other REBT behavioral methods—and borrow some, if you will, from other forms of therapy. Here are some possible suggestions.

RISK-TAKING METHODS

The shame-attacks are in themselves risky, since you put *yourself*, your ego on the line, and may lose social status. But you can also take the risks of losing money, losing a job, losing friends, losing at a sport, and losing various other things or enjoyments. Not too much! Your goal, I hope, is not to defeat yourself for you normally delight in winning. But losing is *also* part of life and if you keep trying, it will inevitably occur. You can't win them all!

ACCEPTANCE OF YOUR PHYSICAL FEELINGS

In the *REBT Resource Book for Practitioners* (Bernard and Wolfe 2000) Jeffrey Brandsma teaches you rational self-acceptance by having you stand naked in front of a full-length mirror and honestly examine your body from all angles. You mainly concentrate on *calmly* accepting all the "bad" or distasteful aspects of your body, especially those you dislike most. You then see what aspects of your body—such as fatness—it would be desirable to change, and you work out an active plan of effecting such change. But you end up by fully acknowledging that your changing your body is limited, that you will never like some aspects of it, you still will fully accept them, and you will live as good a way as you can live *with* these undesirable body parts. You *are* not your physical imperfections!

DESENSITIZING YOURSELF TO PERFORMANCE ANXIETY

When you are afraid to perform a test, an interview, a speech, a sport, or almost any other activity, this usually means that you are afraid to do poorly at it, especially in public, and that you would devaluate yourself, and not merely your performance, if you did so. That old self-downing again!

Behavior Therapy, REBT, and cognitive-behavior therapy (among other therapies) give the answer: Risk it! Do what you are afraid of, accept yourself *with* your failings and keep going. But *doubly* chance it. While risking and failing, and while letting others *know* your "incompetence," use this opportunity to strongly show yourself that you are *not* your performance and that it doesn't brand *you*. Yes, you struck out or dropped the ball and it was your error and your (non)doing. But you have lots more chances—if you don't kill yourself. Keep trying.

It is what you tell yourself *while* striking out or dropping the ball that does the self-acceptance trick: "I failed *this time* and will probably fail some more. Poor catch *this time*! Watch for the next one! No sweat!" You are never a dodo—just a *this time* bungler. No, not even a bung*ler*. A person who missed the ball but gained the opportunity to improve and to fight his performance anxiety. Excellent!

GIVING YOUR WILL DISTINCT POWER

Deciding to act in your interests and conquer your unassertiveness and your inhibitions is easy—you've done so, along with deciding to stop smoking, a hundred times. Implementing your decision is harder! To turn your "decision" into a reality, push yourself through the rough steps leading to will*power*: (1) Clearly and unequivocally decide, "I will be less inhibited and more assertive if it kills me!" (2) Make yourself emotionally *determined* to assert yourself in spite of your difficulty in doing so. "No nonsense! So I'll often get rejected. Tough shit!" (3) Explore some "best" ways to be assertive. "Why don't I try asking for what I want and also keep giving them what they want?" "If you try the movie I like, I'll buy drinks afterward." (4) No matter what, act, act, act on your assertion. "Okay, if you really don't like this movie, let's try that one, or another. Come on, let's go!" (5) *Keep* deciding, determining, exploring ways of asserting, and pushing, pushing, pushing. No rest for the weary!

With all this, remember the *benefits*. You are not just going after what you want (risking) and what you don't want (inhibiting your life). You are keeping in mind your *future* desires—especially your strong desire to be *free*. To fully *accept* yourself, to find some of the things you never dared ask for previously. In a word, to be a much less trammeled *you*.

WELCOMING CHALLENGING AND DIFFICULT PURSUITS AND PEOPLE

Safety-seeking is probably the main human pursuit—sticking with goals, friends, relatives, sports, and pursuits that are easy, that you can win at, that you don't have to go out of your way to encounter. How restricting—and often boring! You only have a limited time to work and to play—so why make it *more* limited?

Again, face performance anxiety and discomfort anxiety. Both often include self-deprecation. Performance anxiety: "I'm no good if I perform poorly at important tasks." Discomfort anxiety: "It's *too hard* to go after the goals I want. I'm much too *inadequate* to achieve them."

Counter-attacking: "I'm okay even when my performance is lousy." "I'm out to enjoy myself even if my game is crummy." "Others may think that I play badly, but I don't have to take their criticisms too seriously." "Yes, I play poorly right now but it is challenging to keep practicing!"

If you stay with difficult pursuits, you fail more but give yourself the opportunity to work on your potential self-downing. If you stay with difficult people, you can risk their criticism and not agree with it, or you can see that their whining about your deficiencies may be partly accurate but, even when they are, they still are no reflection of your worth as a person. The more that you see that others' criticism *isn't* you, the more self-accepting of yourself you will train yourself to be. Your training yourself to bear up under rejections hardens you for the knocks of life. The trick is to *acknowledge* your mistakes and limitations and still forge ahead where less hardy souls then you frequently give up trying.

USING REINFORCEMENTS

Fred Skinner's and Joseph Wolpe's techniques of reinforcement can be used for almost any behavioral methods you apply to self-acceptance exercises. Thus, if you promise yourself to do some shame-attacking homework but actually reinforce your feelings of shame by refusing to do it, you can reinforce yourself with easy and pleasant tasks—such as listening to music or socializing with your friends—*only after* you have done your assigned homework.

Remember, again, however, that your goal had better be, first, to do the shame-attacks and make it *easier* (almost routine) to do them; but, second, to see philosophically how they particularly abet self-acceptance *while* you are under fire. If you can force yourself to do the shame-attacks when difficult and critical people are watching, so much the better! You fight *their* shaming as well as your own at the same time!

USING REINFORCING PENALTIES

Fred Skinner was opposed to your penalizing yourself when you assigned yourself shame-attacking and other onerous homework and failed to carry out your assignments. Be that as it may, I have personally found penalties very practical and, sometimes, almost the only ones that will help you do what you *don't* want to do as well as strongly encourage you to do it.

Like Jack, who *almost* told his best friend, Val, about his passing a rough course in statistics by cheating on the final exam—but never quite confessed doing so after several tries. He then was ashamed of his cheating—and of his blocking on telling Val about it when he wanted to minimize his feelings of shame. He stewed about this, until he gave himself thirty days to do so and burned a fifty-dollar bill every day he went beyond thirty days. When his thirty days were up, he actually burned $250 before he stopped in disgust and told Val about his cheating. He was so relieved to confess that he *welcomed* Val's censure and *then* saw that it was no big deal and that he wasn't a *rotten person* even though his cheating was immoral. Up to the time he refused to shame-attack, he not only felt bad about his unconfessed cheating but also felt bad about *himself.*

Usually, you will probably not have to penalize yourself when you fail to do your self-assigned homework, because your failure *helps* you think of the importance of doing it. When steadily refusing to tell his friend Jack about his cheating, and thereby seeing *what kind of federal case* he made out of confessing, Val realized *how much* he was putting his whole worth on the line by this avoidance, and *how much* he would retain his abysmal guilt, *until* he confessed. So he made his shame-attacking confession *crucial* and (at first) made himself most uncomfortably do it. *After* he confessed, he still thought his *cheating* was immoral—but livable with.

USING SKILL TRAINING

REBT specializes in skill-training in its homework—ever since I began doing sex and love therapy in 1943. No, even before, because I used it unofficially with my friends before I even went to graduate school for my degrees in clinical psychology. From the start, I realized that my sexually inept clients had to *learn* what to do to be proficient—and then practice, practice, practice! So did I, when, with the aid of good sex books, I had to practice getting and staying erect!

Love, too? Ah, yes. I had to skill myself in not being insensately jealous when my first wife, Karyl, was madly in love with me—and also with various So-and-sos.

So I taught, as best I could, sex, love, communication, assertion, and other skills to my poor benighted clients. And, in turn, learned a hell of a lot from them. As in the case of one of my first clients, who taught me that she could reasonably enjoy anal intercourse with her eighteen-year-old lover if she fully faced the dire penalties of her parents finding her pregnant. I agreed—in those days before AIDS—that that was a fairly wise choice.

Anyway, with clients' often enthusiastic consent, I have used considerable skill training in therapy and, being a sexologist, have offered it to many clients. Few shied away! Many took my mere suggestions and built them into talents. Obviously, you can learn from friends, therapists, books, cassettes, and whatnot the skills of social-sexual relations.

To tie up these skills with achieving unconditional self-acceptance, you can develop some of your own skill training in these important ways: (1) Shamelessly admit your ignorance. What you don't know can hurt you. (2) Confess it to your partners. Don't pretend to know much more than you do know. If you are both equally ignorant, good! You can learn what works for each of you. (3) Know something about your partner's sex-love history and, if there are any blocks, find out about them. (4) Inquire about what will probably work best with him or her and try it. Life is an experiment and so is sex. *See* what works—and what doesn't. (5) Keep trying and keep experimenting. (6) Get relevant information from books, cassettes, and from a sex-love therapist. (7) Keep experimenting! (8) Sometimes try something new, but if the old reliables keep working by all means continue to use them.

USING RELAPSE PREVENTION

Not everything in sex and love works for all people all of the time. Sometimes you relapse because you stop looking for and working at what used to work and sometimes you just get tired of old ways. If the latter is the case, back to the drawing board! If you just got bored, try something new. You may try some variety—even a new partner. But, like everything else, that has its advantages and disadvantages. As usual, the question is: Is something nice and different *worth* it? How will you know without trying?

But no perfectionism! You and your partner don't have to be stupendous, ideal lovers. You especially don't have to prove your "worth" by your "success" in bed. Let yourself enjoy yourself and enjoy your partner's enjoyment. That's enough! Winning prizes—especially status prizes—for love and sex is unnecessary—and taxing!

Back to relapse prevention—which usually includes low frustration tolerance (LFT). In REBT and the behavior therapy, this is how you frequently handle your LFT:

1. Acknowledge your relapsing and, above all, accept *you* with *it*. Yes, you may have refused to keep pushing yourself and therefore, have fallen back. Bad—but not *too* bad. You are a *person who* retrogressed, not a *lazy person.*
2. Thoroughly accept yourself, your being, *with* your lapses.
3. Look for your Irrational Beliefs (IBs) that led to your relapsing. "Dammit! Looks like I'll have to keep up fighting my need for approval forever! That's much too hard! Especially when I really *need* it!"
4. Dispute your IBs *vigorously* and *persistently.* "Why *must* I be approved to be worthy? Why is it *necessary*? How does approval *make* me a good person? Where will it get me if I am *convinced* that I need approval? How will it help me get love and approval?"
5. Think of other pleasures you can work at getting and calmly seek to fulfill them. There are more than a few possibilities. Investigate and try them!

THE USE OF HUMOR

Among its many cognitive, emotive, and behavioral techniques to interfere with and Dispute conditional self-esteem (CSE) and to replace it largely with unconditional self-acceptance, REBT uses a good deal of humor. This is because when people lose their sense of humor and become too serious, they defeat themselves and others. So REBT urges people often to lighten up and to take things seriously—but not TOO seriously. It particularly specializes in rational humorous songs, since 1976, when I first used them at the American Psychological Association Annual Convention in Washington, DC. Since then, we have encouraged their use in individual therapy, group therapy, and all kinds of REBT workshops and intensives.

Some of the rational humorous songs that you can use to combat your own taking yourself too seriously and your striving for conditional self-esteem instead of unconditional self-acceptance are these:

PERFECT RATIONALITY
(Tune, *Funiculi, Funicula* by Luigi Denza)

Some think the world must have a right direction—
And so do I!—and so do I!
Some think that with the slightest imperfection,
They can't get by—and so do I!
For I, I have to prove I'm superhuman,
And better far than people are!
To show I have miraculous acumen—
And always rate among the Great!
Perfect, perfect rationality
Is, of course, the only thing for me!
How can I ever be so free
And still exist quite fallibly?
Rationality must be a perfect thing for me!

LOVE, OH LOVE ME, ONLY ME!
(Tune: *Yankee Doodle Dandy*, by George M. Cohan)

Love, oh love me, only me, or I will die without you!
Oh, make your love a guarantee, so I can never doubt you!
Love me, love me, totally—really really try, dear.
But if you demand love, too, I'll hate you till I die, dear!

Love, oh love me all the time, quite thoroughly and wholly!
My total life is slushy slime, unless you love me solely.
Love me with great tenderness, with no ifs or buts, dear.
If you love me somewhat less, I'll hate your goddamned guts, dear!

YOU FOR ME AND ME FOR ME
(Tune: *Tea for Two*, by Vincent Youmans)

Picture you upon my knee
Just you for me, and me for me!
And then you'll see
How happy I will be!
Though you beseech me
You never will reach me—
For I am autistic
As any real mystic!
And only relate to
Myself with a great to-do, dear!
If you dare to try to care
You'll see my caring soon will wear,
For I can't pair and make our sharing fair!
If you want a family,
We'll both agree you'll baby me—
Then you'll see how happy I will be!

GLORY, GLORY HALLELUJAH!
(Tune: *Battle Hymn of the Republic*, by Julia Ward Howe)

Mine eyes have seen the glory of relationships that glow
And then falter by the wayside as love passions come—and go!
Oh, I've heard of great romances
Where there is no slightest lull—
But I am skeptical!
Glory, glory hallelujah!
People love ya till they screw ya!
If you'd lessen how they do ya
Then don't expect they won't!
Glory, glory hallelujah!
People cheer ya—then pooh-pooh ya!
If you'd soften how they screw ya!
Then don't expect they won't!

I WISH I WERE NOT CRAZY!
(Tune: *Dixie*, by Dan Emmett)

I wish I were really put together—
Smooth and fine as patent leather!
Oh, how great to be rated innately sedate!
But I'm afraid that I was fated
To be rather aberrated—
Oh, how sad to be as mad as my mom and my dad!

Oh, I wish I were not crazy! Hooray! Hooray!
I wish my mind were less inclined
To be the kind that's hazy!
I could, you see, agree to be less crazy—
But I, alas, am just too goddamned lazy!

246

CHAPTER 27
Summary and Conclusion

I think that I have said enough about conditional self-esteem (CSE) and its hazards, about unconditional self-acceptance (USA) and its remarkable advantages, and about your choice between them. Something quite important would be missing, however, if I didn't once again stress the rational emotive behavior therapy theme of integration.

As Heidegger, Sartre, and other existentialists have nicely stressed, we humans integrally have a three-in-one inclusion: (1) We are individually alive and kicking as unique persons—for a while and in memory. (2) We have our Being with others, in a give-and-take social context. (3) We exist in the world of animate and inanimate things with which we continually integrate and interact. We influence ourselves, others, and the world—integrally!

We are strongly tempted at times to emphasize our individuality, and our sociality, and our worldliness, forgetting their interaction. I particularly stress, in this book, our courage to be our "unique" selves—along with our courage to be social and worldly.

I say that unless we have three-part courage to hang together, we may well hang separately. The road is rough and treacherous!

Back to basics. As much as you can be you, yourself, you'd better experimentally see what that is like and how it turns out. Fortunately, you can always revise your complicated self. Do so!

While you work—yes, work—at being an ever-changing person, never forget your neighbors. They, too, have the right to be—and to partly be themselves. Your having unconditional acceptance of them goes *with* your unconditional self-acceptance. I hope, integrally.

Simultaneously, you live in a highly complex and complicated world—whether you like it or not. If you choose, you can gracefully lump what you don't like—while still enjoying what you do. If so, you also give yourself unconditional life-acceptance (ULA).

You have three choices—USA, UOA, and ULA. Don't be niggardly—choose them all!

This book has now considered in detail some of the main aspects of conditional self-esteem and unconditional self-acceptance; and has shown how Rational Emotive Behavior Therapy (REBT) and several other noted philosophers have, at least at times, also espoused USA over CSE. It has also tried to clarify what USA is, what advantages it includes, and how you can achieve it by using important cognitive, emotive, and behavioral methods of psychotherapy that are usually employed in REBT and in other forms of cognitive-behavior therapy. Let me hope that I have been fairly convincing in these respects, and that you, the reader, will gain from this material!

An important question remains that up to now has not been fully answered. REBT, as I keep showing, differs from most other therapies in that it clearly distinguishes between your healthy negative feelings of frustration, concern, sorrow, regret, and disappointment when you don't get what you want and do get what you don't want in life and your unhealthy negative feelings of serious anxiety, depression, and anger. REBT also differentiates between your healthy actions—such as persistent self-discipline and action when you act dysfunctionally (e.g., procrastinate and overeat) and unhealthfully addict yourself to injurious behavior.

The question still remains: Even your healthy negative feelings—especially sadness and frustration about Adversities—*are* negative and unenjoyable. If you are healthily sorrowing for a lost relative or friend, that is much better than depressing yourself. But your sadness is hardly pleasurable and "good." So how can you alleviate such healthy feelings? How can you still be happy?

The answer I usually give is: You'd better not eliminate sorrow. For unless you feel suitably sad and regretful about the unfortunate happenings in your life, you will not try to prevent them (e.g., help your friend or relative survive), you will not look for new relationships, and you will not bother to find substitute satisfactions. So healthy negative feelings when you are deprived foster *good* future outcomes. Therefore, you'd better live with them and not eliminate them.

So you have a pretty good rationale for your making yourself healthfully sorry instead of unhealthily depressed, anxious, and angry when you suffer a distinct loss or fail to achieve a desired gain. But I now see that unconditionally accepting yourself, other people, and the world will often bring you even better results than your creating healthy feelings of sorrow and regret. I realized this recently when I was again acknowledging the Buddhist concept of widespread human suffering.

It is, I realized, an indisputable fact that just about all of us frequently suffer—yes, even when we engage in enjoyable pursuits. If we enjoy marital and family life, we also find that it has many restrictions (e.g., putting up with some of our in-laws) and hassles (e.g., disciplining our children). If we really love our work, we also often encounter mean bosses, supervisors, and colleagues. If we like sports, we frequently dislike some of our teammates, umpires, and the hassles of getting to the places where the sports take place. If we thrill to theatrical performances, we have to put up with boring plays, poor directors, crummy performances, and expensive tickets. Whatever we do, there is no rest for the weary! Adversities abound!

If significant amounts of trouble, expense, boredom, and frustration accompany even our most enjoyable pursuits, how can we avoid healthy negative feelings and difficulties about them? No way! Normal life includes pleasure, joy, enthusiasm—*and* suffering.

There is, however, a damned good—hardly perfect—solution for our bad healthy and unhealthy feelings and behaviors; and that is the choice we can take that is espoused in this book—unconditional acceptance.

Let us suppose that you persist at taking and practicing this choice. You largely accept *yourself* with your shortcomings and mistakes; you also accept *others* with their stupidities and unfairnesses; and you distinctly accept the conditions of the world in which you live, with its inefficiencies, injustices, and innumerable other problems. What will happen?

My theory says, though I cannot as yet definitely prove it, several things will in all probability happen: (1) You will unresentfully and peacefully accept you, others, and the world. (2) You will have a profound *philosophy* and *habit* of acceptance. (3) You will not condone your own, others', or your community's destructive thoughts, feelings, and behaviors, even though you fully acknowledge their frequent evils. (4) You may choose to actively oppose and act against these evils. (5) You will minimize and even eliminate your damning philosophies that lie behind your serious anxieties, depression, and rage: for example, "I must perform well and be loved by significant others to be a worthwhile person."

In other words, with your nonacceptance, leading to awfulizing, catastrophizing, and fuming and frothing, you create real rage against yourself, other people, and the world. With this rage, you not only feel disturbed, but very often help to make your own, others', and the world's behaviors considerably worse than before. Rage leads to arguing, fighting, vengeance, feuds, terrorism, wars, and holocausts. Not so good! It also interferes with pleasure, satisfaction, constructiveness, creativity, and progress. Alas! Almost always, it results in return rage, retaliation, and vengeance by those at whom you are raging and warring. As the old proverb goes, love begets love and rage begets rage. Even the most "righteous" anger usually has some grim consequences.

Although I may possibly be overgeneralizing, your anger and aggression may be at the root of most of your severe anxiety, depression, and feelings of worthlessness and hopelessness. Thus, when you are angry at your mistakes and immoralities, your anger may help you ameliorate and correct them. "I hate my foolishness!" may help you to investigate and modify it. But when you hate *yourself* for acting foolishly, you tend to think, "I am a worthless, hopeless fool!" Result: Self-damnation, lack of correction, *more* foolishness.

Similarly with social prejudice, bigotry, and hatred. When you hate what others *think, feel,* and *do,* you are motivated to teach them to behave differently. You try to show them—even crusade for—better standards, customs, and actions. But when you hate *people* for their "misdeeds," you usually meet up with return hatred, resistance, and intentional, retributive "wrongdoing." You're so *insistent* that others change their ways for the "better" that you commonly encourage them to act much "worse." Paradoxical? Yes, but often true.

Finally, when you hate the difficulties, problems, and inefficiencies of your community and the world, you may be motivated to try to reform and improve them. Again, you may constructively crusade against them. But when you make yourself furious against the "terrible" and "horrible" world itself, you may become discouraged, hopeless, purposeless, and severely depressed. You may even, because of these severe feelings, make yourself rabid, destructively rebellious, and murderous. Suicidal terrorists may be a good—though extreme—example here.

Hostility, hatred, fighting, and war are quite the issue—not only in their own right but in their common link to severe anxiety and depression. These disturbed feelings may not always go together; but they frequently do. Hatred, as I have just shown, is just about the opposite of acceptance. If you persistently and strongly work at unconditionally accepting yourself (*with* your failings), unconditionally accepting others (*with* their "wrongness"), and unconditionally accepting the world (with its adversities), you will have great difficulty creating and, especially, maintaining your hostility and rage. You still—I practically guarantee it—will be quite frustrated and disappointed with your own, other people's, and the world's actions. But not enraged and violent.

Then what? Then back to your good—and even your great—choices that you have in life. The tendency to disturb yourself by damning yourself, others, and the world is partly biological and innate, since just about 100 percent of people often do it. But it is also *chosen*, as I have been showing in this book. You don't *have to* hate and can *decide* to refuse to do it. Unconditionally accepting yourself, others, and life can be achieved by your hard and persistent cognitive, emotional, and behavioral *work* and *practice*.

You can—I hypothesize—achieve USA, UOA, and ULA; and they are remarkably worth attaining. Maybe I am wrong, but I say again that your acquiring them stops your raging at anyone, especially at yourself, and sets the stage for many other joyous involvements.

For you, along with your great propensity for anguish, also have a distinct propensity for creative pleasure. It would be rare if you did not. You can enjoy—and usually intensely enjoy—a number of bodily processes (taste, smell, sight, sound, touch, kinesthetic responses). These, together with your thoughts, feelings, and activities, enable you to moderately or ecstatically thrill to art, music, dance, plays, architecture, science, philosophy, sports, and scores of other pursuits. Quite a variety!

Once you make yourself unconditionally accepting, once your unconditional acceptance of yourself, others, and the world is fairly solid, and once it results in considerably reduced anger, depression, and severe anxiety, you can feel free to actualize yourself as REBT recommends (Ellis 2001a, 2001b; Ellis and Becker 1983). This means that you experiment with finding what you really like, what you like more, and what you like still more. You have many adventures to choose from and presumably only one fairly short life in which to relish them. Find out, by experimenting, what truly pleases—and displeases—you. Be open to learn from others; but, surrendering self-damnation, also find out for yourself.

This is one of the real virtues of acceptance. It doesn't in itself guarantee joy, and to some extent it leaves you sad about the unfortunate things that you can't change. Sad, but not angry and horrified. Then your healthy sorrow, free from anguish, frees you to lead a self-actualizing life that includes as many joys as you can challengingly try in your still limited, imperfect existence.

I still, with the Buddhists, say that life has its inevitable suffering and frustration, as well as its satisfactions and pleasures. Approach it by realistically and maturely thinking, feeling, and working to enjoy what you can; by unangrily and unwhiningly accepting (not liking) what you cannot change; and having the wisdom to know (and accept!) the difference. You can then open yourself to much joy. Accepting inevitable pain is unpleasant—but it can lead to self-actualization and fulfillment. If you choose!

APPENDIX 1
Rational Emotive Behavior Therapy for Beginners

Rational Emotive Behavior Therapy (REBT) is the first of the modern cognitive behavior therapies (CBTs) and was developed from 1953 to 1955, after I had abandoned the practice of psychoanalysis, which I had been doing since 1947. I was always skeptical of Sigmund Freud's classical theory and practice of psychoanalysis, and published a monograph in 1950, *An Introduction to the Scientific Principles of Psychoanalysis*.

I was therefore a neo-Freudian—and more of a neo-Adlerian—who followed the procedures of Karen Horney, Erich Fromm, and other analytic revisionists. I also used the humanistic-existentialist teachings of my training analyst, Dr. Richard Hulbeck. I decided in 1953 to stop calling myself an analyst and became much more active-directive and behavioral than I had previously been. So I reviewed the more than two hundred systems of psychotherapy that were being practiced at that time; produced a monograph in 1955, *New Approaches to Psychotherapy Techniques*; and reread many ancient and modern philosophers before formulating REBT. My philosophic leanings went back to 1928, when I was about to enter college at the age of fifteen. I had my own emotional problems —largely with performance anxiety—and I thought that the answer to them could be found in the more rational thinking of the ancient and modern philosophers.

During my teens, I devoured Asian, Greek, and Roman philosophy, especially that of Confucius, Lao-Tsu, Siddhartha Gautama Buddha, Socrates, Epicurus, Epictetus, and Marcus Aurelius, and started formulating my own rational principles. Unfortunately, my psychoanalytic training and practice sidetracked me somewhat. So when I largely abandoned psychoanalysis for more cognitive-behavioral methods, I reread considerable philosophy and came up with REBT, which combines behaviorism with philosophy.

When cognitive behavior therapy started to follow my lead in the mid-1960s, with the writings of Aaron Beck, William Glasser, Donald Meichenbaum, Albert Bandura, and others, it consisted largely of cognitive informational processing and of practical homework assignments, while REBT included these methods but has always been highly philosophical. In addition, REBT always included highly forceful and emotional methods, since I emphasized, in my first major paper on REBT in 1956, that thinking *includes* emotion and behavior, that emotion *includes* thinking and behavior, and that behavior *includes* thinking and feeling. We often falsely see them as disparate processes; but actually, they are combined and integrated; they strongly influence each other; and they *all* have to be changed if people are to minimize their emotional dysfunctioning and live more happily. Recently, the cognitive behavioral therapies are beginning to take integrated thinking-feeling-acting approaches, but REBT has done so for several decades.

My emphasis in REBT on thinking, feeling, and action was probably distinctly influenced by my perusal of Buddhist teachings. For Buddhism first posits Enlightenment or hardheaded conscious thinking about yourself and your dysfunctions. Simultaneously, it encourages you to be emotionally, strongly, and determinedly committed to changing yourself and it gives you evocative-experiential exercises to help you do so. It also recommends your following, being attached to, and having faith in a guru or teacher. Finally, it firmly pushes you to *act* against your passive tendencies, to *practice* rigorous training and retraining, to *do* rather than *stew*. So it is antihabitual and highly behavioral. It actively-directively uses, therefore, all three of your healthy functioning processes—cognition, emotion, and behavior. Even when it uses inactive methods —such as calm meditation—it recommends active elements such as *mindfulness* meditation. You actively *watch* yourself while meditating; and you often achieve a highly emotional state. REBT and Buddhism, of course, also stress perception: You *perceive* "reality" in order to change it.

Although some forms of Buddhism—such as extreme Zen Buddhism—are too mystical and romantic for my realistic leanings, Buddhism's main principles significantly overlap with Rational Emotive Behavior Therapy basic philosophies. This, I have found in recent years, is particularly true of the similarities between Tibetan Buddhism and REBT. Since the 1980s, Tensin Gyatso, the Fourteenth Dalai Lama, has collaborated with psychological, physiological, and social scientists to test and possibly validate some of the main Buddhist hypotheses. He has consistently worked with the psychiatrist Howard Cutler, the psychologist Daniel Goleman, and many other scientists to integrate Buddhism with Western science.

Similarly, Ron Leifer, another psychiatrist; Jon Kabat-Zinn, a physicist; and several other Western scientists have steadily used Tibetan mindfulness meditation in their own life, have studied with reputable Buddhist gurus, and have integrated Buddhism with Western psychotherapy and science. Very good—but also subject to human prejudice. When the followers of one religious or philosophic discipline are converted to another system—such as Paul, reared as a Jew, was converted to Jesus' Christianity—they almost inevitably become overly prejudiced in favor of the new system, and fanatically fail to see its shortcomings. So the faith of the Fourteenth Dalai Lama and other Buddhists is to be viewed with some skepticism when it strongly favors poetic and romantic principles and practices.

My own favoring of Buddhism is—I hope—more impartial. I am certainly not a Buddhist and only lightly practice a relaxing form of meditation that is not Vipashyana or mindfulness meditation. Moreover, I have a long history of being skeptical of psychoanalysis, pure behavior therapy (à la B. F. Skinner and Joseph Wolpe), Gestalt Therapy (of Fritz Perls), Rogerian psychotherapy, extreme postmodern therapy, and even radical constructivist therapy. I use elements of all these systems but am hardly devout in my adherence to or practice of them. I think I am a born and reared skeptic and tolerator. I hope I am also not a devout REBTer, since I do not think it is an unmitigated cure for everyone and do accept its distinct limitations.

I have described what REBT is almost ad nauseam in over fifty books and about five hundred articles, so I shall be brief about its main aspects now. You can get more details, if you wish, in *Overcoming Destructive Beliefs, Feelings, and Behaviors*; *Feeling Better, Getting Better, and Staying Better*; and *The Road to Tolerance*. Assuming that you have not read these books, here in highly summary form, is what Rational Emotive Behavior Therapy is about.

THE TYRANNY OF THE SHOULDS AND MUSTS

I formulated one of the fundamental ideas about how people largely construct their own emotional disturbances and dysfunctioning from combining the stoic philosophy of Epictetus with the idealized image notions of Karen Horney. Epictetus, after serving as a

Greek slave to his Roman master, was freed during the first century CE and founded the Stoic school in Rome. He had many wise things to say, but I was particularly impressed with his statement, "It's never the events that happen that make us disturbed, but our view of them." That is why I practiced psychoanalysis from 1947 to 1953, but never emphasized Freud's theory that your early childhood happenings and experiences make you anxious, depressed, and raging. Epictetus strongly held that your view of these (and later) events disturbed you; and that you could, as an adult, change this view. So he was one of the first constructivists.

In 1950 I read Karen Horney's notion that most of us invent an idealized image or picture of ourselves, and afflict ourselves with "the tyranny of the shoulds." "Right on!" I said to myself—and lost more faith in Freud and in the conditioning theories of J. B. Watson and B. F. Skinner. Horney, I noted, agreed with Epictetus—we humans largely construct our neuroses and can deconstruct and reconstruct them. How? By realistically and logically rethinking our notion of how we make ourselves neurotic; by being *strongly* (emotionally) determined to revise them; and by forcefully and persistently *acting* against them.

There I had it—the first essentials of REBT. So I began to teach this REBT view of good mental health to my clients—together with less and less psychoanalytic interpretations of how they became upset and could, with these insights, manage to unupset themselves. I also—because, from 1943 to 1947, I was an active-directive eclectic therapist—and included some of my prior eclectic techniques into my liberal—very liberal!—psychoanalytic explanations.

Finally, by the end of 1953, I realized that all the talk in the world wouldn't help my clients with severe personality disorders unless they were also determined to take some action—such as in vivo desensitization—against their habitual thoughts, feelings, and behaviors. So I stopped my psychoanalytic practice and began to

develop an *integration* of thinking, feeling, and behavioral methods
that later turned into REBT.

THE VAST DIFFERENCE BETWEEN
DESIRING AND MUSTURBATING

As I began to see that absolutistic shoulds and musts were tyran-
nical and almost always led my clients to construct self-defeating
behaviors, I also saw that their having strong desires could not be
eliminated, since people stay alive and fulfill themselves by
desiring, and often strongly desiring, food, clothing, shelter, love,
sex, and other goals; and therefore, if they had little or no desires,
they could hardly survive and be happy. So I formulated the REBT
proposition that healthy desires and preferences are useful but
destructive desires and obsessive desires can easily create trouble.
Healthy desires include, "I distinctly want such things as sex and
love, and may strongly desire them; but if I am deprived of them, I
will feel frustrated and annoyed, but will hardly die." So I held that
your being thwarted in your desires would usually lead you to
healthy feelings of frustration and regret, but not to the unhealthy,
destructive feelings of anxiety, depression, and rage. "Because I
want sex and love, I also absolutely must get them," is a belief that
frequently will create anxiety, depression, and rage.

Even extreme healthy desires—such as your wanting someone
to solely love you forever—are risky, since they are easily thwarted
and will bring you great sorrow and sadness when they are not fulfilled. So some Buddhist groups view strong desires as foolish,
while REBT views them as risky but okay if you're willing to take
the risk. However, extreme *demands*—for example, "I need you to
love me more than anyone was ever loved"—are *too* risky, and may
lead you to feel depressed.

It is hard to draw an exact line between extreme desires and demands. But you can usually do so by recognizing the obsessive-compulsive quality of the latter. Thus, if you keep joyfully making more money after you have already gained a million, we could say that you are engaging in healthy strong desire. But if you have millions and you still fight others for every extra penny and you have no interest in life other than amassing more money, we could say you were desperately and commandingly greedy. Your desires are frantic and obsessive, and you have probably turned them into *needs* and *insistences.* REBT views nonobsessive desires as healthy even when you have them strongly. Indeed, your strong desire to write the Great American Novel, to help impoverished people, or to be tennis champion may provide a vital absorbing interest that gives you much healthy enjoyment and, if it is not obsessive, little anxiety and depression when you only make second best.

REBT, then, like some forms of Buddhism, encourages your desires but not your dire, exaggerated needs. Like Epicurus, it favors happiness and pleasure but also favors long-range hedonism and discipline that are usually required to achieve your future gains. Moderate eating and drinking may add to your life; addiction to gluttony and alcohol will often sabotage you.

THE PROFOUND DIFFERENCE BETWEEN JUDGING YOUR BEHAVIORS AND RATING YOUR SELF

REBT from the start has favored rational judging and has soundly opposed irrational, global judging. Why? Because I learned from several philosophers—such as Bertrand Russell and Gilbert Ryle—not to make category errors before I graduated from college at the age of twenty. My doing badly in social affairs doesn't make me a *bad person*; nor does my *failing at work* make me a *complete failure.* This notion was reinforced for me in my twenties by my reading Stuart Chase's *Tyranny of Words* and Alfred Korzybski's *Science and Sanity.* Also, my nonreligious views, starting at the age of twelve, got me thinking that the human soul didn't exist and could not be deified or damned.

Obviously, however, human thoughts, feelings, and actions can be evaluated once you set a goal or purpose for them to be assessed by. Thus, if your goal is to earn a comfortable living, you had better rate productive work as "good" for that goal. If your purpose is to get along well with others, you had better treat them with some degree of kindness. So you rate your productivity and kindness as "good" traits and your laziness and nastiness as "bad" ones. That kind of rating aids your goals.

From my childhood onward, however, I saw that I was also rating my self, my being, my totality in terms of my performances—at school, at sports, and in my social life. What child doesn't? So I not only *wanted* to do well in these respects, but thought that I *needed* to do so. Result: I was often anxious and sometimes depressed when I performed "badly." Who isn't?— especially when you tell yourself, "I have to *always* perform well." Which, as an anxious child, I often did. So I sometimes made myself *less* anxious by telling myself, "Well, I failed to perform well *this time*, but maybe I'll do so *next time.*"

I *almost* got rid of my anxiety when I was twenty-four and was madly in love with Karyl, a marvelous girlfriend of nineteen, who was most erratic about her love for me. So I frequently made myself panicked and depressed about her inconsistency. One eventful midnight, however, as I was ruminating in Bronx Botanical Gardens about my beloved's fickleness, I suddenly realized that I didn't merely strongly desire her love. I thought that I completely *needed* it. How idiotic! I obviously *didn't* need what I wanted. I could live and even be reasonably happy without it. I could, I could!

This brilliant insight greatly changed my life; and when I developed it in detail, when I became a practicing therapist fifteen years later, it blossomed into a basic principle of REBT: I and other people do not really *need* what we want, we only foolishly *think* and *feel* that we do! Again, how idiotic! How unrealistic!

From its start, REBT has taught these interrelated propositions: (1) People almost all have the goals of staying alive and being reasonably happy. (2) They therefore have several desires to perform important prospects well, to relate to other people, and to do things that help them reach their goals. (3) When they strongly (emotionally) desire to achieve or to avoid something, they frequently escalate their wishes and insist that they are *needs* or *necessities*. (4) Along with thinking that they *need* what they *want* (and *must* avoid what they *don't* want), people frequently (and falsely) convince themselves, "I *am* what I think, feel, and do. If I perform satisfactorily, I *am* a *good person*, and if I perform poorly, I *am* bad." (5) In addition to globally rating *themselves* as "good" or "bad," they frequently rate other people's behaviors as "good" or "bad" and then rate other *persons* as "great" or "damnable." (6) They also rate world events as "good" or "bad" and then globally rate the world or life as a whole as "good" or "bad."

By thinking, feeling, and acting in these inaccurate ways, REBT hypothesizes, people often healthily fulfill their main goals and purposes, but they also often unhealthily defeat these same goals and purposes and needlessly create emotional-behavioral problems, especially, severe anxiety, depression, and rage.

As long as they have an underlying tendency to rate their performances and their self, which they all seem to some extent to have, they also have underlying anxiety. This is sometimes called existential anxiety because the fact that they exist and want to continue to exist leads them to sensibly rate what they do and inaccurately rate their self for doing it.

PEOPLE'S TENDENCY TO ACT CONSTRUCTIVELY AND DESTRUCTIVELY

REBT hypothesizes that people innately and by their social upbringing have some degree of choice (so-called free will or self-determination) in how they conduct their lives. Their constructivism is hardly complete, since they have biological tendencies that set limits for them. Thus, they have a limited life span and are genetically predisposed to have ailments, diseases, and handicaps. They also live in families, groups, communities, and nations that restrict them and teach them to restrict themselves. Nonetheless, they have some degree of choice or decision making in what they do and don't do; and they can, with some degree of effort, change themselves considerably. Once they behave in a certain way, they often become habituated to keep acting that way. But they also can dehabituate themselves and make themselves prone to behave in other ways. They almost always keep changing and become somewhat habituated to changing. So, again, their "free will" is far from complete!

Because of their constructivism, people can motivate and force themselves to change, and can do so more than other animals. Because they have highly developed language systems, they can think, think about their thinking, and think about thinking about their thinking. Their thinking, feeling, and action often seem to be separate or disparate, but they actually significantly influence each other and are rarely, if ever, pure. When people think, they also feel and act. When they feel, they also think and act. When they act, they also think and feel. They therefore have the ability to push themselves to think, feel, and behave differently.

Consequently, REBT teaches people *many* kinds of thinking, feeling, and acting techniques to investigate their dysfunctional behaviors and to work at changing them. It is multimodal in its methods. It also holds that steady work and practice is usually required to change destructive tendencies and acts and to maintain the desired changes. REBT stresses insight, reasoning, and logic, but holds that these "rational" elements, without strong emotion and action, are not enough.

REBT is highly educational and believes that direct, didactic teaching of its theories and practices often works. So it uses dialogue, arguing, and disputing of irrational beliefs with clients. It also uses other educational approaches, such as articles, books, lectures, workshops, audiocassettes, and videotapes. But it recognizes that indirect teaching methods work best with many people and therefore uses Socratic dialogue, stories, fables, plays, poems, parables, and other forms of communication. It particularly acknowledges that all people are individuals and may have various modalities of learning that work best for them.

MULTIMODAL ASPECTS OF REBT

As noted above, REBT is concerned with the cognitive, emotional, and behavioral aspects of the client's (and other people's) emotional and practical problems. It therefore is widely multimodal in its teachings, as Arnold Lazarus has recommended for effective therapy. It has invented a number of intellectual, affective, and action techniques that it uses regularly; but it also uses and adapts many methods taken from other therapies, such as Rogerian, Existential, Transactional Analysis, Psychoanalytic, and Gestalt therapy. It thereby integrates several of these approaches with REBT.

In its simplest form, REBT teaches people its ABCDE procedures. Whenever any unfortunate event or Adversity (A) happens to them and they feel and behave dysfunctionally at C (Consequence), it shows them that A significantly *contributes* to but doesn't directly *cause* C. Instead, their disturbances (C) are also created by their

Belief System (B). So both A and B "cause" C; or A × B = C. B is largely their Beliefs—but these importantly include their thoughts plus their feelings plus their actions. Why? Because, as I noted above, people think *and* feel *and* act interrelatedly.

People's Belief Systems include functional or rational beliefs (RBs) and dysfunctional or Irrational Beliefs (IBs), and includes them strongly (emotionally) and behaviorally (activity-wise). Their RBs, as I noted above, tend to be *preferences* or *wishes* ("I want to perform well and be approved by significant others or else my *behaviors* are faulty"). Their IBs tend to include absolutistic musts, shoulds, and demands ("I have to perform well and be approved by significant others, else I am worthless!").

To use the ABCs of REBT, clients are taught to distinguish their rational from their irrational Beliefs, to keep their preferences but change their musts by arguing with and Disputing (D) the latter.

Disputing (D) largely consists of three kinds of rational questions:

(1) *Realistic disputing*: "Why must I perform well? Where is it written that I have to be approved by significant others?" Answer: "There is no evidence that I *must* or *have* to, but it would be highly *preferable* if I did."

(2) *Logical disputing*: "Does it follow that if I perform badly and lose the approval of significant others, that will make me an *inadequate person*?" Answer: "No, it will only make my *deeds* inadequate; but my performance isn't *me* or my *total personhood*."

(3) *Pragmatic disputing*: "What results will I get if I believe that I absolutely must perform well and always be approved by significant others?" Answer: "I will make myself anxious and depressed." "Do I want to get these results?" Answer: "No!"

Rational Emotive Behavior Therapy for Beginners

When clients persistently retain their Rational Beliefs (RBs) and Dispute their Irrational Beliefs (IBs), and when they strongly (emotionally) act against them, they tend to wind up with answers that include Effective New Philosophies (ENP), such as: "I never really *need* to do well, but I'd very much *like* to and will do my best to do so." "No matter how badly or foolishly I act, I am never a *bad person*, just a person who acted foolishly this time." "Some conditions in my life are unfortunate right now, but that doesn't mean that the *world* is bad or that my *whole life* is rotten!"

Clients then create other suitable rational coping statements that aid them to enjoy their healthy preferences and surrender their dysfunctional demands. They also agree with their therapists to do cognitive, experiential, and activity homework assignments that will counterattack their dysfunctional behaviors. One of the main cognitive assignments they do is to regularly fill out the REBT Self-Help Form which is shown in figures 1 and 2.

Rachel, a forty-year-old bookkeeper, was angry at her boss for not giving her a raise that she thought she well deserved and at her husband, Jim, for not sympathizing with her "terrible predicament." She contended that both of them were making her angry and wouldn't accept the REBT position that they may have been wrong, but that her demands on them were also making her upset. She and I argued for several REBT sessions about this and I (naturally!) almost won—but Rachel held on to her anger.

I finally gave Rachel several of our REBT Self-Help Forms to fill out and kept correcting them when she filled them out incorrectly. Finally, after four weeks she correctly did her seventh form and got it "right." She delightedly said, "Oh, I see now! The changing my wishes from my husband's and boss's backing me up to an insistent demand that they do so—that is what makes me angry at them. Of course. Hereafter, I'm going to stop my childish demanding."

Rachel's seventh REBT Self-Help Form was as follows:

REBT Self-Help Form

A (ACTIVATING EVENTS OR ADVERSITIES)

- Briefly summarize the situation you are disturbed about (what would a camera see?).
- An A can be *internal or external, real or imagined.*
- An A can be an event in the *past, present, or future.*

IB's (IRRATIONAL BELIEFS)

To identify IB's, look for:

- DOGMATIC DEMANDS (musts, absolutes, shoulds)
- AWFULIZING (It's awful, terrible, horrible)
- LOW FRUSTRATION TOLERANCE (I can't stand it)
- SELF/OTHER RATING (I'm / he / she is bad, worthless)

D (DISPUTING IB'S)

To dispute ask yourself:

- Where is holding this belief getting me? Is it *helpful* or *self-defeating?*
- Where is the evidence to support the existence of my irrational belief? Is it *consistent with social reality?* Is my belief *logical?* Does it follow from my preferences?
- Is it really awful (as bad as it could be?)
- Can I really not *stand* it?

© *Windy Dryden & Jane Walker 1992. Revised by Albert Ellis, 1996.*

C (CONSEQUENCES)

Major unhealthy negative emotions:

Major self-defeating behaviors:

Unhealthy negative emotions include:
- Anxiety
- Depression
- Shame/Embarassment
- Rage
- Hurt
- Low Frustration Tolerance
- Jealousy
- Guilt

E (EFFECTIVE NEW PHILOSPHIES)

To think more rationally, strive for:

- NON-DOGMATIC PREFERENCES (wishes, wants, desires)
- EVALUATING BADNESS (It's bad, unfortunate)
- HIGH FRUSTRATION TOLERANCE (I don't like it, but I can stand it)
- NOT GLOBALLY RATING SELF OR OTHERS (I—and others—are fallible human beings)

E (EFFECTIVE EMOTIONS & BEHAVIORS)

New healthy negative emotions:

New constructive behaviors:

Healthy negative emotions include:
- Disappointment
- Concern
- Annoyance
- Sadness
- Regret
- Frustration

Figure 2. **REBT Self-Help Form**

A (ACTIVATING EVENTS OR ADVERSITIES)

My boss refused to give me a raise which I deserved.
My husband was unsympathetic.

- Briefly summarize the situation you are disturbed about (what would a camera see?)
- An A can be *internal* or *external*, real or imagined.
- An A can be an event in the *past, present,* or *future.*

IB's (IRRATIONAL BELIEFS)

*My boss is very unfair to me and he absolutely **shouldn't be!***

My husband is unsympathetic, as he often is —that louse!

D (DISPUTING IB'S)

*Why **must** my boss be fair?*

What a quaint idea! Who says that my husband has to be sympathetic.? That would be a remarkable change!

To identify IB's, look for:

- DOGMATIC DEMANDS (musts, absolutes, shoulds)
- AWFULIZING (It's awful, terrible, horrible)
- LOW FRUSTRATION TOLERANCE (I can't stand it)
- SELF/OTHER RATING (I'm / he / she is bad, worthless)

To dispute ask yourself:

- Where is holding this belief getting me? Is it *helpful* or *self-defeating?*
- Where is the evidence to support the existence of my irrational belief? Is it *consistent with social reality?*
- Is my belief *logical?* Does it follow from my preferences?
- Is it really *awful* (as bad as it could be?)
- Can I really not *stand* it?

C (CONSEQUENCES)

Major unhealthy negative **emotions:** *Anger at boss and husband.*

Major self-defeating **behaviors:** *Screaming at them.*

Unhealthy negative emotions include:
- Anxiety   • Depression   • Rage   • Low Frustration Tolerance
- Shame/Embarrassment   • Hurt   • Jealousy   • Guilt

E (EFFECTIVE EMOTIONS & BEHAVIORS)

New healthy **negative emotions:**

Frustration.
Disappointment.

New constructive **behaviors:**

Calmed down.

Tactfully told my boss and husband how disappointed I was.

E (EFFECTIVE NEW PHILOSOPHIES)

Bosses are frequently unfair, but mine is only partly so. I can accept him with his unfairness.

*My husband, seeing the way he often is, has a perfect right to his lack of sympathy. He acts lousily but is **not** a lousy person.*

To think more rationally, strive for:

- NON-DOGMATIC PREFERENCES (wishes, wants, desires)
- EVALUATING BADNESS (it's bad, unfortunate)
- HIGH FRUSTRATION TOLERANCE (I don't like it, but I can stand it)
- NOT GLOBALLY RATING SELF OR OTHERS (I—and others—are fallible human beings)

Healthy negative emotions include:
- Disappointment
- Concern
- Annoyance
- Sadness
- Regret
- Frustration

© *Windy Dryden & Jane Walker 1992. Revised by Albert Ellis, 1996.*

REBT EVOCATIVE-EMOTIVE
AND BEHAVIORAL EXERCISES

As noted above, REBT includes several special exercises of an evocative-emotive and behavioral nature. One of its main exercises is my famous shame-attacking exercise, which I invented for myself when I had little money when I was twenty-three and ashamed to eat with my friends in a cafeteria and present an empty receipt to the cashier. I "knew" from my philosophic readings that my shame was self-created and unnecessary, because obviously the cashier was merely going to *think* badly of me and not arrest or kill me. So I vigorously tried to convince myself that I was not a worm, no matter what the cashier thought of me; and I forced myself to go to many cafeterias in New York, take a drink of water, and present a blank receipt to the cashier when I left. Within a few weeks, my shame-attacking exercise made me quite shameless! So, years later, I frequently encourage my clients to perform it.

When, for example, my client Alice was ashamed of speaking poorly in public and showing how anxious she was, I encouraged her to do several "shameful" things and refuse to put herself down when people criticized her doing them. She did two of the REBT main shame-attacking exercises: (1) Yell out several stops in the subway—and stay on the train. (2) Stop a perfect stranger on the street and say, "I just got out of the mental hospital. Will you please tell me what month this is?" She did these "risky" exercises several times, put up with people thinking she was crazy, and wound up feeling unashamed.

Using REBT, I also encourage my fearful clients to do various other "dangerous" exercises that help them overcome their anxieties—such as going for difficult job interviews, dancing badly in public, speaking about a topic that they are not prepared to present, and being assertive with difficult people. They thereby desensitize themselves to criticism by seeing that their actions may indeed be uncomfortable but they are hardly fatal.

REBT has also created a number of emotional-evocative exercises, like Maxie Maultsby's 1971 creation of rational emotive imagery. Soon after Maxie created it, I used it with a client, Rob, who wouldn't risk having sex with a new woman because he might not get and keep an erection and might be rejected by her. I showed him, first, using regular REBT that he was telling himself, "I absolutely must be perfectly potent with all women I go to bed with, and I am a complete loser if I am unarousable!" When he changed this to, "I'd *like* to be fully potent with every woman, but I don't *have to be*," he became much less anxious about failing sexually. But he still was afraid to fail.

So as an emotive-experiential technique, I gave Rob rational emotive imagery. With his eyes closed, he was to imagine risking intercourse with a new woman, failing to get an erection, and having her bawl him out for being so hopelessly inept. "Maybe," he was to imagine her saying, "you'd better give up sex and join a monastery!"

"As you vividly imagine this woman's damning you," I asked Rob, "how do you honestly feel?"

"Very depressed and almost suicidal."

"Good! You're really using this rational emotive imagery (REI) technique well. Okay, allow yourself to feel very very depressed. Feel it as deeply as you can. Feel very depressed and suicidal. Get fully in touch with your feelings. Don't suppress, but feel them."

"Oh, I do. I really do!"

"Fine. Now, keeping the same vivid image of the woman's putting you down, make yourself feel the healthy negative emotions of regret and frustration, but not the unhealthy ones of depression and suicidalness. Feel only healthily regretful and frustrated but not depressed and suicidal."

"I'm trying to do what you say, but I can't do it. I can't!"

"You damned well *can*! Anyone can change his feelings. Because you *create* them yourself, you always can *choose* to change them. Now do it! You can!"

Rob did so, and as I predicted, made himself feel regretful and frustrated but *not* depressed and suicidal.

"Great!" I said. "*How* did you change your feelings? What did you *do* to change them?"

"First, I said to myself, "To hell with her! She's very hostile." Then I said, "That's *her* opinion. I'll find another woman who's not like her and can be sexually satisfied even if I never get an erection! That really made me unhostile and unanxious. Just sorry and frustrated."

"Beautiful!" I said. "I told you that you could do it."

Anyone can change his disturbed feelings to healthy ones if he only changes his irrational *musts* and *shoulds* into realistic *preferences*.

As usual, since Rob only lightly believed that it was *good* to be erect with the women but it wasn't *necessary*, and that he could accept *himself* in spite of a woman's putting him down for his *failing*, I encouraged him to practice rational emotive imagery once a day for thirty consecutive days until he *solidly* believed and felt his new philosophy. He did so and after twenty days of using this method, he lost his fear of going to bed with new women.

In addition to this imagery technique, I use several other highly emotional-evocative methods with my anxious, depressed, and raging clients—such as role playing. Thus, they role-play taking an important interview, let themselves feel anxious about its outcome, stop the role-play to discover what they are telling themselves to make themselves anxious, correct their anxiety-creating *shoulds* and *musts*, and then practice going on with the role-play.

Let me repeat: Though REBT uses a good many behavioral and emotive-evocative exercises, it simultaneously cognitively discovers the absolutistic *shoulds* and *musts* brought out in these exercises, actively and persistently disputes them, and thereby employs *combined* thinking, feeling, and action methods to help people minimize their disturbances. Again: All three!

TEACHING THE BASIC PHILOSOPHY OF UNCONDITIONAL SELF-ACCEPTANCE (USA), UNCONDITIONAL OTHER ACCEPTANCE (UOA), AND UNCONDITIONAL LIFE-ACCEPTANCE (ULA)

To help my clients (and others) achieve the three basic REBT philosophies of unconditional self-acceptance, other-acceptance, and life-acceptance, I use all the cognitive, emotional, and behavioral therapy methods described in this book. But, so that they will change the important habits of thinking-emoting-behaving dysfunctionally, I constantly keep reminding people that they can easily fall back to dangerous self-rating, other-rating, and life-rating. Buddhism seems to be just as skeptical of its adherents as I am of REBT followers and it never lets them forget how vulnerable they are to re-neglecting its four basic truths even after they have presumably accepted them and healthfully used them for years.

It has just occurred to me as I think about this point that that is probably why all the major religions have their monastic side. Thus, the Jewish religion has its rabbis and its Talmudic scholars and its saints (such as David and Job), The Christian religion has priests, ministers, and saints (such as St. Augustine and Joan of Arc). The Muslim religion has its priests, prophets, true believers, and of course Mohammed. These accredited and holy teachers serve as good models for the normal followers of the religion, who frequently fail to maintain devout observance of their basic tenets, and who therefore have to be reminded by outstanding models to avoid retrogressing.

In other words, when a religion has core philosophers that people can "agree with" but still inconsistently follow (because they require much self-discipline), a few devout followers are practically deified so that they can serve as models for its more lax and inconsistent adherents.

This goes for Buddhism, too. Most Buddhists seem to have a hard time consistently following its Four Noble Truths. So Buddhism has a long training program for establishing gurus who are its elite members and who only comprise one out of several thousand Buddhists. Tibetan Buddhists also have the Dalai Lama, who is selected from scores of possible candidates, rigorously trained from childhood onward, and is the recognized head of Buddhism. In addition, it has a few outstanding scholars who are widely read and quoted for centuries after their writings first appear. Quite a hierarchy! And some unusual models for the Buddhist laity to follow.

Parenthetically: The field of psychotherapy has its prophets, too—such as Freud, Adler, Jung, Reich, Rogers, and Perls. But most of their followers do not exactly see them as saints. Let me hope that Albert Ellis does not achieve sainthood either! For sainthood implies absolute truth—which doesn't really exist.

Returning to the basic philosophies of REBT, they are often held in a slippery manner and get confused with and contaminated by *conditional* self- and other-esteem. For it seems *right* to hold yourself and others as *responsible* for their crimes and to denounce wrongdoers for their evil *deeds*. They, as REBT says, are not their antisocial acts. But they still *do* them—and often wreak great harm. How can we *not* blame them?

Answer: By applying REBT forgiveness and Buddhist compassion—and still not condoning human wrongs and injustices. REBT and Buddhism agree on this. Both philosophies steadily reveal and *accept* human fallibility.

REBT teaches, first, unconditional self-acceptance (USA). You damn your misdeeds—but not your *self.* You revile your sins but not you as the sinner. You denigrate some of your thoughts, feelings, and actions—but not your totality, your you-ness.

Second, REBT teaches you to unconditionally *accept* all other humans (and animals)—especially when they act evilly. Again, they often *sin* but are not *damnable sinners.*

Third, you unconditionally accept life and the world—that frequently provide rotten conditions. You deplore and try to better the conditions; but you gracefully accept—no, not *condone*—what you cannot presently change. Yes, gracefully, unresentfully.

Pretty simple, isn't it? Yes and no: For REBT philosophy has its complications. Therefore, it has to be taught and retaught. But I—prejudicedly—say it's worth it!

APPENDIX 2

The Role of Irrational Beliefs in Perfectionism

The importance of perfectionism in helping people become anxious, depressed, and otherwise emotionally disturbed was at least vaguely seen by the Stoics and Epictetus (Epictetus 1899; Xenakis 1969) and has been pointed out by pioneering cognitive therapists such as Alfred Adler (1926), Paul Dubois, and Pierre Janet for more than a century. It also was noted by the non-Freudian psychoanalyst Karen Horney (1950) in her concept of the idealized image.

I was the first cognitive-behavioral therapist to specifically include perfectionism as an irrational, self-defeating belief in my original paper on rational emotive behavior therapy (REBT), presented at the annual convention of the American Psychological Association in Chicago on August 31, 1956 (Ellis 1958). Thus, among twelve basic irrational ideas that I included in this paper, I listed *perfectionism* as

Reprinted from G. L. Flett and Paul L. Hewitt, eds., *Perfectionism: Theory, Research, and Treatment* (Washington, DC: American Psychological Association, 2002), pp. 217–29. Used by permission.

The idea that one should be thoroughly competent, adequate, intelligent, and achieving in all possible respects—instead of the idea that one should *do* rather than desperately try to do well and that one should accept oneself as an imperfect creature, who has general human limitations and specific fallibilities. (p. 41)

In my first book on REBT for the public, *How to Live with a Neurotic* (1957), I included among the main irrational ideas leading to disturbance,

A person should be thoroughly competent, adequate, talented, and intelligent in all possible respects; the main goal and purpose of life is achievement and success; incompetence in anything whatsoever is an indication that a person is inadequate or valueless. (p. 89)

I also noted, "*Perfectionism.* . . . Excessive striving to be perfect will invariably lead to disillusionment, heartache, and self-hatred" (p. 89).

In 1962, after practicing, lecturing, and writing on REBT for seven years, I included in my first book for the psychological profession, *Reason and Emotion in Psychotherapy*, among eleven main irrational ideas that cause and maintain emotional disturbances:

The idea that one should be competent, achieving, and adequate in all possible respects if one is to consider oneself worthwhile. . . . 4. The idea that it is awful and catastrophic when things are not the way one would very much like them to be. . . . 11. The idea that there is invariably a right, precise, and perfect solution to human problems and that it is catastrophic if this perfect solution is not found. (pp. 69–88)

Obviously, REBT has particularly stressed the irrationality and self-defeatism of perfectionism from the start. Scores of REBT articles and books have made this point endlessly, including many of my own publications (Ellis 1988; Ellis and Dryden 1997; Ellis, Gordon, Neenan, and Palmer 1997; Ellis and Harper 1997; Ellis and Tafrate 1997; Ellis and Velten 1988) and publications by other leading REBTers (Bernard 1993; Dryden 1988; Hauck 1991; Walen, DiGiuseppe, and Dryden 1992). Following REBT's identification of perfectionism as an important irrational belief, the vast literature has been devoted in recent years to the findings and treatment of perfectionism; cognitive-behavioral therapy also has frequently emphasized the psychological harm and the treatment of perfectionism. A. Beck (1976) and Burns (1980) particularly emphasized its importance, and many other cognitive behaviorists have described it and its treatment (J. Beck 1995; Flett and Hewitt 2002; Hewitt and Flett 1993; Lazarus, Lazarus, and Fay 1993; Lazarus 1997).

Although I have been one of the main theorists and therapists to emphasize the importance of perfectionism in emotional and behavioral disturbance, I now see that I have never described what the rational or self-helping elements in perfectionism are, how they accompany the irrational and self-defeating elements, and why they probably "naturally" exist and impede humanity's surrendering its strong perfectionistic tendencies. Because this entire book is about perfectionism, it might be good if I were more specific than I have been about these important aspects of it.

The main idea of rationality and irrationality in human behavior stems from the ancient notion that humans, in order to stay alive and well-functioning, have several basic desires, goals, and preferences—which are often incorrectly called *needs* or *necessities*—that help them do so. Thus, people are commonly said to survive better and be more effective when they:

1. have a sense of self-efficacy or self-mastery (ego-satisfactions);

2. actually succeed in getting what they want and avoiding what they don't want (goal or accomplishment satisfaction);
3. get approval and minimal disapproval of other people whom they consider important (love and approval satisfaction); and
4. are safe and sound, and not likely to be diseased, hurt, or killed (safety satisfaction).

It is not that people *cannot* exist or *must be* completely miserable if they don't fulfill any or all of these desires and goals; therefore, we had better not call them *needs* or *dire necessities*. But it is usually agreed—and we can tentatively accept for the sake of the following discussion—that humans tend to be better off (happier) and live longer (survive) when they achieve those four goals than when they fail to achieve them.

Assuming—for the sake of discussion and not to posit any absolute truth—that people are more likely to survive and to be glad they're alive if they satisfy the four basic urges or wants mentioned above, then they can probably justifiably take the first of these urges or goals—ego satisfaction—and rationally reach the following conclusion:

If I have self-inefficacy and view myself as only being able to function badly, and definitely to function imperfectly, I actually will tend to function less well than I am theoretically able to function. Therefore,

1. I will probably actually get less of what I want and more of what I don't want as I go through life (because I think I am unable to perform well).
2. I will probably get less approval and love from significant other people (because, again, I think I am unable to get it).

3. I will probably be in more danger of being harmed and killed by dangerous conditions (because I think I am unable to take precautions and cope with threat).

If, in other words, failing to perform well or perfectly well and succeeding in performing badly or imperfectly *will* likely get you less of what you want; less approval from others; and make you less likely to be safe from disease, harm, and death, and if your sense of self-inefficacy will impede you from performing well or perfectly well, then it is quite rational (i.e., self-helping) to have a sense of self-efficacy—as many studies by Bandura (1997) and his followers tend to show. Your *wish* or *desire* to have a sense of self-efficacy, and thereby improve your chances of performing well, being approved by others, and being safe from harm or death, is therefore a rational belief, not an irrational belief.

You also may have an irrational, self-defeating belief about self-efficacy, however, such as, "Because I *desire* to have a sense of self-efficacy, I *absolutely must* have it, else I am a worthless, unlovable, hopelessly endangered person!" To go one step further, your irrational belief about self-efficacy may be, "Because I desire to have it, I *absolutely must*, under all conditions at all times perfectly have it!" Lots of luck with that belief!

What I have said about the goal of self-efficacy also goes for the desire to *be* efficacious, productive, efficient, and accomplished. Such aims are usually rational in that if you perform well and, perhaps, perfectly well, you will *in all likelihood* in most of today's world (although who knows about tomorrow's) get more of what you want, greater approval (and also envy and jealousy!), and more security and longer life. So under most conditions—although hardly all—if you want to achieve those goals, you try to achieve them. As long as you merely *wish for*, but not *demand*, their achievement, you will (says REBT theory) feel frustrated, sorry, and disappointed but not depressed, anxious, or angry when you do not achieve them.

Escalating your *desire* for success and accomplishment to a *demand*, and especially to a *perfectionistic* demand, is quite another matter! Listen to this: "I *absolutely must*—under all conditions at all times—*perfectly achieve* my goals!" Or else? Or else you will tend to conclude that you'll *never* get what you want. Or else you'll be *totally* unworthy of approval and love by significant others. Or else you will be in *continual danger* of harm and annihilation. Quite a series of "horrors" you've predicted—and helped bring on yourself.

If what I have been saying so far is correct, you can easily and legitimately have rational, sane, self-helping *desires* for success and achievement—and even for perfect achievement. For example, you can wish for a 100 percent grade on a test and the approval of all the people you find significant. That would be nice. But don't make it necessary.

Once again, you can have desires—even strong desires—for others' approval. It probably would be great if you acted the way they wanted you to act—and if they always, under all conditions, perfectly favored you. They might well give you more of what you want and less of what you dislike. Fine! But if you *need* others' approval, and especially if you need their undying, perfect approval, watch it! Raising your want to a necessity is your irrationality. Quite a difference!

What about your striving for safety, security, good health, and longevity? By all means strive—but not desperately, compulsively. If you distinctly want security measures like these, you will, perhaps, also notice their disadvantages and restrictions. The safer you make yourself, the more you may sacrifice adventure and experimentation. So you have a choice. A safe, long life is not necessarily a merry one. Caution and concern, as wants and choices, may have real value for you. But to *absolutely need* safety is to make yourself anxious and panicked. And, quite probably, it is likely to bring on some needless dangers.

What I have been saying so far shows that having self-efficacy, competence, lovability, and safety tend to aid human living. Not always, of course, and with some exceptions. For most of the people most of the time, they are characteristics that seem to have more advantages than disadvantages. Therefore, few individuals and groups do not strive for these goals. If they are, in fact, more beneficial than harmful, you are rational or self-helping when you aim for them. Why, then, should you irrationally and self-sabotagingly do yourself in by frequently escalating your desires to unrealistic and often perfectionistic demands? Why do you often turn them into foolish, absolutistic musts?

The usual answer psychologists give to this paradox is a combination of innate, biological tendencies of humans and their early conditioning or rearing. First, for evolutionary, survival reasons they are born wishers *and* demanders, instead of mere wishers. Second, their parents and teachers reinforce their wishing and demandingness and often help make them worse. Third, they practice both wishing and demanding and become habituated to and comfortable with both behaviors; hence, they continue desiring and insisting for the rest of their lives.

These are all probably good reasons why both rational preferring and irrational demanding are so common among practically all people and lead to great benefits and detriments. Over the past sixty years of doing psychotherapy with thousands of people, I have figured out some more specific reasons why humans are "demanders" and "musturbators" when they would probably be much less disturbed if they were mainly "preferrers" and "unimperative goal seekers." Let me present the following ideas as hypotheses that are yet to be tested but will possibly add to our understanding of perfectionism if they are tested and receive some creditable empirical support:

1. People have little difficulty in distinguishing their weak or moderate desires from their demands, but they frequently have great difficulty distinguishing their strong, forceful wishes from insistences. When they have a weak or moderate desire to succeed at an important task, to gain social approval, or to be safe from harm, they rarely or occasionally think that they *absolutely must* achieve those goals, but when they have strong desires to do those things, they frequently insist that they *have* to have them. *Why* they have weak or strong desires depends on many factors, both biological and environmental. But my theory says that once, for any reason, they *do* have powerful wishes—or what Wolcott Gibbs, a *New Yorker* writer, called "a whim of iron"—they frequently think, and especially *feel*, that they *must* attain them.

2. A mild or moderate preference to perform well or win others' approval implies the legitimacy of alternative behaviors. Thus: "I would moderately like to win this tennis match *but* if I lose it's no big deal, and I can probably go on and win the next one." "I would moderately prefer to have Mary like me, *but* if she doesn't, I can live without her approval and probably get Jane, who is not much different from Mary, to like me." If you *mildly* want something and don't get it, there is a good chance that you can get something almost equally desirable instead.

   A strong preference, however, often leaves few alternative choices of equal valence. Thus: "I *greatly* want to win the tennis match, and thereby become champion, so if I lose it I will lose the championship—which I also *strongly* want to win—and never gain it at *all*. Therefore, I *must* win this match to get what I *really* want." "I greatly want to have Mary like me, because she is a *special* person with whom I could be *notably* happy. Therefore, if Mary doesn't like me, and I could be close to Jane instead of her, this is a poor alternative, and it will not really satisfy me. Therefore, I *must* get Mary to like me"

Strong preferences, consequently, leave little room for alternative choices—or, at least, *equally* satisfying ones—and imply that because alternatives don't exist, you *must* have your strong preferences fulfilled. By their very *strength*, they prejudice you against alternative choices and make your particular choice seem mandatory instead of preferential.

3. Strong desires encourage you, just because of their strength, to focus, sometimes almost obsessively-compulsively, on *one* choice or a *special* choice and to ignore or disparage alternative choices. Thus, if you *mildly* want to win a tennis match, you are free to think of many other things—such as the pleasure your opponent will have if he or she wins instead of you or the fact that he or she will dislike you if you win. So, you consider, again, alternative plans to winning the match and may even deliberately lose it. Or you may decide to play golf instead of tennis.

If, however, you *strongly* desire to win the tennis match—as well as, perhaps, win the championship along with it—you will tend to focus, focus, focus on the gains to be achieved by winning and the "horrible" consequences of losing, and your (obsessive-compulsive?) focus will discourage alternative thoughts and selectively prejudice you against seriously considering such alternatives. Strong desires, in other words, frequently lead to focused thinking and to prejudiced overgeneralizations—not always, of course, but significantly more frequently than mild or moderate desires do. If so, the prejudiced overgeneralization that strong desire encourages leads to the belief that because some other performance goal, approval aim, or safety seeking is *highly* preferable, it is also necessary. Overfocusing on its desirability encourages seeing it as a dire necessity.

Assuming that my hypothesis that strong desires more often lead to demandingness and musturbation than do weak desires is supported by empirical findings, what has all this got to do with perfectionism? My theory goes one step further and says that the beliefs "I would *like* to perform well and often to perform perfectly well" are rational and self-helping in human societies that define certain performances as "good" and then reward the performer—which seems to be the case in practically all cultures that survive. But the beliefs "I *absolutely must* perform well and indeed *must* perform perfectly well" are often irrational and self-defeating because, being a fallible human and living with social restrictions, you frequently will *not* perform well (according to personal and social standards) and you certainly won't be able to function perfectly well.

Moreover, your demand for a guarantee of good or perfect performance may well create feelings of anxiety about performing that will interfere with your succeeding; your demand for a guarantee, "I must not be anxious! I must not be anxious!" will likely make you even more anxious. So demanding, rather than preferring, again won't work too well to aid your purpose. To insist that you *must* get something you desire seems "logical" (in terms of motivation). Paradoxically, it is illogical and tends to create anxiety.

My theory about desire hypothesizes that your strong, rather than weak, desires (a) make you more likely to think that those desires *absolutely must* be fulfilled and (b) make you more likely to think that they must be *perfectly* fulfilled. If their successful fulfillment is rationally beneficial to you and if perfect fulfillment is also rationally beneficial to you—as I have noted above—then it is logical for you to jump from "I absolutely *must* fulfill my strong desires just because they are so strong"—which actually is a complete non sequitur—to "I *absolutely must* fulfill my strong desires perfectly just because they are so strong"—which again, is a complete non sequitur.

I am theorizing, then, that strong desires, rather than weak desires, are profound prejudices—that is, they are cognitive-emotional biases—that for various reasons often encourage people to think, "Because I *strongly* want success, approval, or safety, and it would be beneficial for me to have them, I *absolutely must* have them." This is a fairly grandiose and perfectionistic idea itself, because you and I obviously don't run the universe, so whatever we desire, no matter how strongly we prefer it, doesn't have to exist.

Humans are, however, prone to grandiosity, to demanding that their strong desires absolutely must be fulfilled. They often think wish-fulfillingly—as Freud and his psychoanalytic followers have pointed out. More to the point, they often think and feel wish-demandingly: "Because I *strongly* want it so, it *should* be that way!" Once they escalate their powerful wishes to dire necessities, they frequently take them one step further: "Because my most important desires are sacred and *absolutely must* be fulfilled, they must be thoroughly, completely, and perfectly fulfilled!" Then they really have emotional and behavioral problems!

PERFECTIONISM, IRRATIONAL BELIEFS, AND ANXIETY SENSITIVITY

Let me consider one more important point. I noted in *Reason and Emotion in Psychotherapy* (Ellis 1962) that people who are anxious, particularly those who experience panic, frequently make themselves quite anxious about their anxiety and thus have a secondary disturbance about their original disturbance. Why is this so common among humans? According to REBT theory, they are forcefully thinking "I must not be anxious! It's terrible to be anxious! I am an inadequate person for being anxious!"

For several years, Reiss and his coworkers (Reiss and McNally 1985) have theorized that some people have unusual sensitivity to their own feelings of anxiety, as I hypothesized in 1962. They have conducted many studies of this secondary symptom of anxiety, which they called *anxiety sensitivity*, and have confirmed some of my observations and other clinicians' observations about it (Cox, Parker, and Swinson 1996; Taylor 1995; Wachtel 1994). Reiss's theory of anxiety sensitivity somewhat overlaps with my theory of strong desire in that it implies that some people who experience anxiety about anxiety find their anxious feelings *so* uncomfortable that they "awfulize" about them and thereby produce panic states. Their desire for relief from anxiety is so intense that they *demand* that they not have it and thereby escalate it.

What, we may ask, makes anxiety-sensitive people so *demanding* about their anxiety? My theory answers this question as follows:

1. Anxiety, and particularly panic, is uncomfortable. It feels bad, disrupts competence, may lead to social disapproval, and often brings on physical symptoms—such as shortness of breath and rapid heartbeat—that make you think you are in real physical danger, even that you are dying.
2. Because it is *so* uncomfortable, you *strongly* wish that it not exist—disappear—and that all its disadvantages disappear with it.
3. Because you *strongly* desire it to go, you insist and demand "I must not be anxious! I must not be panicked!"
4. Then, logically (and perversely enough), you make yourself anxious about your anxiety, panicked about your panic.

The Role of Irrational Beliefs in Perfectionism

5. Consequently, you increase your uncomfortable symptoms—especially your physical symptoms of suffocating and heart pounding.
6. You become more panicked than ever.
7. Your vicious cycle continues.
8. Finally, because your slightest feelings of panic bring on *great* discomfort, you may frequently conclude "I must never panic *at all*! I must be *perfectly* free from anxiety and panic!" The moral: By being *acutely aware of your discomfort* (and other disadvantages) of your feeling of panic, you may demand *perfect* freedom from panic and may therefore increase the likelihood of your panicking.

My explanations of anxiety about anxiety and panic about panic in the preceding paragraph fit nicely into my theory about strong desire and its relationship to demandingness and perfectionism. However, beware! The explanatory power of my theory is interesting but may have little connection with empirical findings. Many psychoanalytic theories fit brilliantly together and support their derived postulates, but they appear to be little connected with hard-headed facts.

So I believe in and present this theory that when people's weak desires are thwarted, they commonly lead to healthy negative feelings of disappointment, regret, and frustration, but when their strong desires are thwarted, they more often lead to absolutistic musts and demands and thereby to unhealthy feelings of anxiety, depression, rage, and self-pity. It seems to me a plausible and testable theory. It also seems to explain some reasons for human perfectionism. Now all we have to do is check my theories and explanations to see if any evidence backs them. Theorizing is fun. Evidence gathering is harder.

PERFECTIONISM AND
IRRATIONAL BELIEFS IN COUPLES

So far in this chapter I have considered individualistic demands for achievement, approval, and safety but, of course, they exist in couples, in families, and in social respects as well. Take couples therapy, which I have done extensively along REBT lines for more than forty years. Are husbands, wives, and other partners as demanding and perfectionistic about their mates as they are about themselves? Frequently, yes, and with frightful results for their relationships.

John, a thirty-six-year-old accountant, gave himself a perfectionistic hard time about his work and made himself exceptionally anxious if it wasn't wholly accurate. He excused his perfectionism in this respect by saying that of course it had to be perfectly accurate—because it was accounting and that *meant* accuracy. But John was also perfectionistic about his dress, his tennis game, and several other aspects of his life. Because, however, he worked mightily to keep his accounting, his appearance, and his tennis game in order, he succeeded fairly well in doing so and was only temporarily anxious when things got a bit beyond his control. His compulsive striving kept things pretty much in line.

John, however, was equally perfectionistic about his wife, Sally, and his two accounting partners. They, too, had to—yes, had to—perform well, dress well, and even play tennis well. And often they didn't, those laggards! John, of course, couldn't control others as he strove for his own perfection, so he was frequently enraged against his "careless" wife and partners, much more than he was anxious about his own performances.

I saw John for therapy because his wife and partners insisted that he go—or else. He was set for a double divorce. I had a rough time, at first, showing him the folly of his own performance-oriented perfectionism, because he was willing to strive mightily to achieve it and suffer occasional panic attacks when he didn't. It was easier to show him that his demands on others just wouldn't work. He had little control over others, and they were going to continue to be just as abominably unperfectionistic—not to mention downright sloppy—as they chose. They *shouldn't* be that way—but they were.

After several sessions of REBT, John was able to *prefer* without *demanding* perfect behavior from Sally and his partners and therefore to be keenly disappointed but not enraged when they made accounting, tennis, or other errors. He lived with their imperfections, and no one divorced him. He only slightly gave up his own perfectionistic demands on himself and continued to perform well in most ways, but he was decidedly more anxious than he need have been.

John's wife, Sally, whom I also saw for a few sessions, was nondemanding of herself for the most part but *couldn't stand* the obsessive-compulsiveness of John and their twelve-year-old daughter, Electra. They were both carved from the same perfectionistic family block (as were John's father and sister) and had to do many things absolutely perfectly. Sally couldn't take their frantically pushing themselves to achieve (which was bad enough) and their insistence that she, too, be faultlessly on the ball (which was impossible!). Although usually easygoing, in this respect she kept inwardly demanding "They *must not* be that scrupulous! They *have to* be more tolerant! I can't bear their intolerance!"

I showed Sally—and she was much easier to work with than was John—that her intolerance of John's and Electra's intolerance was not going to work. Her rage was going to be exceptionally self-upsetting, was not going to change John or Electra, and might lead to her divorcing John (not so bad) but also to her divorcing Electra (not so good!) and to her own psychosomatic horrors (still worse!).

Sally saw the light and soon gave up her intolerance of John's and Electra's intolerance. She still *wanted* them to but didn't insist that they be more reasonable, and she worked with me to change her own demands that her family be less perfectionistic. So John improved in his demands on Sally (and his own partners), and Sally distinctly improved in her perfectionistic demands on John and on Electra. John kept some of his perfectionistic demands on his own performance but did not let them interfere too seriously with his family and business relationships.

PERFECTIONISM AND HYPERCOMPETITIVENESS

One reason John kept insisting that he must perform outstandingly was because he was fixated on the kind of competitiveness that I described about perfectionists in the original edition of *Reason and Emotion in Psychotherapy* (1962). I said at that time,

> The individual who *must* succeed in an outstanding way is not merely challenging himself and testing his own powers (which may well be beneficial); but he is invariably comparing himself to and fighting to best *others*. He thereby becomes other- rather than self-directed and sets himself essentially impossible tasks (since no matter how outstandingly good he may be in a given field, it is most likely that there will be others who are still better). (pp. 63–64)

After practicing REBT for almost fifty years and after studying the results obtained in scores of studies of irrational beliefs, I find this hypothesis more tenable than ever. Hypercompetitiveness is a common trait of "normal" musturbators and especially of perfectionists. They mainly have unhealthy *conditional* self-acceptance instead of healthy *unconditional* self-acceptance. Their main condition for being a "good person" is notable achievement, and to be a "better person" than others requires outstanding achievement.

Actually, to strive desperately to best others and thereby to gain "better" worth as a person is an undemocratic, fascistlike philosophy. Fascists like Hitler and Mussolini are seen by many of their followers to be not only better (i.e., more competent) in some traits, such as physical prowess or blondeness, but are viewed as being superior *people*. Their *essence* is supposedly outstandingly good. They are almost diametrically opposed to the concept of unconditional self-acceptance, which means fully accepting and respecting yourself *whether or not* you are achieving (Ellis 1962, 2004a, 2004b; Ellis and Harper 1997; Ellis and Velten 1998; Hauck 1991).

Perfectionists, then, tend to be highly conditional self-acceptors who base their worth as persons on hypercompetitively besting others—and, in the process, often lose out on discovering what they personally want to do—and who tend to fascistically denigrate others. These hypotheses, for which I have found much clinical evidence over the years, merit considerable research efforts.

PERFECTIONISM AND STRESS

How are perfectionists affected by stressful conditions? More so, I would say, than are run-of-the-mill nonperfectionists. First, they may demand that stress be minimal—or perfectly nonexistent. Second, they may insist that they get perfect solutions to practical problems that create stress—such as how to have a perfect job interview, how to get a perfect job, how to deal with bosses or employees perfectly well, and so forth. Third, when stressful conditions—such as business difficulties—occur, they may demand that they have perfect solutions to them. They not only greatly prefer these conditions of solutions to them but require that they be easily and quickly available—which they normally are not. Therefore, under conditions that are equally stressful to others, perfec-

293

tionists "find" more stress, less satisfactory solutions, and more prolonged difficulties than nonperfectionists find. Their perfectionism contradicts realistic and probabilistic expectations about the number and degree of stressors that should exist and often results in their making a hassle into a holocaust.

About the stressors of their lives, they have the usual irrational beliefs of disturbed people but hold them more vigorously and rigidly. Thus, they tend to believe that stressful situations *absolutely must not* exist; that it is *utterly awful and horrible* (as bad as it could be) when they do; that they *completely can't stand them* (can't enjoy life *at all* because of them); are *quite powerless* to improve them; and rightly should damn themselves and other people for not removing them or coping beautifully with them.

According to REBT theory, practically all disturbed people *at times* hold these self-defeating beliefs. But perfectionists seem to hold them more frequently and insistently—and cling to them as *fixed ideas*. Consequently and, they often require long-term treatment—as Blatt (1995) showed—and, if REBT is used with them, will frequently require several cognitive, emotive, and behavioral methods before they will surrender their beliefs. Why? Because a single method of disputing and acting against their irrational beliefs doesn't seem convincing enough. So a therapist's use of several techniques may finally work better.

By the same token, I have found that if perfectionists who react badly to stressful conditions are placed in cognitive-behavioral group therapy, in which several group members in addition to the therapist actively try to help them give up their rigid beliefs and behaviors, it works better than if they are in individual therapy with only a single therapist to counter their perfectionism. Again, the issue seems to be that compared with nonperfectionists, perfectionists have (a) a stronger desire or preference to do well; (b) a stronger and more rigid demand that they do well; (c) a stronger insistence that they do perfectly well under one or more conditions; and (d) a long-term habit of perfectionistic thinking, feeling, and behaving that resists short-term change. For all these reasons, they frequently are difficult customers, who can use intensive, prolonged therapy.

My hypothesis, then, is that perfectionists are more rigid and persistent in their irrational beliefs than what I call the "nice neurotics." Many of them—not all—have severe personality disorders. They have *idées fixes* (fixed ideas), as Pierre Janet said of many severely disturbed people over a century ago. And let us honestly admit this before we try to fix them.

APPENDIX 3

Showing People that They Are Not Worthless Individuals

erhaps the most common self-defeating belief of disturbed people is their conviction that they are worthless, inadequate individuals who essentially are undeserving of self-respect and happiness. This negative self-evaluation can be tackled in various ways—such as by giving them unconditional positive regard (Carl Rogers), directly approving them (Sandor Ferenczi), or otherwise giving them supportive therapy (Lewis Wolberg). I prefer, as I have indicated in my books *Reason and Emotion in Psychotherapy* and *How to Stubbornly Refuse to Make Yourself Miserable About Anything—Yes, Anything!* an active-directive discussion of the clients' basic philosophy of life and teaching them that they can view themselves as okay *just because* they exist, and *whether or not* they are competent or loved. This is a central teaching of rational emotive behavior therapy (REBT).

As may well be imagined, I often have great difficulty in

Originally published in *Voices: The Art and Science of Psychotherapy* 1, no. 2 (1965): 74–77. Revised, 2001. New York: Albert Ellis Institute.

showing people that they are merely *defining* themselves as worthless. For even if I show them, as I often do, that they cannot possibly empirically prove that they are valueless, they still may ask, "But how can you show that I *do* have value? Isn't that concept an arbitrary definition, too?"

Yes, it is, I freely admit: For, philosophically speaking, *all* concepts of human worth are axiomatically given values and cannot be empirically proven so (except by the pragmatic criterion that if you *think* you're worthwhile—or worthless—and this belief "works" for you, then you presumably become what you think you are). It would be philosophically more elegant, I explain to people, if they would not evaluate their *self* at all but merely accept its existence while only evaluating their *performances*. Then they would do better to solve the problem of their "worth."

Many people resist this idea of not evaluating themselves for a variety of reasons—particularly because they find it almost impossible to separate their selves from their performances and therefore insist that if their *deeds* are rotten *they* must be *rotten* people. I maintain that no matter how inefficient their *products* are, they are still an ongoing *process*, and their process or being (as Robert Hartman and Alfred Korzybski have shown) simply cannot be measured the way their products can be.

I have recently added a cogent argument for convincing people that they are much more than their acts. Instead of only showing them that their *self* is not to be measured by the criterion used for assessing their performance, I also demonstrate how their (or anyone's) *good* creations are not a measure of their self.

"Did you ever realize," I ask a person, "that almost all emotional disturbance comes from inaccurate or unoperational definitions of our terms about ourselves and our deeds and that it could be minimized if we would force ourselves vigorously to define our self-descriptions?"

"How so?" she usually asks.

"Well," I reply, "let's take Leonardo da Vinci. We usually call him a *genius* or even a *universal genius*. But that's nonsense—he of course wasn't anything of the sort."

"He wasn't?"

"No. To call him—or Michelangelo, or Einstein, or anyone else—a *genius* is to indulge in slipshod thinking. Leonardo, admittedly, had *aspects of genius*. That is, *in certain respects* and for a *specific era of history* he did remarkably well."

"But isn't that what a genius is—one who does unusually well in certain ways?"

"That's what we carelessly say. But, actually, using the noun *genius* clearly implies that a person to whom this title is given is *generally* an outstanding performer; and of course no one, including Leonardo, is. In fact, he did many silly, asinine things. He fought with several of his patrons and frequently depressed himself and made himself very angry. So he often behaved stupidly and uncreatively—which is hardly what a true genius should do. Isn't that right?"

"Well—uh—perhaps."

"Moreover, let's even consider his best work—his art. Was he really a thoroughgoing genius even in *that* respect? Were all, or even most, of his paintings great examples of color *and* composition *and* draughtsmanship *and* contrast *and* originality? Hardly! Again, if the truth is admitted and accurately described, we'd better admit that only *certain aspects* of Leonardo's art were masterful; his work *as a whole* was not."

"Are you saying, then, that there are *no* real geniuses?"

"I definitely am. Nor are there any heroes or heroines, any great people. These are fiction, myths which we fallible humans seem determined to believe in order to ignore the fact that we presently *are*, and probably always will be, highly inefficient, mistake-making animals. So if we want to be sensible, we'd better honestly admit that there *are* no geniuses or extraordinary *people*; there are merely individuals with exceptional deeds. And we'd better sensibly evaluate their acts rather than *deifying*—or, as the case may be, devil-ifying—their personhoods. People are always *human*, not gods or devils. Tough!—but that's the way it is."

So I now continue, demonstrating as best I can to people that they will never, except by overgeneralized definition, be a hero or an angel—or a louse or a worm. Does this new tack always convince them that they are not the worthless, hopeless slobs they usually think they are? Hell, no! But it has so far proved to be a useful tool in rational emotive behavior therapy (REBT).

DISCUSSION BY DR. BINGHAM DAI:

1. This approach does not help a person to work through his original experiential bases for his sense of worthlessness;
2. It tends to encourage people to avoid responsibility for the guilt that may be involved;
3. It overemphasizes the therapist's intellectual prowess and may enhance a client's sense of inadequacy;
4. It fails to stimulate a client's own potentialities for health or to make use of his own ability to think through his problems; and
5. One has reason to doubt that an individual's sense of personal worth can really be enhanced by the sort of arguments presented here. Since this is claimed to be a report of effective psychotherapeutic techniques, perhaps the reader may want to see some evidence of the effectiveness which is entirely missing.

Showing People that They Are Not Worthless Individuals

REPLY TO DR. DAI BY DR. ALBERT ELLIS:

Dr. Dai's discussion of my paper is brief but highly pertinent. Let me see if I can briefly answer it.

1. No, my approach does not help people work through their original experiential bases for their sense of worthlessness; and in my estimation it is only an unverified (and almost unverifiable) assumption that it is necessary or even desirable to do this. Whatever the *original* cause of their self-deprecation, the *present* cause is largely their belief that they are *still* slobs because they are, and *should* and *must not* be, imperfect. I think that they were born with a predisposition to think this nonsense and then were raised to give into this predisposition. No matter! They *are* capable of giving it up—or else psychotherapy of any sort is useless. The belief that they can only change their ideas about their worth by understanding the *complete origin of these ideas* is only a theory, hardly a fact.

2. Teaching people that they are worthwhile just because they exist does not encourage them to avoid responsibility for any immoral act they may have committed. On the contrary, by showing them that they are not bad *people*, even if some of their *acts* are wrong, encourages them to be responsible for their acts, to admit that they have been mistaken, and to focus on changing their behavior for the better in the future. Guilt or self-blame encourages repression and depression. Unconditional self-acceptance (USA) *even* when one is fallible encourages honest confession and greater responsibility in the future.

3. Clients who feel more inadequate because their therapist displays intellectual prowess do so precisely because they

falsely believe that they are worthless if someone else, even their own therapist, excels them. The technique advocated in REBT teaches them that they are never no good, no matter how bright their therapist (or anyone else) is. It thereby helps appreciably to decrease their feelings of inadequacy.

4. It is Dr. Dai's hypothesis that teaching people how to think straighter fails to stimulate their own potentialities for health or make use of their own ability to think through their problems. The entire history of education would tend to show otherwise. If Dr. Dai were correct, every client (and every high school and college student) should be left to muddle through on his or her own rather than be helped to acquire various kinds of helpful knowledge.

5. Dr. Dai is quite right in asking for evidence of the effectiveness of my briefly stated technique. I can only say that I have now used it on about twenty thousand clients; that about 20 percent seemed to be little affected by it and 80 percent seemed to be significantly helped. One young female patient was so greatly helped by a single session consisting almost entirely of this kind of material that she seemed to surrender her deep-seated feeling of worthlessness, got out of a severe state of depression, and began to function much better in her love life and her work.

Case histories, however, are not very good evidence for the efficacy of any kind of psychotherapy, because the "effectiveness" is mainly evaluated by the therapist, who is obviously biased in favor of her or his methods. Moreover, only "successful" cases are usually presented, while less successful ones are commonly omitted.

Psychotherapy research, however, studies groups of clients who have been treated with one method of therapy and another control group who were not treated or with whom therapists used another method. REBT, along with Aaron Beck's cognitive therapy (CT), Donald Meichenbaum's cognitive behavior therapy (CBT), Arnold Lazarus's multimodal therapy (MT), and several other similar kinds of treatment that follow some of the main principles and practices of REBT have been tested in over two thousand studies of people with anxiety, depression, and other aspects of self-deprecation. The great majority of these studies have shown that REBT-oriented techniques have significantly helped people to feel less worthless and more self-accepting.

Try REBT and see for yourself! This brief article only describes a few of its methods. Others will be found in the books and tapes which can be obtained from the Albert Ellis Institute in New York.

For starters, however, let me repeat in more detail two of the main REBT solutions that you, as an individual, can use to make yourself feel worthwhile or that you, as a therapist, facilitator, or teacher can teach others to help them achieve unconditional self-acceptance (USA):

1. Decide to define yourself as a "good" or "worthwhile" person just because you exist, just because you are alive, just because you are human. For no other reason or condition! Work at—that is, think and act at—unconditionally accepting yourself *whether or not* you perform "adequately" or "well" and *whether or not* other people approve of you. Acknowledge that what you *do* (or don't do) is often mistaken, foolish, or immoral, but still determinedly accept *you*, your *self*, with your errors and do your best to correct your past behavior.

2. Don't give *any* kind of global, generalized rating to your *self*, your *essence*, or your *being*. Only measure or evaluate what you think, you feel, or you do. Usually, evaluate as "good" or "healthy" those thoughts, emotions, and behaviors

that help you and the members of the social group in which you choose to live and that are not self-defeating or anti-social; and rate as "bad" those that are self-defeating and socially disruptive. Again, work at changing your "bad" behaviors and continuing your "good" behaviors. But stubbornly refuse to globally rate or measure your *self* or *being* or *personhood* at all. Yes, at all!

Will USA solve all of your (or your clients') emotional problems? Most likely not, because rational emotive behavior therapy sees you and other people as having three basic neurotic difficulties: (1) Damning or deprecating your self, your being, and thereby making yourself feel inadequate or worthless. (2) Damning or putting down other *people* for their "bad" behaviors and thus making yourself enraged, hostile, combative, or homicidal. (3) Damning or whining about conditions under which you live and thereby producing low frustration tolerance (LFT), depression, or self-pity.

If, as this article suggests, you work at achieving unconditional self-acceptance (USA), you will have an easier time also achieving unconditional acceptance of others (but not of what they often do!). And you can achieve unconditional acceptance of poor external conditions that you do your best to change but are clearly not able to change. For anger at yourself sometimes comes first and is basic to rage at other people and at the world. Thus, if you demand that you *absolutely must* do better than others do at work, relationships, or sports, you will tend to strongly hate yourself when you don't perform as well as you presumably must. But because damning yourself leads you to feel highly anxious and/or depressed, and because you may easily horrify yourself about having such feelings by insisting, "I *must not* be anxious! I'm no good for being depressed!"—you will then feel anxious *about* your anxiety, depressed *about* your depression, and will be *doubly* self-downing.

Sensing this, you may choose to think, instead, "Other people *must not* make me fail, and *they* are no good!" If so, you will make yourself enraged at these others. Or you may think, "The conditions under which I live are so lousy, and *must* not be. It's *awful* that they are so bad! I *can't* stand it!" You will then create low frustration tolerance (LFT).

So conditional self-acceptance and consequent feelings of worthlessness may encourage (1) damning yourself for your failures, (2) feelings of severe anxiety and/or depression, (3) downing yourself for having these disturbed feelings, (4) defensively damning others who "make" you fail, and (5) defensively damning conditions that are "responsible" for your failing. Quite a kettle of (rotten) fish!

Feelings of worthlessness are not worth it. You largely bring them on yourself, and you can choose—and help your clients choose—to replace them, when you behave "badly," with healthy feelings of sorrow and regret. Then, as a "goodnik" rather than a "no-goodnik," you are in a much better position to change what you can change. By unconditionally accepting yourself you increase your chances of being able to change harsh reality or, as Rheinhold Niebuhr said, to have the serenity to *accept*, but not to *like*, bad conditions that you cannot change.

APPENDIX 4

Comments on David Mills's "Overcoming Self-Esteem"

I am delighted that David Mills has taken off from some of my main ideas about human worth and self-esteem and has written this important essay. If people follow the views that he has presented, I cannot give them a guarantee but can give them a high degree of probability that they will make themselves less anxious and, as he shows, more achieving. Even if they achieve little during their lives, they will enable themselves to live more peacefully and happily with themselves and others. Again, in all probability!

However, the solution to the problem of self-worth that David Mills gives—rating only one's deeds, acts, and performances and *not* one's self, being, or essence—is what I call the *elegant* solution. Because most humans seem to be born with a strong tendency to make misleading *global* evaluations of their "self," as well as to make fairly accurate *specific* evaluations of their performances, I have found clinically that my rational emotive behavior therapy (REBT) clients often have great difficulty in *not* rating their self and in *only* rating their thoughts, feelings, and behaviors in regard to the results they achieve by creating and engaging in these responses. I therefore teach most of them the "elegant" philosophic solution that David Mills has beautifully outlined; but I also give them the choice of "inelegant" or practical solution to their self-concept. Thus, somewhere during the first few sessions of REBT I say something like this to my clients:

> *You very likely were born and reared with both self-actualizing and self-defeating tendencies and you can use the former to overcome the latter. Self-actualizingly, you are born to think, to think about your thinking, and to think about thinking about your thinking. Consequently, whenever you defeat yourself, you can observe your conduct, think differently, and free yourself to change your feelings and your habits. But it's not easy—and you'd better keep working at it!*
>
> *Perhaps your main self-helping tendency is to sanely rate or evaluate what you do—that is, whether your acts are "good" and helpful or "bad" and unhelpful. Without measuring your feelings and acts, you would not repeat the "good" and not change the "bad" ones. Unfortunately, however, you are also biologically and socially predisposed to rate your self, your being, your essence as "good" or "bad" and, by using these global ratings, to get yourself into trouble. For you are not what you do, as general semanticist Alfred Korzybski pointed out in 1933. You are a person who does millions of acts during your life—some "good" and some "bad" and some "indifferent." As a person, you are too complex and many-sided to rate yourself (or rate any other pluralistic human) and to do so totally, globally, or generally. When you make this kind of global rating of your "you-ness," you end up as a "good person," and presumably better than other people—and that is a grandiose, godlike view. Or, more frequently, because you are indubitably fallible and imperfect, you view yourself as a "bad person," presumably undeserving, worthless, and incapable of changing your behaviors and of*

doing *better. So* self-*rating leads to deification or devil-ification.*
Watch it!—and go back to only measuring what you do *and not*
what you supposedly are.

If, however, you have difficulty refusing to rate your self, *your*
being, *you can arbitrarily convince yourself, "I am 'good' or*
'okay' because I exist, because I am alive, because I am human."
This is not an elegant solution to a problem of self-worth,
because I (or anyone else) could reply, "But I think you are 'bad'
or 'worthless' because you are human and alive." Which of us is
correct? Neither of us: because we are both arbitrarily defining
you as "good" or "bad," and our definitions are not really prov-
able nor falsifiable. They are just that: definitions.

Defining yourself as "good," however, will give you much
better results than believing that you are "bad" or "rotten."
Therefore, this inelegant conclusion works and is a fairly good
practical *or* pragmatic *solution to the problem of human "worth."*
So if you want *to rate your* self *or your* being, *you can definition-*
ally, tautologically, or axiomatically use this "solution" to self-
rating. Better yet, however, as I have pointed out in Reason and
Emotion in Psychotherapy, Humanistic Psychotherapy, A New
Guide to Rational Living, *and a number of my other writings,*
and as David Mills emphasizes in this essay, you can use the
"elegant" REBT solution to rating yourself. That is, give up all
your ideas about self-esteem, stick only to those of unconditional
acceptance, and choose to accept your self, your existence, your
humanity whether or not *you perform well,* whether or not *you*
are loved by significant others, and whether or not *you suffer*
from school, work, sports, or other handicaps.

This is what I usually say to my therapy clients. As David Mills
aptly points out, you can recognize that your absence of self-image
is possible and, in fact, preferable to frequent anxiety and inhibi-
tion. Your goal can be to *enjoy* rather than to *prove* yourself—for
the rest of your unself-esteeming life!

APPENDIX 5
Intellectual Fascism

I f fascism is defined as the arbitrary belief that individuals possessing certain traits (such as those who are white, Aryan, or
male) are intrinsically superior to individuals possessing certain
other traits (such as those who are black, Jewish, or female), and
that therefore the "superior" individuals should have distinct
politico-social privileges, then the vast majority of American liberals and so-called antifascists are actually intellectual fascists. In
fact, the more politico-economically liberal our citizens are, the
more intellectually fascistic they often tend to be.

Intellectual fascism—in accordance with the above definition—
is the arbitrary belief that individuals possessing certain traits (such
as those who are intelligent, cultured, artistic, creative, or
achieving) are intrinsically superior to individuals possessing certain other traits (such as those who are stupid, uncultured,
unartistic, uncreative, or unachieving). The reason why the belief of
the intellectual fascist, like that of the politico-social fascist, is arbitrary is simple: there is no objective evidence to support it. At

bottom, it is based on value judgements or prejudices which are definitional in character and are not empirically validatable, nor is it falsifiable. It is a value chosen by a group of prejudiced people—and not necessarily by a majority.

This is not to deny that verifiable differences exist among various individuals. They certainly do. Blacks, in some ways, are different from whites; short people do differ from tall ones; stupid individuals can be separated from bright ones. Anyone who denies this, whatever his or her good intentions, is simply not accepting reality.

Human differences, moreover, usually have their distinct advantages—and disadvantages. Under tropical conditions, the darkly pigmented blacks seem to fare better than do the lightly pigmented whites. At the same time, many blacks and fewer whites become afflicted with sickle-cell anemia. When it comes to playing basketball, tall men are generally superior to short ones. But as jockeys and coxswains, the undersized have their day. For designing and operating electric computers, a plethora of gray matter is a vital necessity; for driving a car for long distances, it is likely to prove a real handicap.

Let us face the fact, then, that under certain conditions some human traits are more advantageous—or "better"—than some other traits. Whether we approve the fact or not, they are. All people, in today's world, may be created free, but they certainly are not created equal.

Granting that this is so, the important question is: Does the possession of a specific advantageous endowment make an individual a better human? Or more concretely: Does the fact that someone is an excellent athlete, artist, author, or achiever make him or her a better person? Consciously or unconsciously, both the politico-social and the intellectual fascist say yes to these questions.

This is gruesomely clear when we consider politico-social or lower-order fascists. For they honestly and openly not only tell themselves and the world that being white, Aryan, or male, or a member of the state-supported party is a grand and glorious thing; but, simultaneously, they just as honestly and openly admit that they despise, loathe, consider as scum of the earth individuals who are not so fortunate as to be in these select categories. Lower-order fascists at least have the conscious courage of their own convictions.

Not so, alas, intellectual or higher-order fascists. For they almost invariably pride themselves on their liberality, humanitarianism, and lack of arbitrary prejudice against certain classes of people. But underneath, just because they have no insight into their fascistic beliefs, they are often more vicious, in their social effects, than their lower-order counterparts.

Take, by way of illustration, two well-educated, presumably liberal, intelligent people in our culture who are arguing with each other about some point. What, out of irritation and disgust, is one likely to call the other? A "filthy black," a "dirty Jew bastard," or a "black-eyed runt"? Heavens, no. But a "stupid idiot," a "nincompoop," a "misinformed numbskull"? By all means, yes. And will the note of venom, of utter despisement that is in the detractor's voice, be any different from that in the voice of the out-and-out fascist with his racial, religious, and political epithets? Honestly, now: will it?

Suppose the individual against whom a well-educated, presumably liberal, intelligent person aims scorn actually is stupid, or misinformed. Is this a crime? Should he, perforce, curl up and die because he is so afflicted? Is she an utterly worthless, valueless blackguard for not possessing the degree of intelligence and knowledge that her detractor thinks she should possess? And yet—let us be ruthlessly honest with ourselves, now!—isn't this exactly what the presumably liberal person is saying and implying—that the individual whose traits she dislikes doesn't deserve to live? Isn't this what we (for it is not hard to recognize our own image here, is it?) frequently are alleging when we argue with, criticize, and judge others in our everyday living?

The facts, in regard to higher-order fascism, are just as clear as those in regard to lower-order prejudice. For just as everyone in our society cannot be, except through the process of arbitrary genocide or "eugenic" elimination, Aryan, or tall, or white, so cannot everyone be bright, or artistically talented, or successful in some profession. In fact, even if we deliberately bred only highly intelligent and artistically endowed individuals to each other, and forced the rest of the human race to die off, we still would be far from obtaining a race of universal achievers: since, by definition, topflight achievement can only be attained by a relatively few leaders in most fields of endeavor, and is a relative rather than an absolute possibility.

The implicit goals of intellectual fascism, then, are, at least in today's world, impractical and utopian. Everyone cannot be endowed with artistic or intellectual genius; only a small minority can be. And if we demand that all be in that minority, to what are we automatically condemning those who clearly cannot be? Obviously: to being blamed and despised for their "deficiencies"; to being lower-class citizens; to having self-hatred and minimal self-acceptance.

Even this, however, hardly plumbs the inherent viciousness of intellectual fascism. For whereas lower-order or politico-economic fascism at least serves as a form of neurotic defensiveness for those who uphold its tenets, higher-order fascism fails to provide such defenses and actually destroys them. Thus, politico-social fascists believe that others are to be despised for not having certain "desirable" traits—but that they are to be applauded for having them. From a psychological standpoint, they compensate for their own underlying feelings of inadequacy by insisting that they are super-adequate and that those who are not like them are subhumans.

Intellectual fascists start out with a similar assumption but more often than not get blown to bits by their own homemade explosives. For although they can at first assume that they are bright, talented, and potentially achieving, they must eventually prove that they are. Because, in the last analysis, they tend to define talent and intelligence in terms of concrete achievement, and because outstanding achievement in our society is mathematically restricted to a few, they rarely can have real confidence in their own possession of the values they have arbitrarily deified.

To make matters still worse, intellectual fascists frequently demand of themselves, as well as others, perfect competence and universal achievement. If they are excellent mathematicians or dancers, they demand that they be the most accomplished. If they are outstanding scientists or manufacturers, they also must be first-rate painters or writers. If they are fine poets, they not only need to be the finest, but likewise must be great lovers, drawing room wits, and political experts. Naturally, only being human, they fail at many or most of these ventures. And then—O, poetic justice!—they apply to themselves the same excoriations and despisements that they apply to others when they fail to be universal geniuses.

However righteous their denials, therefore—and even though those readers who by now are not squirming with guilt are probably screaming with indignation, I will determinedly continue—the typical politico-social "liberals" of our day are fascistic in several significant ways. For they arbitrarily define certain human traits as "good" or "superior"; they automatically exclude most others from any possibility of achieving their "good" standards; they scorn, combat, and in many ways persecute those who do not live up to these capricious goals; and, finally, in most instances they more or less fail to live up to their own definitional standards and bring down neurotic self-pity and blame on their own heads.

Let me give a case in point which I deliberately take not from my psychotherapeutic practice (since, as one might expect, it is replete with cases of all kinds of self-haters) but from my presumably less neurotic acquaintanceship. It is the case of an individual I have known for many years who, partly because of his long-standing union connections and the fact that his parents were killed by the Nazis, prides himself on his antifascist views. This individual, however, not only tries to avoid associations with people whom he considers unintelligent (which, of course, is his privilege, just as it is the privilege of a musician to try to associate mainly with other musicians), but goes into long diatribes against almost everybody he meets because they are "so terribly stupid" or "real idiots" or "utterly impossible." He gets quite upset whenever he encounters people who turn out to be below his accepted standards of intelligence, and says that he cannot understand "why they let people like that live. Surely the world would be much better off without such dopes."

This same individual, as I would have predicted from seeing many clients with similar views, has for many years been completely ineffective in his own desires to write short stories. Every time he reads over a few paragraphs he has written, he finds them to be "stupid," "inconsequential," or "trite," and he stops right there. He obviously is trying to write not because he enjoys doing so, or feels that he'd like to express himself, but mainly because he has to be admired, accepted, thought intelligent by other people, particularly by other writers. His intellectual fascism not only prejudices all his human relationships, but also sabotages his own creativity and potential happiness. His name, I contend, is legion.

What is the alternative? Assuming that intellectual fascism exists on a wide scale today, and that it does enormous harm and little good to people's relations with themselves and others, what philosophy of living are they to set up in its place? Surely, you may well ask, I am not suggesting an uncritical, sentimental equalitarianism, whereunder everyone would fully accept and hobnob with

316

everyone else and where no one would attempt to excel or perfect himself at anything? No, I am not.

I feel, on the contrary, that significant human differences (as well as samenesses) exist; that they add much variety and zest to living; and that one human may sensibly cultivate the company of another just because this other is different from, and perhaps in certain specific respects superior to, others. I feel, at the same time, that one's worth as a human being is not to be measured in terms of one's popularity, success, achievement, intelligence, or any other such trait, but solely in terms of one's humanity.

More positively stated: I espouse the seemingly revolutionary doctrine, which actually goes back many hundreds of years and is partially incorporated into the philosophies of Jesus of Nazareth and several other religious leaders, that people are worthwhile merely because they exist, and not because they exist in an intelligent, cultured, artistic, achieving, or other way. If any particular person decides to pursue a certain goal, such as excelling at basketball, astrophysics, or Terpsichore, then it may be better for this purpose that he or she be tall, intelligent, supple, or something else. But if the main purpose of humans is, as I think it can be, living in some kind of satisfactory way, then it is highly desirable that they live and enjoy simply by acting, doing, being, and not by acting, doing, or being anything special.

Let us get this matter perfectly straight, since it is the easiest thing to muddle and confuse. I am not in any manner, shape, or form opposed to people's trying to achieve a given goal, and to this end consistently practicing some task and trying to keep bettering their performances. I believe, in fact, that most men and women cannot live too happily without some kind of goal direction or vital interest in solving problems or completing long-range projects.

I still maintain, however: the fact that people achieve, produce, solve, or complete anything is not to be used as a measure of their intrinsic value. They may be happier, healthier, richer, or more confident if they successfully paint, write, or manufacture a useful product. But they will not be, nor is it desirable that they see themselves as, better people.

In Rational Emotive Behavior Therapy (REBT), we encourage you to refrain from rating your **self**, your **totality**, your **essence**, or your **being** at all—but instead to **only** rate your acts, deeds, and performances.

Why had you better not rate your **self** or your **essence**? For several reasons:

1. Rating your **self** or your **you**-ness is an overgeneralization and is virtually impossible to do accurately. You **are** (consist of) literally millions of acts, deeds, and traits during your lifetime. Even if you were fully aware of all these performances and characteristics (which you never will be) and were able to give each of them a rating (say, from zero to one hundred), **how** would you rate each one? for what **purpose**? and under what **conditions**? Even if you could accurately rate **all** your millions of acts, how could you get a **mean** or **global** rating of the **you** who performs them? Not very easily!

2. Just as your deeds and characteristics constantly change (today you play tennis or chess or the stock market very well and tomorrow quite badly), so does your **self** change. Even if you could, at any one second, somehow give your **totality** a legitimate rating, this rating would keep changing constantly as you did new things and had more experiences. Only after your death could you give your **self** a final and stable rating.

3. What is the **purpose** of rating your **self** or achieving **ego** aggrandizement or **self**-esteem? Obviously, to make you feel better than other people: to grandiosely deify yourself, to be

holier than thou, and to rise to heaven in a golden chariot. Nice work—if you can do it! But since self-esteem seems to be highly correlated with what Albert Bandura calls self-efficacy, you can only have stable ego-strength when (a) you do well, (b) know you will continue to do well, and (c) have a guarantee that you will always equal or best others in important performances in the present and future. Well, unless you are truly perfect, lots of luck on **those** aspirations!

4. Although rating your performances and comparing them to those of others has real value—because it will help you improve your efficacy and presumably increase your happiness—rating your **self** and insisting that you must be a good and adequate **person** will (unless you, again, are perfect!) almost inevitably result in your being anxious when you may do any important thing badly, depressed when you do behave poorly, hostile when others outperform you, and self-pitying when conditions interfere with your doing as well as you think you **should**. In addition to these neurotic and debilitating feelings, you may suffer from serious behavioral problems, such as procrastination, withdrawal, shyness, phobias, obsessions, inertia, and inefficiency.

For these reasons, as well as others I have outlined elsewhere, rating or measuring your **self** or your **ego** will tend to make you anxious, miserable, and ineffective. By all means rate your **acts** and try (undesperately!) to do well. For you may be happier, healthier, richer, or more achievement-confident (confident that you **can** achieve) if you perform adequately. But you will not be, nor had you better define yourself as, a better **person**.

If you insist on rating your **self** or your **personhood** at all—which REBT advises you **not** to do—you had better conceive of yourself as being valuable or worthwhile just because you are human, because you are alive, because you exist. Preferably, don't rate your **self** or your **being** at **all**—and then you won't get into any philosophic or scientific difficulties. But if you do use inaccurate, overgeneralized self-ratings, such as "I am a good person," "I am worthwhile," or "I like myself," say "I am a good person because I exist and not because I do something special." Then you will not be rating yourself in a rigid, bigoted, authoritarian—that is, fascistic—manner.

Human traits are good for a purpose; are not, in, or, by, and for themselves, good or bad, virtuous or evil. Intelligence is good for problem solving; aesthetic sensitivity for enjoyment; persistence for achievement; honesty for putting others at their ease; courage for facing dangers with equanimity. But intelligence, aesthetic sensitivity, persistence, honesty, courage, or any other purposeful trait is not, except by arbitrary definition, an end in itself, nor an absolute good. And as soon as such a trait is defined as a good thing in itself, all nonpossessors of that trait automatically are labeled as evil or worthless. Such an arbitrary, labeling, again, is fascism.

What, then, can be taken as a valid measure of a person's worth? If being intelligent, or artistic, or honest, or what you will does not render him or her "good" or "worthwhile," what does?

Nothing, actually. All human "worth" or "value" is simply a **choice**, a **decision**. We **choose** to rate our **selves** or to not do so. Almost always (because that seems to be our nature or innate predisposition) we **decide** to give ourselves global ratings. And we **select** standards to use for this rating. Thus, we **choose** to rate ourselves as "good people" because (1) we perform well; (2) we have good, moral character traits; (3) we win the approval of others; (4) we are members of a favored group, community, or nation; and (5) we believe in some deity (e.g., Jehovah, Jesus, or Allah) whom we are convinced created us and loves us.

All these "criteria" of our "worth" or "value" or "goodness" are actually arbitrary and are valid because we **choose** to believe them so. None of them, except by our **belief** in them, is empirically confirmable or falsifiable. Some work well and some badly—that is, bring us more or less happiness and greater or lesser disturbance. If we are wise, therefore, we will select those criteria of our "worth" or "value" that bring us the best results.

According to REBT, the best or most effective criterion of our human worth would probably be **no** self-rating—yes, **no** measure of our **self** or our **ego**. For then we would **only** rate our behaviors and traits, and thereby strive for continued aliveness and enjoyment—and not for deification or devilification. And, because self-ratings are overgeneralizations that are impossible to validate, we would be philosophically sounder.

If you do, however, choose to rate your **self** or your **totality**, why not rate it in terms of your **aliveness** and your **enjoyment**? Try, for example, this philosophy: "I am alive and I choose to stay alive and to try to enjoy my existence. I will rate my **aliveness**, my **existence** as 'good' because that is my choice; and if my aliveness truly becomes too painful or unenjoyable I may rationally **choose** to end it. Meanwhile, I value my existence (my be-ing) simply because I am alive and, while so alive, I can sense, feel, think, and act. This I select as my 'real' worth: my humanity, my aliveness, my present cheating of nonexistence."

From choosing to value your aliveness, your existence, you can also choose various subvalues. You can decide, for example, to be happily, vitally, maximally, or freely alive. You can judge if it is good for you to be alive and happy it is also good if you help others enjoy their existence (and to enjoy yours with them). You can plan to live healthfully, peacefully, and productively. Once you **choose** to see living as "worthwhile," you will probably also choose to live in a social group, to be intimate with some others, to work productively, and to engage in several recreational pursuits. These choices and the actions you take to implement them are frequent concomitants of your decision to value your aliveness and the enjoyments that may go with it. But all these values and their derivatives are not only given to you (by your heredity and your environment) but are also **accepted** and **chosen**. They are "good" because you (consciously or unconsciously) **decide** that they are. And even when you think that outside forces foist them on you or devoutly believe that God loves you (and that He or She **makes** you "good" or "worthwhile") you obviously **chose** to believe this and thereby **select** the criteria for your human worth. If you are wise, therefore, you will admit that you make this choice and will consciously and honestly (from here on in) continue to make it.

To return to our central theme: If you insist on rating your **self** instead of merely rating your acts and traits, choose to see yourself as worthwhile simply because you exist. And try to see all other humans as "good" because they are human, because they are alive and have potential for enjoyments. If you, for purposes of your own, prefer to be with intelligent, or cultured, or tall, or any other kind of individuals, that is your privilege—go be with them. But if you insist that only intelligent, cultured, tall, or any other kind of individuals are good or worthy humans, you are, except by your personal and arbitrary definition, wrong, since you cannot present any objective, scientific evidence to support your preference. Even if you induce the majority to agree with you—as, presumably, Mussolini, Hitler, and various other dictators have done—this merely proves that your view is popular, not that it is correct.

People, then, can be viewed as good in themselves—because they are people, because they exist. They may be good for some specific purpose because they have this or that trait. But that purpose is not them. Nor is this or that trait. If you want to use people for your purpose—for having cultured conversations, for example, with them—then you can legitimately specify that they be intelligent, aesthethic, well-educated, or what you will. But please don't, because you desire them to have certain traits, insist that they are worthless for not possessing these traits. Don't confuse their worthlessness to you with worthlessness in themselves.

This is the essence of intellectual fascism. It is a belief about humans which convinces not only the believers, but usually their victims as well, that people acquire intrinsic worth not from merely being, but from being intelligent, talented, competent, or achieving. It is politico-social fascism with the trait names changed—the same hearse with different license plates.

SELECTED REFERENCES

Many of the references that were included in the first articles and books mentioned in this book are outdated, so only selected ones are included in the following list. Many up-to-date and classic references on self-esteem and self-acceptance have been included, but no comprehensive listing, which would be endless, will be found here. Most of the items on Rational Emotive Behavior Therapy (REBT) and on methods on achieving unconditional self-acceptance (USA) and unconditional other-acceptance (UOA) are listed in the regular free catalogue of the Albert Ellis Institute, 45 East 65th Street, New York, NY 10021; (212) 535-0822; FAX (212) 249-3582. A catalogue may be obtained by writing or calling the institute and sending your mailing address.

Adler, A. 1926. *What Life Should Mean to You*. New York: Greenberg.

Baird-Windle, P., and E. J. Bader. 2001. *Targets of Hatred: Anti-Abortion Terrorism*. New York: Palgrave.

Bandura, A. 1997. *Self-Efficacy: The Exercise of Control*. New York: Freeman.

SELECTED REFERENCES

Baron, J. 2000. "What Can We Learn from Individual Differences?" *Contemporary Psychology* 45: 253–55.

Baumeister, R. F. 1997. *Inside Human Violence and Cruelty*. New York: W. H. Freeman.

Beck, A. T. 1976. *Cognitive Therapy and the Emotional Disorders*. New York: New American Library.

Beck, J. S. 1995. *Cognitive Therapy: Basics and Beyond*. New York: Guilford.

Bernard, M. E., and J. L. Wolfe, eds. 2000. *The REBT Resource Book for Practitioners*. New York: Albert Ellis Institute.

Bourland, D. D., Jr., and P. D. Johnston. 1991. *To Be or Not: An E-Prime Anthology*. San Francisco: International Society for General Semantics.

Branden, N. 1969. *The Psychology of Self-Esteem*. New York: Bantam.

Burns, D. D. 1995. *Ten Days to Self-Esteem*. New York: Morrow.

———. 1999a. *Feeling Good: The New Mood Therapy*. Rev. ed. New York: Morrow, Williams & Co.

———. 1999b. *Feeling Good Handbook*. Rev. ed. New York: Plume.

———. 2003. *Worried Sick: Defeat Your Fears and Lead a Happier Life*. New York: Riverhead.

Coopersmith, S. 1968. "Studies in Self-Esteem." *Scientific Monthly* 118, no. 2: 96–106.

Dacey, A. 2001. "Metaphors, Minds, and the Fate of Western Philosophy." *Free Inquiry* (Spring): 39–41.

Dalai Lama, and H. C. Cutter. 1998. *The Art of Happiness*. New York: Riverhead.

Danielsson, D. 1956. *Love in the South Seas*. New York: Random House.

Dryden, W., R. DiGiuseppe, and M. Neenan. 2003. *A Primer on Rational Emotive Behavior Therapy*. Lafayette, IL: Research Press.

Dweck, C. S. 1992. "The Study of Goals in Psychology." *Psychological Science* 3, no. 3 (May): 165–67.

Ellis, A. 1957a. *How to Live with a Neurotic: At Home and at Work*. New York: Crown.

———. 1957b. "Outcome of Employing Three Techniques of Psychotherapy." *Journal of Clinical Psychology* 13: 344–50.

Selected References

———. 1962. *Reason and Emotion in Psychotherapy*. Secaucus, NJ: Citadel.

———. 1999. *How to Make Yourself Happy and Remarkably Less Disturbable*. Atascadero, CA: Impact Publishers.

———. 2000a. *How to Control Your Anxiety before It Controls You*. New York: Citadel Press.

———. 2000b. "Spiritual Goals and Spirited Values in Psychotherapy." *Journal of Individual Psychology* 56: 277–84.

———. 2001a. *Feeling Better, Getting Better, and Staying Better*. Atascadero, CA: Impact Publishers.

———. 2001b. *Overcoming Destructive Beliefs, Feelings, and Behaviors*. Amherst, NY: Prometheus Books.

———. 2002. *Overcoming Resistance: A Rational Emotive Behavior Therapy Integrative Approach*. New York: Springer.

———. 2003a. *Anger: How to Live with and without It*. Rev. ed. New York: Citadel Press.

———. 2003b. *Ask Albert Ellis: Straight Answers and Sound Advice from America's Best Known Psychologist*. Atascadero, CA: Impact Publishers.

———. 2004a. *Rational Emotive Behavior Therapy: It Works for Me—It Can Work for You*. Amherst, NY: Prometheus Books.

———. 2004b. *The Road to Tolerance*. Amherst, NY: Prometheus Books.

Ellis, A., and I. Becker. 1982. *A Guide to Personal Happiness*. North Hollywood, CA: Melvin Powers.

Ellis, A., and S. Blau, eds. 1998. *The Albert Ellis Reader*. New York: Kensington Publishers.

Ellis, A., and T. Crawford. 2000. *Making Intimate Connections: 7 Guidelines for Great Relationships and Better Communication*. Atascadero, CA: Impact Publishers.

Ellis, A., and W. Dryden. 1997. *The Practice of Rational Emotive Behavior Therapy*. New York: Springer.

Ellis, A., J. Gordon, M. Neenan, and S. Palmer. 1998. *Stress Counseling*. New York: Springer.

Ellis, A., and J. Gullo. 1972. *Murder and Assassination.* New York: Lyle Stuart.

Ellis, A., and R. A. Harper. 1961a. *A Guide to Rational Living.* Rev. ed. North Hollywood, CA: Melvin Powers/Wilshire Books.

———. Harper. 1961b. *A Guide to Successful Marriage.* North Hollywood, CA: Wilshire Books.

———. 2002. *Dating, Mating, and Relating: How to Build a Healthy Relationship.* New York: Citadel Press Books.

Ellis, A., and W. Knaus. 1977. *Overcoming Procrastination.* New York: New American Library.

Ellis, A., and H. Robb. 1994. "Acceptance in Rational-Emotive Therapy." In *Acceptance and Change,* edited by S. C. Hayes, N. S. Jacobson, V. M. Follette, and M. J. Dougher, 91–102. Reno, NV: Context Press.

Ellis, A., and C. Tafrate. 1998. *How to Control Your Anger before It Controls You.* New York: Citadel.

Ellis, A., and E. Velten. 1992. *When AA Doesn't Work for You: Rational Steps for Quitting Alcohol.* New York: Barricade Books.

———. 1998. *Optimal Aging: Getting over Getting Older.* Chicago: Open Court.

Ellis, A., J. Young, and G. Lockwood. 1987. "Cognitive Therapy and Rational-Emotive Therapy: A Dialogue." *Journal of Cognitive Psychotherapy* 1, no. 4: 137–87.

Farson, R. H. 1966. "Praise Reappraised." *Encounter* (January): 13–26.

FitzMaurice, K. E. 1997. *Attitude Is All You Need.* Omaha, NE: Palm Tree Publishers.

———. 2000. *Planet Earth: Insane Asylum for the Universe.* Omaha, NE: Palm Tree Publishers.

Flett, G. L., and P. L. Hewitt. 2002. *Perfectionism: Theory, Research and Training.* Washington, DC: American Psychological Association.

Flett, G. L., P. L. Hewitt, K. R. Blankstein, M. Solnik, and M. Van Bronschot. 1996. "Perfectionism, Social Problem-solving Ability, and Psychological Distress." *Journal of Rational-Emotive and Cognitive-Behavioral Therapy* 14: 245–75.

Froggatt, W. 2003a. *Choose to Be Happy.* Rev. ed. Auckland, NZ: Harper Collins.

————. 2003b. *Fearless: Your Guide to Overcoming Anxiety.* Auckland, NZ: Harper Collins.

Glasser, W. 1965. *Reality Therapy.* New York: Harper.

————. 1998. *Choice Therapy.* San Francisco, CA: Harper Collins.

Goleman, D. 2003. *Destructive Emotions: How Can We Overcome Them? A Scientific Dialogue with the Dalai Lama.* New York: Bantam Books.

Gunaratana, M. 2002. *Mindfulness in Plain English.* Boston: Wisdom Books.

Haaga, D. A. F., and G. C. Davison. 1993. "An Appraisal of Rational-Emotive Therapy." *Journal of Consulting and Clinical Psychology* 61: 215–30.

Hajzler, D., and M. E. Bernard. 1991. "A Review of Rational-Emotive Outcome Studies." *School Psychology Quarterly* 6, no. 1: 27–49.

Hartman, R. S. 1967. *The Measurement of Value.* Carbondale: University of Southern Illinois Press.

Hauck, P. A. 1991. *Overcoming the Rating Game: Beyond Self-Love—Beyond Self-Esteem.* Louisville, KY: Westminster/John Knox.

Hayakawa, S. I. 1990. *Language in Thought and Action.* 5th ed. New York: Harcourt, Brace, Jovanovich.

Hayes, S. S., N. S. Jacobson, V. M. Follette, and M. J. Dougher. 1994. *Acceptance and Change.* Reno, NV: Context Press.

Hayes, S. C., K. Strosahl, and K. G. Wilson. 1999. *Acceptance and Commitment Therapy.* New York: Guilford.

Heidegger, M. 1962. *Being and Time.* New York: Harper and Row.

Henry, J. 1963. *Culture against Man.* New York: Simon & Schuster.

Hoffer, E. 1951. *The True Believer.* New York: Harper and Row.

Hollon, S. D., and A. T. Beck. 1994. "Cognitive and Cognitive-Behavioral Therapies." In *Handbook of Psychotherapy and Behavior Change,* edited by A. E. Bergin and S. L. Garfield, 428–66. New York: Wiley.

Horney, K. 1950. *Neurosis and Human Growth.* New York: Norton.

Jacobson, N. S. 1992. "Behavioral Couple Therapy: A New Beginning." *Behavior Therapy* 23: 491–506.

Kelly, G. 1955. *The Psychology of Personal Constructs.* New York: Norton.

Korzybski, A. 1933. *Science and Sanity.* Reprint, Concord, CA: International Society for General Semantics, 1990.

Lazarus, A. A. 1997. *Brief Comprehensive Therapy.* New York: Springer.

Lecky, P. 1943. *Self-Consistency.* New York: Doubleday/Anchor.

Leifer, R. 1999. "Buddhist Conceptualization and Treatment of Anger." *Journal of Clinical Psychology/In Session* 55: 339–51.

Low, A. A. 1952. *Mental Health through Will Training.* Boston: Christopher.

Maultsby, M. C., Jr. 1971. "Rational Emotive Imagery." *Rational Living* 6, no. 1: 24–27.

May, R. 1969. *Love and Will.* New York: Norton.

Mills, D. 2000. *Overcoming Self-Esteem.* In *The REBT Resource Book for Practitioners*, 2nd ed., edited by M. E. Bernard and J. L. Wolfe, 14–15. New York: Albert Ellis Institute.

Mruk, C. 1995. *Self-Esteem: Research, Theory, and Practice.* New York: Springer.

Nietzsche, F. 1959. *The Portable Nietzsche.*

Rand, A. 1957. *Atlas Shrugged.* New York: New American Library.

Robertiello, R. 1964. *Sexual Fulfillment and Self-Affirmation.* Larchmont, NY: Argonaut Books.

Rogers, C. R. 1951. *Client-Centered Therapy.* Boston: Houghton Mifflin.

———. 1957. "The Necessary and Sufficient Conditions of Therapeutic Personality Change." *Journal of Consulting Psychology* 21: 93–103. Reprinted, *Journal of Consulting and Clinical Psychology* 60: 827–32.

Rogers, C. 1961. *On Becoming a Person.* Boston: Houghton Mifflin.

Russell, B. 1965. *The Basic Writings of Bertrand Russell.* New York: Simon & Schuster.

Spinoza, B. *A Spinoza Reader: The Ethics and Other Works.* Edited and translated by Edwin Curley. Princeton, NJ: Princeton University Press, 1994.

Tillich, P. 1953. *The Courage to Be.* Cambridge: Harvard University Press.

Walen, S., R. DiGiuseppe, and W. Dryden. 1992. *A Practitioner's Guide to Rational-Emotive Therapy.* New York: Oxford.

Watzlawick, P. 1978. *The Language of Change.* New York: Basic Books.

ABOUT THE AUTHOR

Albert Ellis, born in Pittsburgh and raised in New York City, holds MA and PhD degrees in clinical psychology from Columbia University. He has held many important psychological positions, including chief psychologist of the state of New Jersey and adjunct professorships at Rutgers and other universities. He is currently president of the Albert Ellis Institute in New York City; has practiced psychotherapy, marriage and family counseling, and sex therapy for sixty years; and continues this practice at the Psychological Center of the institute in New York. He is the founder of Rational Emotive Behavior Therapy (REBT), the first of the now-popular Cognitive Behavior Therapies (CBT).

Dr. Ellis has served as president of the Division of Consulting Psychology of the American Psychological Association and of the Society for the Scientific Study of Sexuality, and he has also served as officer of several professional societies, including the American Association of Marital and Family Therapy; the American Academy of Psychotherapists; and the American Association of Sex Educators, Counselors, and Therapists. He is a diplomate in clinical psychology of the American Board of Professional Psychology and of several other professional organizations. Professional societies that have given Dr. Ellis their highest professional and clinical awards include the American Psychological Association, the Association for the Advancement of Behavior Therapy, the American Counseling Association, and the American Psychopathological Association. He was ranked as one of the "most influential psychologists" by both American and Canadian psychologists and counselors. He has served as consulting or associate editor of many scientific journals and has published over eight hundred scientific papers and more than two hundred audio- and video-cassettes. He has authored or edited over seventy books and monographs, including a number of best-selling popular and professional volumes. Some of his best-known books include *How to Live with a "Neurotic"*; *The Art and Science of Love*; *A Guide to Rational Living*; *Reason and Emotion in Psychotherapy*; *How to Stubbornly Refuse to Make Yourself Miserable about Anything—Yes, Anything!*; *Overcoming Procrastination*; *The Practice of Rational Emotive Behavior Therapy*; *How to Make Yourself Happy and Remarkably Less Disturbable*; *Feeling Better, Getting Better, Staying Better*; *Overcoming Destructive Beliefs, Feelings, and Behaviors*; *Anger: How to Live with It and without It*; *Ask Dr. Ellis*; *Anger: How to Live with It and without It* (revised edition); *Overcoming Resistance: The Rational Emotive Behavior Therapy Integrated Approach*; *The Road to Tolerance*; *Sex without Guilt in the Twenty-First Century*; and *Rational Emotive Behavior Therapy—It Works for Me, It Can Work for You*.

INDEX